THE NEW SUPERVISOR

FIFTH EDITION

MARTIN M. BROADWELL
with CAROL BROADWELL DIETRICH

THE NEW SUPERVISOR

How to Thrive in Your First Year as a Manager

FIFTH EDITION

PERSEUS BOOKS

Cambridge, Massachusetts

Library of Congress Cataloging-in-Publication Data
Broadwell, Martin M.
    The new supervisor : how to thrive in your first year as a manager
   / Martin M. Broadwell with Carol Broadwell Dietrich.—5th ed.
     p.   cm.
    Includes index.
    ISBN 0-201-33992-7
    1. Supervision of employees.   I. Dietrich, Carol Broadwell.
II. Title
HF5549.12.B77   1998
658.3'02—dc20   98-14806
                                                                   CIP

Perseus Books is a member of the Perseus Books Group

Cover design by Tom Tafuri/One + One Studio
Text design by IPA
Set in 10-point Palatino by Pagesetters

EBC 02 03 04 05   15 14 13 12 11 10 9

Perseus Books are available at special discounts for bulk purchases in the U.S. by corporations, institutions, and other organizations. For more information, please contact the Special Markets Department at HarperCollins Publishers, 10 East 53rd Street, New York, NY 10022, or call 212-207-7528.

Find us on the World Wide Web at
http://www.perseusbooks.com

To the men in my life:
My father
My brother
My two sons
My seven grandsons

—M.M.B.

To my husband, Eric
My sons, Connolly and Cavan
My mother, Patricia
Most especially, to my
father — thanks, Dad!

—C.B.D.

CONTENTS

PREFACE TO THE FIFTH EDITION

We lived in the same house for nearly twenty years then trained together for nearly twenty years. It seems only natural that we should write a book together. We wrote a number of articles together and discovered that even we couldn't tell which of us wrote what part. That's true for this revision. We hope the readers will appreciate that the lack of different styles shows how much we think alike.

It's been seven years since the last revision. Even though some changes have been introduced into supervisory skills, the job of the new supervisor hasn't changed much, unless it's been to get even more difficult. The chapter on managing and monitoring stress should help. Since this is really a survival book, we decided that delegation needed more emphasis—after all, getting the work done through others is the real job of the supervisor—so we've added a chapter to make that easier. Much has been said about team building in the last seven years, so we've tried to simplify it a little for the reader. For the new supervisor, the idea of a massive program on team building is a frightening thing. We've tried to take some of the sting out of it by saying that it can be done on a much simpler level, within the supervised group.

Finally, we've both enjoyed the last seven years and more of training mostly new supervisors, or at least first-level ones, and we've always had fun doing it. We wrote this book with a smile, so the authors urge that the readers read it without a furrowed brow!

M.M.B.
Decatur, Georgia, 1998

C.B.D.
Atlanta, Georgia, 1998

ACKNOWLEDGMENTS

Anyone who reads a book may say, "My, how smart the authors are!" Anyone who writes a book must say, "I hope no one ever realizes how much of this we got from someone else!" Let the reader of this book know that the authors don't ask those who have contributed so much to it to accept the blame for the way it came out, only to take credit for heading us in the right direction. In this book each will recognize the part that once was his idea, his manner of expressing the old thing in a new way or of making the new idea sound not too far out:

Cabot Jaffee	Ruth House
Dugan Laird	Dave Loeser
Brother Bill	Nina Hollingsworth
Joel Ramich	Denny Crumpler
Bob Rock	Brother/son Tim
Irv Scherman	Husband Eric
Norm Stanton	

M.M.B.

PROLOGUE

All the books in the world won't prepare a person adequately for that first day—or even the first few weeks—as a supervisor. The first time we have responsibility not only for the job but also for the people doing the job can be an awesome thing. But the job becomes rewarding when it is done properly, and it can be done that way if we avoid certain mistakes.

The purpose of this book is to help keep the new supervisor from doing wrong some things that others did wrong when they became new supervisors. This book contains very little theory, but it does illustrate the practical application of many theories. People do not act theoretically; neither can they be supervised theoretically. The new supervisor has gone too far to be satisfied with mere theories, no matter how good they are or how practical they have proved to be. What he or she wants to know is, "What do I do right now with *this* problem?"

We hope this book will help answer that question.

THE NEW SUPERVISOR

FIFTH EDITION

Chapter 1

A NEW ATTITUDE TOWARD THE JOB

A NEW ROLE

Supervising others can be fully understood only by those who do it. This doesn't mean it is mysterious or deep, it just means it's hard to explain—like describing chocolate cake to someone who has never eaten cake. That first day on the job can be frustrating, and many new supervisors have been heard to say, "I didn't know how well off I was. At least I knew what I was doing." And therein lies the problem. When we become supervisors, we must realize that we've taken on a new role, one for which we have the qualifications—but for which *we probably haven't been trained.*

There was one thing about the old job—we knew what to do and when to do it. In fact, that's probably why we got our new job in the first place; we could do our job better than anyone else. Someone looked at us and decided we were pretty good at our job and seemed to have the qualities that would make a good supervisor. So we were promoted to supervisor. Now we have the job, but what do we do? In the old job we were trained. We were never given a job to do and left with no more instruction than "Just do what comes naturally to you." But that's the situation right now. We have people working for us, and we really can't do their work for them. Our job is to see that *they* do the work. No matter how slow they seem to be, or how bad their attitude may be, or how much they foul up the job, our role is still to get work done by them, *not do it ourselves*.

Remember when we used to gripe about the boss doing things wrong? Remember those sessions around the coffeepot when we and the rest of the workers used to really let the boss have it (behind his or her back, of course)? Well, we're the boss now, and we're the one being talked about around the coffeepot. This means we are going to have to start looking at things differently. *Our job is to worry about the job*. This doesn't mean our people aren't important—we've already seen that they are the ones who do the work for us—but it does mean that we must learn to think about both the people and the job, not letting either one become more important than the other. And that's pretty difficult, as we will see time and again in this book.

Let's look at a simple example: Susan comes in red-eyed and obviously has a problem. As the story unfolds, it looks something like this.

Susan's having family problems. She and her husband haven't been married very long, and this morning they had an argument. The husband was pretty hateful and said some pretty mean things. Susan has decided to go home to Mother and wants to take the afternoon off so she can go home and pack before her husband gets there. The only thing is, she can't afford to lose the pay (now that she's on her own), and she wants to come in on a Saturday to make it up. This means actually showing her time as worked this afternoon, but showing nothing on the Saturday she works. She is willing to work all day for the halftime off so as not to lose the money. The truth is, we can't afford to let her go—even without pay—because of the heavy workload today. But as distraught as she is, there's no telling how she'll react if we tell her she can't go. Also, if we say no, she'll think it's just because we weren't willing to let her make the time up on a Saturday. She's waiting now for an answer and needs it immediately so she can call her mother.

Well, *what do we do?* The problem is real and important to Susan. As a supervisor, we are expected to make the right decision. Suppose we let her go, with or without pay; what will we tell Artie Angler when he comes in next Friday to do the same thing so he can go fishing with the guys for the opening of trout season? How will we explain to Artie the difference in our handling of the two situations? Suppose we don't let Susan go; how much production can we expect to get out of her for the rest of the day? How will we explain the loss in production to our boss? What will our decision do to morale in the office? Does it matter?

NEW WORDS—NEW MEANINGS FOR OLD ONES

As we go along, we will see better approaches to solving this kind of problem than just doing what comes naturally. But for now, let's say that we must learn a new vocabulary. At least, we must learn new meanings for old words. They are going to be key words and key meanings for years to come. They are going to be the things that we spend our time thinking about, worrying about, and making decisions about. Words like *management* take on a different look now. Also, *money* and *time* aren't bad words anymore. We can't make decisions based only on emotions or even based on the feelings of the people involved. We make decisions based on good job management. We make them in light of what's good for the organization—which *includes* the feelings of the people but *is not limited to* the feelings of the people.

All of this says that the word *production* should take on a new meaning for us. We aren't responsible just for things anymore; people and money and time and production have suddenly become inseparable. And remember, what we were best at—getting the job done—we are no longer supposed to do (at least not with our own hands). And remember, too, we may not have been trained to do this new job of supervising people. Of course, there are some basic rules: treat them as we would like to be treated; remember that they are human beings—the basic human courtesies still apply. But we may not even be sure how we would like to be treated in a similar situation. Also, knowing as much as we do about production needs and work scheduling and profits and the bosses' demands means that we would want to be treated differently from those who don't know about these matters. And suppose we decide that Susan and Artie *are* human beings—so what? That's a nice thought, but what do we do with their problems now that they've become human beings? What do we do about getting the job done?

Though this may sound a bit heartless, it really isn't. It just means that being a supervisor changes things for us. It changes our outlook and presents us with new problems. It changes our perspective and gives us a bigger picture to look at. It doesn't take the human element out; it puts other elements in. It gives us more factors to consider when we make decisions. It does, in fact, give us the right and opportunity to make decisions that were not ours to make before. As we said earlier, the *job* becomes important now, and all these other considerations are part of getting the job done. It doesn't make us any less interested in people; it makes us interested in them because they are the ones who make us look good or bad. They have been entrusted, in a sense, to our hands, and we have an obligation to see that things go well for them. But the job has been entrusted to us also, and we have an obligation to the organization to see that the work is done so that *all concerned* will profit.

A DIFFERENT GANG NOW

The supervisory role has been referred to as the lonely role. It looked simple enough when we were working for the boss and he or she was making all the decisions. It didn't seem too bad when the boss just seemed to hang around doing very little but getting in the way. As a matter of fact, we remember when we used to say, "Boy, that's really having it made. We do all the work, and the boss gets the credit and the money and the office!" This job looked pretty easy when we were the Susans and Arties. But somehow it doesn't look now the way it did then. Susan and Artie even look different to us now. But they haven't changed. And we haven't changed. So what's different? The *job* is different. The responsibility has changed. Our viewpoint has changed. And let's face it, our loyalties have probably changed, too. Whether we like it or not, the people working for us don't see us the same way, either. A few supervisors have been able to make a go of it by telling the old gang that nothing has changed. They have continued to go on break and eat lunch with them and gripe with them and criticize the organization with them and knock the big boss with them and still get the work done and handle discipline problems and fire some and promote some and not get into trouble with the group—but there aren't many successes who took this route, and there are plenty of failures to show that it is a dangerous route to take. Being a regular guy is nice, and it's all right, too—but only if the phrase means that even though you are the *boss*, you're still a regular guy. You can't give up being the boss just to stay a regular guy.

The important thing is that we belong to a different gang now. We have to give up some of the pleasures of being part of the old gang and accept our position as the boss. As the boss, we belong to the gang that is made up of the other bosses. We don't have to associate with them, but we do have to communicate with them, on their level (which is our level, too). We still have to communicate with those who work for us, and on their level, too (which is *not* our level). And as we look out over the group that works for us, we've got to say, "We are a group that must stick together, perform as one unit, and meet the organization's goals. But even though we work as one, I must be the leader. I must set the pattern of leadership by letting them be a part of the goal setting; I must lead by giving them as much authority as possible so they can do their job with a minimum of interference from me; I must see that they develop their full potential; I must see that their needs are met; *but*—I must do these things as the boss, not as just one of them."

BEWARE OF POWER

Moving to the supervisor's role has the hazard of giving us power. In this new role, we have all the marbles. We can say, "Do, because I'm the boss," and generally it will get done. We didn't like that approach before we made supervisor; our people aren't going to like it in us when we become their supervisor. How could we ever get like that, as much as we hated it when we were nonsupervisors? The answer isn't complicated: we do it because it works. When we aren't trained in people skills, including how to get the work done through others, we tend to become like our supervisors. If we had autocratic ones, we tend to grasp that as a role model. If our bosses were more democratic in their treatment, we pick up those traits. Because the job of a new supervisor is often so strange to us, we are desperate to find something that works.

Remember, we got this job because we were the best worker, the best *doer*. Now we aren't supposed to be a doer. We're supposed to get others to *do*, and we're going to be measured on how well we get others to perform. Unfortunately, we seldom have received any training on how to do all of this, so we make some mistakes. We aren't very good at delegating. We aren't very good at motivating. We aren't very good at people skills. We aren't very good at communicating. We aren't very good at interviewing. *We aren't very good at being a supervisor!* After some near disasters in trying to use our common sense—without the skills or knowledge of people—we start to try to find something that works. It begins to dawn on us that we have some *power!* We can issue edicts and things get done. If we aren't careful, we'll find ourselves in the following situation:

SUPERVISOR: *Alice, we're about to miss another deadline with that report you're working on. How are you doing?*

ALICE: *I don't know if I'm going to finish it on time or not. There's a lot of things that need to be done, and it's not the most exciting thing I've ever worked on, you know. You used to have to do this, remember?*

SUPERVISOR: *Yeah, I remember. I also remember that I used to get it done on time, too!*

ALICE: *Well, maybe you should do this one, if it's so important. I'm not sure I can finish on time.*

SUPERVISOR: *Come on, Alice! This is your job. There's no reason you can't get it done.*

ALICE: *Okay, I might get it done if you'd quit bugging me. I can't get anything done if you keep screaming at me.*

SUPERVISOR: *Alice, are you going to get this job done or am I going to have to find someone else to do it?*

ALICE: *Why me? Why should I have to meet these unreal deadlines?*

SUPERVISOR: *You want to know why? I'll tell you why. You'll do it because I'm the boss and I'm telling you to do it. That's why!*

ALICE: *So what does that mean? You going to fire me if I don't?*

SUPERVISOR: *I'm not saying that, but you realize there are a lot of*

people out there who would jump at getting your job. You make
good money for the little bit of work you do around here!
ALICE: *Well, listen to Mr. Big Shot. You used to be part of the gang.*
Now you're Mr. My-way-or-the-highway!

So, how did it go? We certainly didn't mean to end up at this
point. We've backed ourselves and Alice into a corner. We don't
want to fire Alice. We aren't trying to be a big shot. We just finally
had to resort to the use of our power to try to get the job done. It
was a mistake, and we'll pay for it for a long time. Our relationship
with Alice is in the pits, and it won't take long for everyone else
to hear about this. Whatever motivation Alice had is shot, and
soon the others will be in the same shape. We've dug a deep
hole, thrown ourselves into it, and haven't taken a ladder with
us. One thing we hope to do in this book is to prevent just such
situations from arising. Certainly we can prevent them from ending as this one did!

The bad part of all of this is that when we're in a situation like
this, we tend to take ourselves seriously and think we're doing the
right thing. The first reaction we have is, "Well, what else can you
do with the kind of people we have to hire these days?" We make
Alice the bad person. And it becomes a self-fulfilling prophecy.
She actually becomes a bad employee. Her motivation is down,
her interest in the job is diminished, and she gets all the blame. If
something doesn't happen to change our behavior, we're going
to become just what Alice said we were: "Mr. My-way-or-the-
highway" supervisor. That alone should be enough for us to avoid
using our power as long as we can!

How do we accomplish this without being snobbish or con-
ceited or overbearing? It isn't easy, but it isn't impossible, either. In
the next chapter we will see some examples of how it can be done
successfully.

CONCLUSION

The role of a new supervisor is quite a change from whatever else
we have been doing. Coming from within the organization will
cause one kind of problem, coming from outside will cause another. In either case, though, things are going to be different from

now on. The *purpose* of the job is different. Viewpoints are different. Like it or not, we're part of a different group now; we're part of the managing effort, rather than part of the hourly worker effort. Our job now is to get the work done through others, not to do it ourselves. Instead of griping about the boss, we are the boss. Instead of griping about policy, we must implement the policy. Instead of just waiting for someone to appraise us, we must do appraisals of others. This list goes on and on, because we've assumed this new role. It takes some getting used to, but we can do it. Many have before us, and they're better for it. We will be, too!

EXERCISES

1. Individual activity: Let each person write down how he or she got to be a supervisor. (What were the processes—in the minds of the decision makers—that he or she thinks led to the promotion? If the person was *hired* into the organization as a supervisor, what led the organization to choose this person over another—as a *supervisor*?)

2. Half-group activity: Divide the group into two subgroups. Have one subgroup list what might be typical viewpoints of hourly workers toward the job of supervision and the other subgroup list how a newly appointed supervisor might feel about supervision the first week after taking the job. Record the lists in separate places.

3. Let each person vote "Agree" or "Disagree" on each item in each list from exercise 2. Do the majority of the group members agree with the hourly workers or with the supervisors?

4. Group discussion: Have the group come up with a list of factors that ought to be taken into consideration in selecting a person for the job of supervisor. Let the whole group reach agreement on as many factors as possible. (The dissenters should be answered by those who are in favor of the item under discussion.)

5. Small-group activity: Form several small groups and give the subgroups two or three of the factors from exercise 4. Have

each subgroup decide how its factors could be measured. (Be sure that each factor is measured well enough—by the subgroup's suggestions—so that each person's work can be distinguished from that of the others.)

6. Half-group activity: Divide the group into two subgroups. Have one group represent typical hourly workers and the other group represent typical first-line supervisors. Have them look at the following terms and give their "feelings" about each of them. After each individual does this, each subgroup should try to come up with a consensus on each term. In discussion afterward, see why there is a difference in the definition of the terms themselves between the groups. The terms to be discussed are:

time off	money	production
management	work	overtime
profit	the boss	union

Chapter 2

A NEW ATTITUDE TOWARD THE SUBORDINATE

As a new supervisor, one of the most difficult things for us to accept is the fact that those under us might be able to do our job just as well as we can do it. In fact, in different circumstances, one of those under us might well have been the boss instead of us. What made the difference? Brainpower? Probably not. In sheer ability to think, most of us come out very close to the middle range, even though we like to think of it otherwise. The fact that we are the boss doesn't reduce the brainpower of those we supervise or mean that we necessarily have more than they have. What about knowledge of the job? This varies, of course, because many new supervisors know their former job better than anyone else (which may well be the reason they were selected for the supervisory job in the first place). On the other hand, as a new supervisor, we may know less about the job we're supervising than anyone else (having been promoted from some other job or hired into the supervisory job). Overlooking luck or influence, the only thing we can say for sure is that the new supervisor gets the job because somebody in higher management thinks he or she can handle the job of getting work done by directing the activities of others.

RECOGNIZE SUBORDINATES' ABILITIES

So what, then, should be our attitude toward those who work for us? The important thing to remember is that it is to our—and the company's—advantage to use their talents as much as possible, leaving less and less of their job for us to do! It's rather poor management of time, people, and talent to let brainpower go unused, or to let experience and knowledge of the job be wasted. And the chances are pretty good that our people will use these things or not use them *as a result of what we do or don't do*. In a sense, we can think of our people as being a huge storehouse of brainpower and knowledge of the job. The only catch is that we must find the right keys to give us access to this tremendous asset. Not every key will work every time, nor will every key work on every individual. We spend much of our time looking for the right keys and trying them out when we find them. (All of which adds to the fun and challenge of being a supervisor!)

SUBORDINATES HAVE NEEDS

Those who work for us have more than brainpower, job knowledge, and experience—they have certain needs and anxieties that work against them for a while but can be made to work for us. For example, if their needs are being met on the job, then we have found a good source of motivation. On the other hand, if their needs are very strong and are *not* being met on the job, then no matter how hard we work at motivating, we aren't likely to have much success. It isn't enough to say, "Well, I have problems, too, and I don't let them influence my performance." That may or may not be true, but in any case, we still have to recognize the problems that employees bring to work with them. This doesn't mean we have to excuse poor performance caused by outside problems, but it does mean we have to accept the fact that employees have those problems and those problems may affect their work.

But outside problems aren't the only things that cause

employees to have anxieties; many things right on the job will bother them and cause them to develop additional problems. For example, the simple fact that we're new to the job of supervisor will cause certain anxieties. The employees don't know how they will relate to us. They don't know how they will fit into our thinking. They will worry about our opinion of them and the impression we will get of their work. They will have to start all over again competing with the others in the organization to establish a position in our esteem. These aren't necessarily large problems, but they are real and must be considered by us as new supervisors.

Not only will employees worry about how we will see them, but they will also be watching us to see how we act under certain conditions. What will it be like when there is a rush job to be done? Will we be the kind of supervisor who puts the screws on tight, or will we just relax and not worry about deadlines? What will happen when an employee does something wrong? Will we be tolerant and just say, "Forget it"? Or will we blow our stack and embarrass him or her in front of everyone? What will happen when other departments or groups interfere with our activities or don't meet their deadlines? Will we stand up for our "rights," or will we let them walk all over us? Our employees want to know these things about us and will be anxious about it until the questions are resolved (or until we have acted in such a way as to assure them that they don't have to worry about these things).

AMBIVALENCE—LOVE AND HATE

One of the strange things about being a supervisor is that we have to learn that it's possible for our people to love us and hate us at the same time. Perhaps these terms are too strong, but they identify the problems brought about by the phenomenon of ambivalence. Because we represent two different things to employees, it's possible for them to feel two different ways about us. As a supervisor, we represent authority—something that tells them what to do and what not to do; hence, a threat to their satisfaction. As a supervisor, we represent employees' means of getting ahead, of getting a raise, of solving their problems, of being recognized, of being told how to do things more easily; hence, real security. Just as we are simultaneously a comfort and a threat to them, so they can like us for what we do for them and dislike us for what we represent. This ambivalence shows in employees' reactions to the ways in which we give them assignments. If we just make assignments and don't give the employees much direction, they complain because we haven't explained to them how we want the job done. If we give them instructions, they're apt to complain because we lean over their shoulders all the time and don't let them do anything on their own. Again, our job as a supervisor is to recognize that this phenomenon exists and to look for ways of using it to our advantage.

BOSSES ARE NICE PEOPLE

Often we find ourselves in the peculiar position of seeming to defend our "bosshood." Very early in the game we must realize that *there is nothing wrong with being a boss*. We should never feel the need to apologize for it or defend it. Every organization, at almost any level, must have someone who is in charge: the boss. For whatever reason, we are that person in this situation, and it's up to us to act the part. As a matter of fact, if we find ourselves trying to defend our job as the boss, it is probably a good indication that we aren't being a very good one. ("Look, fellows, I hate to sound like the boss, but we've got to get this job out today.")

Interestingly enough, while we may try to hide it or avoid it, our employees never really get over the obvious fact that we are the boss. Whether or not we act like it is our choice; they still know we are, in spite of whatever we do. All this means is that we should get the work done by being the boss, not by trying to be a friend or a buddy or trying to bribe the employees into doing what they are being paid to do. The problems of supervision arise not because we are the boss but because we don't act like a boss or perhaps because we exploit the job of being the boss. While we have every right to be the boss, we have no right to use this fact as the only means of getting the work done. We can't demand that the employees respect us, and although we can get work out for a while by demanding it, sooner or later such action breeds disrespect that comes back to haunt us. This sort of haunting commonly occurs when we've acted this way for some time, then suddenly find ourselves in a situation in which it's up to the employees to pull our chestnuts out of the fire—and of course they "innocently" let these chestnuts burn! So how do we act? Later in this book we will deal with some specific behavior that has proved to be very satisfactory in setting up the right relationship between the boss and the subordinate. Right now we are just suggesting that somewhere between the two extremes of trying to hide the fact of being boss and exploiting it lies the happy ground of being successful at being the boss.

The fact is, our employees know we are the boss, even if we try to hide it. They used to go on break with a *coworker*; now, when we go on break with them, they're going with the *boss*. One of the best approaches is to remember two rules:

1. Never threaten anything we aren't willing (and able) to carry out.

2. It's a lot easier to go from being strict to being easy than it is to go from being easy to being strict.

The worst thing we can do is try to please and appease all of them. If we aren't wise enough to avoid it, we will end up taking part in the following conversation:

CHARLIE: *You wanted to see me, Chief?*
SUPERVISOR: *Yes, Charlie. Thanks for coming in. I wanted to talk about your working up the budget details for the next quarter.*
CHARLIE: *Aw, come on! Why me? That's a dumb, dumb job. Why don't you give it to Betty? She's good at it and I hate it.*
SUPERVISOR: *Huh! I know what you mean. I used to hate it when I had to do it. But it has to be done, so we ought to take turns.*
CHARLIE: *Yeah, but let me miss a turn. I won't complain!*
SUPERVISOR: *Well, maybe just this once I can give it to Betty again. She's had it the last two times. I feel sort of bad giving it to her, but she never complains.*
CHARLIE: *Naw, she never complains about anything. She'll probably like it. Just keep on giving it to her every time. She won't mind, and it'll make everybody else happy, too. You're a good guy, Chief!*

So, what did that buy us? We probably just shot ourselves in the foot. The fact that Charlie called us "Chief" might have been a clue for us to watch out, especially if he hadn't been calling us that before we made supervisor. What we've just seen is that while we apparently made Charlie happy, we actually gave in to someone who will now take advantage of us every chance he gets. He knows we will cave in pretty easily, so he'll try it the next time and the next time, too. At some time we'll have to take a stand, and it will be harder each time we let Charlie get away with not doing his job. On top of that, we've taken advantage of an employee who has a good attitude toward her work. It won't be long until Betty finds out we're dumping all the jobs on her that the others don't like. We'll find it hard to deal with her, too. Why did this happen? Because we didn't start out being strict enough. If it was Charlie's turn to do the job, then Charlie should have been the one to do it. We didn't need to make any points with Charlie, and we lost some points with Betty. Even if Betty didn't mind and would keep on doing the project, we probably should have given it to Charlie just to let him know he needs to do what we ask him to do. A better conversation would be:

CHARLIE: *You wanted to see me, Chief?*

SUPERVISOR: *Yes, Charlie. Thanks for coming in. I wanted to talk about your working up the budget details for the next quarter.*

CHARLIE: *Aw, come on! Why me? That's a dumb, dumb job. Why don't you give it to Betty? She's good at it and I hate it.*

SUPERVISOR: *Actually, she is good at it, but we need to spread the tasks around. It's your turn to do this project, isn't it?*

CHARLIE: *Yeah, I guess so, but you used to hate it, too. Remember how you used to gripe about having to do it?*

SUPERVISOR: *You're right, I did. But I went ahead and did it. I'm glad I did, because it gave me a better understanding of what the budget is all about. You can use that, too. I'd like to see you get good at all these things so you can move up in the operation.*

CHARLIE: *Okay, but do I really have to do this one? How about skipping a turn with me and letting Betty do it? She never complains and she's really good at it.*

SUPERVISOR: *You're right, she is good at it and she never complains. Now if I can just get you good at it . . . and get you where you don't complain, we'll be in good shape! How about it?*

CHARLIE: *Well, okay, but you sure are making it hard for me to move up in the business. Well, not really. You're not such a bad guy.*

Maybe they won't all turn out this way, but at least we can see what it means to start out being strict and maybe ease up later.

The issue of not making a threat we aren't willing—and able—to carry out follows the same lines. Let's use the same example, but go back to the first conversation and see how we might have gotten into even more trouble.

CHARLIE: *You wanted to see me, Chief?*
SUPERVISOR: *Yes, Charlie. Thanks for coming in. I wanted to talk about your working up the budget details for the next quarter.*
CHARLIE: *Aw, come on! Why me? That's a dumb, dumb job. Why don't you give it to Betty? She's good at it and I hate it.*
SUPERVISOR: *Huh! I know what you mean. I used to hate it when I had to do it. But it has to be done, so we ought to take turns.*
CHARLIE: *Yeah, but let me miss a turn. I won't complain!*
SUPERVISOR: *Come on, Charlie. You know you're supposed to do this when it's your turn!*
CHARLIE: *Now wait a minute! I don't see it written down anywhere that I've got to do stuff like that when somebody else is better. I'm good at other stuff and you let me do it over and over again!*
SUPERVISOR: *Now don't get smart with me, Charlie. If I tell you to do it, it doesn't have to be written down.*
CHARLIE: *So, are you telling me I have to do it or else?*
SUPERVISOR: *Well, uh, yes. I'm telling you you have to do it.*
CHARLIE: *And if I don't?*
SUPERVISOR: *Uh, well, if you don't, then I'll just have to get someone around here with a better attitude!*
CHARLIE: *So, you'll fire me if I refuse?*
SUPERVISOR: *I wouldn't have any choice.*

We'll stop here before it gets worse! Of course, it should never have gotten this far. We backed ourselves into a corner. We don't want to fire Charlie. We threatened him when we didn't even mean to. What's worse, we may not even have the authority to fire him. There are probably some company procedures, some steps in the disciplinary process we have to go through that we've missed. There may even be some union involvement. What's happened is that we made a threat we aren't willing to carry out, and may not even be able to carry out.

There is one thing we could have done that often works. There's a way to turn this around and get Charlie on our side. It's a simple little process that will work over and over again as we learn to fit into this new role of the supervisor. *We ask for help!* The scenario could go like this:

CHARLIE: *You wanted to see me, Chief?*

SUPERVISOR: *Yes, Charlie. Thanks for coming in. I need your help on something. I wanted to talk about the budget details for the next quarter.*

CHARLIE: *Oh, boy! How I hate to do that!*

SUPERVISOR: *I know what you mean. I used to hate it, too. That's why I called on you. I need your help in solving this thing that comes up every month. You know Betty seems to end up doing it more than anyone else.*

CHARLIE: *Yeah, but she's really good at it and never complains.*

SUPERVISOR: *That's right, but there are a lot of things she doesn't do and I need her to learn other things. I'd like for her to be able to learn some of the things you do. If you can learn to do the budget thing, maybe get her to help you, then you could teach her the things you do well. It sure would help me out, being new on the job. I know I can trust you to train her right . . . and it would make you more valuable to the organization.*

CHARLIE: *Wow, that sure took a strange turn. But I see what you mean, and I know you always did it, even if you did gripe about it. It won't kill me, I guess. Maybe I'll get your job some day and never have to do the budget again!*

So, maybe all the conversations won't turn out like this, but the idea is worth a try. When the boss asks for help it carries a message of vulnerability. It's hard for employees to turn the boss down, even if they don't like either the job or the boss! One word we used is very powerful, too—*trust*. When we tell an employee we know we can trust him or her, we are revealing some humanism on our part. The word shows that we don't have all the answers nor do we think we're the only one in the organization who can be trusted. Together, the ideas of help and trust can be an extremely effective motivator. We will certainly go a lot farther toward getting Charlie to do this unsavory job than we would by using threats or by giving in to Charlie and handing the job over to Betty.

WE DEPEND ON OUR PEOPLE

Whether we like it or not, we must depend on our people to accomplish the long-range goals of the organization. We can do only a certain amount ourselves, and the more of the work we do, the poorer the job of supervision we're doing. Sooner or later we must get the work done through the people the organization has given us to do it with. That is why our attitude toward these people is so important. We may not think we have enough people, or the right people, or enough time, or enough training, but it is still up to us as the supervisor to get the work done with these people at this time under these conditions.

And this brings us to another critical thought: these are also the people who will make us look good or bad. These are the people who—to a large degree—can make us or break us as a supervisor. Our ability to use their skills, our ability to motivate them to perform, our ability to get them to think and act the way the organization wants are the things we will be rated on when appraisal time rolls around. So their performance will have a direct and important bearing on our rating as a supervisor.

Delegation Is the New Key Word

The hardest thing for us to learn in this new job is that we really aren't doing *our* job if we don't get other people to do the work. We came from doing things; now we are in the role of getting others to do things. It isn't natural for us, nor is it all that comfortable. It isn't even very satisfying! We've always gotten our satisfaction from a job well done, but that job has been measurable, observable, and very tangible, usually. Now we are only able to measure our success by what our subordinates are able to accomplish. All of this means that we're going to have to see them in a new light.

We must see their work, their progress, their attitudes as *our accomplishments*. We'll have to work that out to where it is measurable and observable and tangible.

Whatever our hesitation about assigning work to others, we'll need to get over it in a hurry, because that's our job. We cannot see our workers as people we are imposing on when we give them work. They are in the same situation we were in when we were in that job; they are there to do the tangible things. They are the production people. We are the *supervisor* of the production people. We aren't there to apologize for delegating work to them. We are there to develop their skills, use their skills. We are there to see that everybody comes as close to working at full capacity as possible, and that means developing people's talents to do more, if possible. We have to remember that if employees resent being given work to do, that's a problem they'll have to overcome—with our help, perhaps, but overcome nevertheless. The general rule is that work should be done at the lowest level in the organization where the competency exists. It's our job to see that that happens.

SUBORDINATES GET OUR JOB

Finally, our attitude toward our people is important because we have an obligation to the organization to see that those who work for us develop the right attitude. It is from their ranks that our job, or others like ours, must be filled, and the way we train them, use them, and treat them will determine whether or not the organization has enough properly trained supervisors to replace us and others like us when we move on to better things. Our attitude toward our people may well determine the attitude they have toward their subordinates when they are promoted. Equally important, it may determine their attitude toward the organization as a whole, both right now and when they become supervisors. It is just as shortsighted to think of our people only in the jobs they fill as it is to think of ourselves only in the job we fill. And it is certainly an indictment of us if we have failed to develop anyone under us who is capable of handling much, if not all, of our work when we are out of the office or when we are moved to another assignment.

CONCLUSION

What have we said about our attitude toward our subordinates? We have said that we must realize that they have a storehouse of brainpower and experience for which the successful supervisor will find keys. It is through the abilities of the subordinates that the job must get done. We've seen that subordinates have certain needs and anxieties, which they brought to the job or may have developed after they got there. In fact, we are part of the problem, because we represent both a threat and a source of security to them. In the process of getting the job done, we must be careful not to try to defend being the boss. We don't need to defend it or hide it, nor do we want to exploit it, because the people who work for us are the means by which the organization will meet its objectives. These are the same people who will determine to a large degree just how well we do when we are appraised, because our job is really one of getting the work done through them. Finally, these are the people who should be able to move into our job when we are moved on to other jobs. Our *attitude* toward these people will largely determine our *actions* toward them; hence, it will determine how well they are able to take over when we leave.

EXERCISES

1. Group discussion: Have the group brainstorm problems that nonsupervisors or hourly workers have that are exactly the same as those faced by supervisors. This discussion isn't limited to job activities, but includes home life, community, future planning, money, etc. Record the ideas and then discuss why supervisors often tend to think their people shouldn't have personal problems—or at least shouldn't let them interfere with the job.

2. Using the list from exercise 1, have the group decide whether these common problems actually *do* interfere with supervisors and their jobs.

3. Group discussion: Have the group brainstorm problems that nonsupervisors or hourly workers have that are *not* like those of typical supervisors. Record these ideas and decide whether

these problems interfere with work. Do supervisors let their nonsimilar problems interfere with their work?

4. Individual assignment: Let each person make a list of ways in which ambivalence is displayed in the workplace. Find situations in which the boss is criticized by the workers for doing something but would also be criticized for failing to do it. We discussed one instance of ambivalence in this chapter—close supervision versus not enough direction.

5. Half-group activity: Divide the group into two subgroups. Have one subgroup think of ways in which supervisors can and should use their positions as *bosses* to their advantage. The other subgroup should think of how and when it can be harmful for supervisors to let it be known that they are bosses. One group is listing the advantages of using the position of boss, and the other is listing the disadvantages, both with specific examples.

6. Group discussion: Discuss ways in which the job couldn't get done if the workers decided to do just what they were told to do and *no more*. Give some specific examples.

Chapter 3

A NEW ATTITUDE TOWARD THE BOSS

BOSSES HAVE THEIR OWN PROBLEMS

One of the things that confronts us soon after we become a new supervisor is the fact that our problems are often compounded by our people coming in with *their* problems, which gives us less time for our own. This really ought to be a very loud message for us: if it's true for us, it must surely be true for *our* boss! In fact, it is very true. Even though we don't like to admit it sometimes, the boss is usually working on problems of greater magnitude than ours. In a sense, our problems are really our boss's, too, and so are all the problems of the other people who work for him or her. Even if our boss hasn't got more important problems, he or she at least has *more*. It behooves us, then, to avoid adding our problems to our boss's burdens, or at least to avoid adding any more than we can help.

The thing we want to do is make very sure that we understand the boss's role and our own role and where the dividing line is between them. We need to remember that just as it's our job to get a certain portion of the work done through other people, so it is the boss's job to get things done through us. If we get the idea that the boss is just sitting around giving us work so he or she won't have anything to do, let's stop and realize that our people may feel the same way about us! Another thing we need to remember is that since our boss has the accountability for our decisions—as well as the decisions of his or her other subordinates—any bad decisions he or she makes have more important consequences than ours would. This doesn't mean that we can forget about using good judgment or that since our boss is going to check everything we do anyway, we don't need to worry about doing it right. It means just the opposite. It means that the better judgment we use and the better job we do, the better job the boss can do. We help our boss handle the bigger, broader problems with better judgment because we have bought him or her a little more time (now that our boss doesn't have to worry about our mistakes and poor judgment). And the better our boss does, the better the final results will be for us. Even if we don't get the credit for a job well done, we are still in the *group* that got the good results, and it will pay off in the long run.

BOSSES HAVE FEELINGS, TOO

Most of our supervisory training will tell us that our people have feelings, anxieties, problems, needs, etc.—a fact we all readily acknowledge. But sometimes the implication is that we as the boss *don't* have any feelings or problems, or at least that we aren't supposed to let them show. Actually, no one argues that bosses don't have problems, and most agree that we need to be careful about letting these problems affect our behavior. Even so, we have to admit that they *do* show sometimes. We can't help it, perhaps. But wait—if we admit that we have feelings that show sometimes, shouldn't we admit, too, that our boss must also have problems and feelings that may show in his or her behavior from time to time? As a matter of fact, our boss has just about every problem and anxiety that we might have: worries about home, family, money, chances for promotion, relationships with others on the same level, and whether or not he or she is being a good boss. And of course, like us, our boss is concerned about the relationship with his or her own boss. We're kidding ourselves if we think we have a monopoly on problems, either personal or office.

We tend to forget that the boss has a boss, too. As much as we'd like to think that our boss always worries about us first, we'd be more honest to admit that *we don't even do that for our people.* When the going gets rough around the office or shop, we can't help but think, "How's this going to affect *me*?" We don't start to worry about those under us until after we've answered that question. So it is with most bosses, including our own, most likely. But that's all right, as long as we recognize that our boss is only acting human and is reacting about the same way we would under similar circumstances. That's no excuse for our boss to treat his or her people wrongly in such situations, but at least we recognize the reason for the behavior and so may know how to act in response.

THE BOSS IS ONE STEP REMOVED

One problem that confronts our boss is that of being one step removed from the job and activity of our people, just as we're one step removed from our boss's boss. This means there's a chance our boss is not getting a full view of the situation, just as we may not be seeing things from the same angle as someone up the line. The chances are pretty good that our boss won't see things the same way we see them, especially when it comes to our people and their work. Our boss must see all of this through the information we provide and from personal observation, then relate it to the bigger organizational picture he or she is looking at. Also, our boss has certain charges from his or her boss, certain objectives that he or she has set, and other people to worry about besides us and our people—all of which cause our boss to see things quite differently from the way we do. So there shouldn't be any great mystery if our boss's interpretation of these things differs from ours.

Take the matter of appraising our people. Being one step removed, our boss may fail to see the potential we see in some of our people. Our boss may judge them on past performance and fail to realize how well they are developing. Since we see our people every day, we have a much better chance to observe their development and how much better they handle responsibility than they did a few weeks ago. Our boss's opinion of the person we have in mind may be based on past performance that created an unfavorable impression, so our boss can't believe that there has been a change. By the same token, our boss may find it hard to believe that a person isn't performing as well as he or she should be. We may have an employee who was rated as satisfactory at one time but for some reason is just not performing up to the standard we expect. Our boss may be dubious about our evaluation because the previous record doesn't bear us out. To make matters worse, since our boss has less information than we have, he or she may form opinions based on incorrect information or even emotional reasons. He or she may base an opinion on something overheard on the elevator or something heard about the employee through someone else. While such information is not reliable, it may be all that our boss has, especially if we have failed to keep him or her properly informed. We all form opinions based on the information we have to work with—the boss is no exception.

WE ARE ONE STEP REMOVED, TOO

The boss isn't the only one who is apt to form opinions on limited amounts of information. We, too, are often guilty. We must be careful not to pass judgment on policies too quickly, before getting the whole story. Policies that are set one or more steps above our boss will likely lose some of their meaning and reason for existence by the time they get to us. Not only that, but the boss sees them in relation to his or her job and subordinates; we see them in relation to *our* job and subordinates. Each of us has a particular window to look out of, so each sees something a little different from what the other sees.

Policies that are not fully explained may appear unreasonable. When we fail to get the whole picture, we may say that the organization is making bad decisions. If we don't know all the facts, we just don't see things as we should. Does this mean that the boss ought to tell us everything he or she knows and the reasoning behind every decision that is made? Of course not, although we often act as though we expect it. At some point we need to develop enough confidence in the boss and the organization to realize that they are making decisions on the basis of more and better information than we have. If we still have some doubts, then we should try to find out more about the reasons behind what is happening. This is the time to *request* the information, though, not *demand* it. The boss is obligated to help us as much as possible, but not to spend all his or her time trying to justify everything the organization does. We ought to realize that we wouldn't want our people using up our time in this manner. We don't mind explaining; in fact, we should make an effort to tell as much as we can about the rationale behind policies. But this doesn't mean that the only way to motivate our employees is to spend most of our time defending and justifying the organization's policies.

One problem we have as a new supervisor is that we are sort of starting from scratch in finding out just what the organization's goals really are. Because we are new, we naturally are missing quite a bit of background on why the organization does certain things in certain ways. This will work a hardship on us because we may find we are going off in the wrong direction without even realizing it, then have to reverse ourselves and perhaps lose face in doing so. There aren't many orientation programs that will bring us up to date on all the things we need to know about the background of the group, the department, and the organization as a whole—so we must hit the ground running in order to catch up. We can't just sit back and say, "Well, now that I'm a supervisor, it's up to the organization to train me in all the things I need to know." When we accepted the job as supervisor, we also accepted the responsibility for a large amount of our own development, including finding out about how and why things are run the way they are. The task is a difficult one, but it must be accomplished if we are to make a success of the new job.

MAKING THE BOSS'S JOB EASIER

One thing we can get into the habit of doing as a new supervisor is making the boss's job easier by being a good subordinate. How do we do it? It is a lot easier than we think. All we have to do is imagine that we work for ourselves, then ask, "What kind of employee would I like to have working for me?" The answer to that question gives us a standard to work and live by as a subordinate. Let's look at some of the qualities most of us would really like to see in our employees. From this list we can make up our minds what we now have going for us and what improvements we should make.

- *Supportive.*   We talk a lot about loyalty, but all we're really saying is that we want the people who work for us to be supportive both of the organization and of us as we try to carry out the organization's policies and procedures. We should be just as supportive of our boss. The boss is passing down policies that he or she probably didn't set and maybe didn't even have much say in. Our first reaction should be, "How can I see that the boss gets these policies carried out?" It isn't that the boss is always right; it's that we want what's best for the organization, and as long as we work there we should try to support it. That usually means doing as well as we can what the boss asks us to do. Our loyalty, then, is to the organization first, the boss second, our own people third.

- *Positive.*   We all like to have positive people around us, especially working for us. Our boss is no different. We should maintain the position that what the boss says is right until it is proved wrong. We should react first in a positive way, assuming that what we are asked to do and what we are asked to tell our people make sense. We assume that our boss knows what he or she is doing, even if on the surface it doesn't appear so. We like our people to assume that we have reasons for what we're doing; our boss deserves the same consideration.

- *Demonstrates Good Work Habits.*   If we don't like it when people come in late, leave early, take too long for breaks, or stay out too long at lunchtime, there's a good chance our boss feels the same way. So we take a good look at our work habits and try to become what we want our people to be. There's more to it than just being on time. There's also the matter of being neat—avoiding sloppy desks, untidy working places, and bad work habits.

- *Willing and Eager to Learn.*   Imagine the employee who comes to us whenever he or she doesn't understand something or when he or she wants training on some new development in the workplace. Think how nice it is when one of our people shows a willingness to spend time learning something new, even if it isn't an immediate part of the assigned job. Thinking about this should cause us to want to learn as much as we can about the job, even before the boss asks us to. We should be on the doorstep waiting eagerly to learn a new process—with the positive attitude that this new thing is good for the organization and we're glad it's happening!

• *Completes Staff Work.* When we assign people tasks, we expect them to be done properly. We also expect them to be done thoroughly and on time. We don't like to be given unfinished or partially completed work. We like what is often called completed staff work. This simply means that the employees have gone as far as they can with the assignment. They have done everything we've asked them to do, and as far as they're concerned, what we've gotten from them is reliable and finished. So let's do the same for our boss. When we receive an assignment, let's determine that when we bring it back, it will be done as nearly the way the boss wants it as we can make it and that it will be as nearly complete as we can make it.

• *Cooperates with Others.* There is no place in any organization for bickering and infighting, yet we still see it. We don't like it, but we sometimes engage in it. Without thinking about it very much, we find ourselves arguing with our coworkers, having small guerrilla wars, being jealous over petty things, taking rumors for facts then fighting with people about them, and cutting people down when they get a little credit we would have liked. We do all of this without realizing that if we don't like it in our people, it's certain that our boss doesn't like it in us, either. We need to be sure that we avoid being that way, so our boss doesn't have to referee *our* battles.

• *Creative.* If we're good supervisors, we like people around us who think for themselves. We admire people who are creative and use their initiative to come up with better ways of doing things but don't get their feelings hurt if we don't agree with their every idea. Some would have us believe that there is a better way of doing everything, but that doesn't mean that everything has to be done differently. We should always be looking for ways of improving the job and should give our boss the benefit of our thinking. At the same time, we should realize that the boss cannot and will not accept every idea we have. Though pride in our ideas is admirable, that pride shouldn't get in the way of our job. We can't afford to get our feelings hurt every time the boss turns down a "good" idea. Maybe we should just determine to come up with a better one the next time.

- *Nonmoody.* As we've just said, there is no place in any organization for people to get their feelings hurt over small things, but it happens anyway. We are all guilty. We really get upset when our people take things personally and imagine that we're trying to hurt them, make fun of them, or belittle them. Yet we may turn right around and commit the same crime with our boss. We get upset because the boss gives a good assignment to another supervisor; we pout because somebody got a little credit for doing something we feel was our job to do; we worry when somebody gets recognition for a job we did or contributed to. Instead of discussing our problems openly, we let them smolder. We make problems bigger than they really are, then sit around and let them grow into a full-blown fire. We need to remember that our boss has enough to worry about without our adding to his or her problems with things that are more matters of personal feelings than significant issues, more imagined than real.

Altogether, we're saying that the best way to become a good employee of our boss is to think about how we'd like our employees to act toward us. We need to remember that our boss has the same anxieties, the same hang-ups, the same kinds of problems on and off the job as we do. Our boss also has bigger areas of responsibilities and more problems of deeper consequences. He or she certainly doesn't need *us* as an additional problem!

DEALING WITH BAD BOSSES

What do we do if we don't have a very good boss? Suppose our boss is poorly organized or a poor delegator or not very good at communicating? What if we have a boss who is unjust or unfair or insensitive or who plays politics with our work? These are all pretty bad things to have to deal with. How can we straighten out a bad boss? The truth is, *we don't*. That's not really our job. It's the organization's job—specifically, the job of our boss's boss. We'll have our hands full trying to get our own job done and get our people to do their work without taking on the problems of straightening out someone a level above us.

Certainly our job will be harder because of these things. We won't be able to accomplish as much, and we'll have some motivation problems. As we saw in the preceding chapter, we still have to protect the organization and our boss. Our boss is a part of the same management team as we are. We will need to defend our people and protect them from our boss, perhaps, but not at the expense of talking openly about our boss to our people.

There is another side to this. While we're seeing all the faults in our boss, we have to face the fact that our people just might have some of the same feelings about us! The whole purpose of this book is to make us better because we are new and have a lot to learn. What are our people supposed to do while we're learning (and practicing) on them? They're going to have to endure some bad times while we get better. They're going to have to put up with what appear to be unfairness and poor judgment and bad time management on our part, just because we're new and have a lot to learn. It might be a good time for us to develop some tolerance toward our boss, since we're asking for the same tolerance from our people.

CONCLUSION

As a new supervisor, we must develop the proper attitude toward our boss and his or her job. We must recognize that our boss has to worry not only about us and our job but also about the others working for him or her. At the same time, our boss is human and will have many of the same problems and anxieties that we have, and they may show on the job. Our boss also works for someone else and so is likely to worry some about his or her own position in the organization. And since our boss is one step removed from our people and their work, he or she gets much less information about our people than we do, and so may reach different or even wrong conclusions about which of our people are good and which are doing well on the job. At the same time, we are one step removed from our boss's supervisors, so we may get the wrong impressions about the policies and decisions that are made at their level. We can't expect our boss to explain every detail and every reason for every act, so we must develop confidence in those who make the policies and question only those things we need to know more about in order to explain them to our people. Finally, we will find it hard to learn all that we need to know about the background of the organization and its people when we first make supervisor. While the organization should provide as much training as possible, the responsibility is still ours to develop as much as we can. Because there is so much to be learned and not much time in which to learn it, a good relationship with our boss will go a long way toward building mutual confidence to sustain us across the gaps in our knowledge.

EXERCISES

1. Small-group activity: Break the group into several small groups and have them discuss and list ways in which supervisors cause their bosses problems, without even realizing it sometimes. Don't think only in terms of one person working for another; rather, think in terms of a first-line supervisor working for the next level of supervision. This information should then be shared with the entire group, with a discussion of how these problems can be avoided.

2. Small-group activity: In the same small groups, make a list of ways in which the next level of supervision makes problems for the first line of supervision, without realizing it. Again, discuss ways in which these problems could be overcome.

3. Group discussion: Come up with a list of problems that the second level of supervision has—in being the boss—that the first line of supervision does not have. Remember, the second level of supervision has problems that are *people* problems, too. In many ways there are similarities, but in some ways there are differences. Don't list only the people problems,

though; think in terms of organizational problems, too. These should be recorded and kept for further discussion.

4. Small-group activity: Have small groups discuss some of those problems discovered in exercise 3, with the idea of finding ways in which the first level could make life easier for the next level. What could people do at the first level to ease some of the problems listed here?

5. Group discussion: Communicating up and down the line in any organization is always a problem. The first level of supervision is at the bottom of the ladder as far as management is concerned and thus will often be the last to get information about policy, reorganization, problems, and goals. The group should generate a list of things that are likely not to be communicated to the first line of supervision until after they've been implemented—and maybe not until they've begun to affect the organization. The idea is to look for things that happen or are decided upon that actually go into effect before the lowest level of supervision finds out about it in the *normal* operation of the business. For example, the budget is set, promotions are made, there is a reorganization at the top level. List these things for later discussion.

6. Half-group activity: Divide the group into two subgroups. Have one half of the group debate the other on each of the items identified in exercise 5, with one side taking the position that there is no reason for sharing this information with the first-line people before going ahead, and the other taking the position that it is essential that first-line people be aware of proposed changes or other decisions before they are implemented.

Chapter 4

SUPERVISORS' RELATIONS WITH THEIR COORDINATES

GROWING UP IS ESSENTIAL

It sometimes surprises new supervisors that there is so much bickering and infighting going on among the other supervisors—their coordinates. If we're smart, we'll react by saying to ourselves, "Why don't they grow up?" That's the real problem. The ability to get along in a work situation where everyone has the same general working conditions, the same boss, and the same organizational policies to work with is a measure of our maturity. It all seems pretty ridiculous, because most of us would rather work in a situation where everyone got along with everyone else, where everyone did his or her job and nobody complained about anything. But that's a dream world that simply doesn't exist. Do we just give in, then, and prepare for battle?

Not if we want to get our job done and help the organization toward its goals. The important thing is that all of our ultimate goals are the same (or should be). We want the organization to prosper, goals to be met, more money to be made available (through our efficient use of what we have) so that there will be raises and promotions. The problem is that while we may have the same long-range goals, the short-range ones seem to differ—even to be opposed to one another. Each supervisor is assigned a task, people to do that task, money to carry out the job, etc. Each task seems different in its purpose and goals. So conflict soon arises. We each become intent on reaching *our* goal with *our* money and *our* people. We all have our own problems to solve and our own means of solving them. The conflict arises when we get so intent on our *own* problems that we lose sight of the organization's goals and problems. We resent anyone who seems to get in our way while we are striving to get where the organization wants us to go. We forget that the organization wants us to get there *together* with the other supervisors, not with their bodies strewn out behind us!

GET THE JOB DONE, BUT . . .

Sooner or later, someone will emerge as the leader of a "Let's-get-along" movement. Why shouldn't we be that leader? We can do our part in seeing that things run smoothly and still get the job done. We really don't have many choices in our relationships with our coordinates. We can get our job done by walking all over them, caring little for how they look or feel. Or we can get our job done by issuing edicts such as "Forget about them. Let's get the job done"; in other words, we can just ignore the supervisors we are supposed to be working with. Or, finally, we can get the job done through a cooperative effort, taking everything into consideration. When we think about how ridiculous it is to spend our time bickering, it's easy to see that the last alternative is the only practical one. To get the job done over the dead bodies of the ones we should be working with will produce some ghosts that can haunt us pretty badly. We may think we've done our job well, but, unfortunately, most people resent being walked over and can get vindictive in a hurry. And when they hit back, it's usually with a much harder blow than we gave them in the first place.

Ignoring the others is sometimes very tempting. "If they don't want to cooperate, just let them go their way. I'll go mine." It seems so simple, but it rarely works. All it takes is for the boss to say, "Did you check this out with George?" or "Will this fit into the time slot with Helen's project?" Now we've got problems. We've either got to admit that we failed to check it out, or try to alibi ("a lie by I"), or go back and take the chance of having to do much of our job over and this time *having* to work with those whom we've deliberately ignored.

All of this talk about cooperating sounds fine, but it really isn't that easy. There are some built-in traps, for instance. We want our people to be loyal. We want them to respect us as their leader. We would like to hear them say that they work for the best group in the organization. That's great—or is it? Loyalty is fine, but it can also work against us. People often find it easier to be loyal to a small group than to a large organization, so they develop strong feelings about the work group, even refusing promotions to other groups or being disgruntled when they are moved somewhere for the betterment of the organization. This means their loyalty really isn't to the organization but to a supervisor or a group of fellow workers. This isn't necessarily bad; it just becomes bad when it causes the organization's overall goals to suffer. When our people begin to compete with other groups to the extent that there are hard feelings or one group takes advantage of another, then it is bad.

Another problem is that resentment builds among supervisors, which is often the beginning of jealousy. We don't like to admit that we are jealous, but let the boss spend too much time with some of our coordinates and we begin to wonder if the boss likes them or their work better than ours. Again we see the immaturity coming out. Lack of confidence will produce the same results. We may feel that we can't really compete on the performance level, so we start to look for other things to make up the difference in our relationship with the boss. We may start a whispering campaign against a fellow supervisor; we may resort to infighting; we may even find ways of telling the boss that the other supervisors have some weaknesses. We may tell the boss about foul-ups that he or she might have missed if we hadn't brought them up. Of course, the boss shouldn't think better of us for doing such a thing, but even if he or she does, we have probably weakened our position in the organization. One of these days we are going to find ourselves needing some help from someone we reported to the boss or hoping that the boss doesn't find out about a mess we've made and may be desperately trying to get straightened out. At that time, we may look longingly for a friend and not find one!

MAKE IT WORK

How do we get the job done? How do we get the cooperation needed to get along and get the work out at the same time? Perhaps the one word that comes closest to being the key is *communication*. The old saying "We're usually down on what we're not up on" is just as true here as anywhere else. We need to know what's going on in the other groups, and it's worth our time to find out. We'll appreciate our fellow workers' jobs a lot more if we know something about their problems and the reasons for what they're doing. And the same is true about their appreciating what we're trying to do—they need to know where we're trying to go, how we plan to get there, and whom we have working to get us there.

We need to anticipate possible conflicts and problems before they have gone too far to be stopped. We need to get into the habit of giving out as much information as possible to those with whom we work. We should learn to *communicate*. When we say to someone, "But I told you . . . ," we're actually admitting that we don't know very much about communicating. Telling rarely is communicating. One good habit to get into is to write memos and notes to our colleagues, letting them know of projects we are working on that might need their help or might either complement theirs or conflict in some way. The obvious result is that they will be in a better position to help us if they know what we're doing. Equally important, if they know something of what we're doing, they will be better able to answer questions that arise from their subordinates about our work.

Another simple habit to get into is checking with our coordinates when there is something we don't understand about their job. If one of their employees is at cross-purposes with one of ours, rather than jumping down someone's throat, we should go calmly to get some facts. We aren't obligated to start a fight whenever one of our people has a problem with someone outside the group. That's building the wrong kind of loyalty. Our people may think we're great for doing it, but we aren't really helping them, ourselves, or the situation by storming around from office to office telling people off. And remember, we shouldn't even pretend that we're "going to get this straightened out once and for all," implying that we will jump on somebody about this. That, too, builds the wrong kind of loyalty. In the long run, our people will respect us more if we provide a smooth working environment for them and fairly harmonious relations with the others with whom they must associate.

AVOID LEARNING THE WRONG THING

One more problem we have to deal with as a new supervisor is what we do around those people who have been in the organization for a long time and for one reason or another have grown bitter. There is a sort of bitterness syndrome that affects some people. They don't like certain policies that affect them; they don't like the way promotions are handled; they don't like the way their raises have been coming or the amount; they feel they should be higher in the organization or should be consulted more or should be making more money. Perhaps even worse, they may see us as a threat to their own security. They may feel that the new people have a better chance than they do, so they resent us and make life a little hard for us. Most of us can handle that because we see through it easily enough. It's the same problem we faced in school when we made better grades than a classmate who had been considered the better student for a long time or when we outran an older or usually faster person in a race for some reason on one occasion. The people who will give us the most trouble are those who do know their jobs and who are respected for their knowledge; one of them may even be the person we've been assigned to, to learn the ropes. When this person has a tainted streak or is bitter, it affects us a lot more.

What can we do about such a situation? To start off, the best thing to do is to *ignore it*. Certainly we shouldn't try to correct these people or try any mind changing. To begin with, we're going to lose the argument on the basis of experience and knowledge alone. These people will know more arguments and more ways to counter ours than we'll ever be able to handle. So we just leave that idea alone. We could try to present another side of the picture as we see it or as we've been treated, but this approach has the same problem. In showing us where we've misinterpreted the data, they may even "convert" us to their way of thinking. In the beginning, the best thing for us to do is simply listen and *not respond*.

Later, as we get more confidence or more facts, we might try to deal with the people who are like this—but at first, let them alone. There is always the possibility that they're right, but in the beginning we really can't tell, so saying nothing will serve us better than anything else we might do. Sooner or later we've got to stand on our own feet. We've got to come to our own conclusions about the organization, about the boss, about our particular work group, and about the specific job we're working on. The sooner we do it, the better, but we ought to make sure that it's our own thinking we're doing, not that of the older and "wiser" heads around us. Just as they have more information, they also have more biases. At least we ought to wait until we've developed our own biases before we become bitter or start to disapprove of the way the organization is run.

Another thing we're going to have to do someday is develop our own standard of behavior. We may not realize it, but at first we really don't have a standard. We act like the people around us; we ask them how we should feel about things, how we should act, and even what kind of action is preferable. At some point we need to ask ourselves, "Is this really me, or am I still just parroting what I've heard?" We need to decide for ourselves how we feel about the boss, the organization, etc., and our decision ought to be based on as much fact and experience as possible. Above all, *it ought to be our own*.

BUILD A LATERAL TEAM

Team building is more than a catchy phrase. Team building implies that everyone is playing on the same side, against the same obstacles. Everyone wants everyone else to win because everyone is on the same team. When we see the infighting that goes on or the jealousy or the politics, we wonder what would happen if all this energy went into production or were directed against the competition. Good team building is based on several things. First and foremost is *trust*. Trust is more than just believing in somebody's intentions or motives, though it includes this. It is building respect as a result of demonstrating that trust is justified. *Trust comes from history!* There have to be some events that justify the trust. For a new supervisor, there is no history to go on, either way. Our coordinates have no history of dealing with us, and we have no history of dealing with them. From the beginning, we have to deal ethically with our peers; we have to show that our word is our bond. We have to let them know that we have a feeling of mutual interest in getting the job done. If a sacrifice on our part—giving up some time or some money in the budget or lending some people—will get the job done better, then we don't play games; we do our part.

Ultimately, we'll have to build a team including our own workers. That will be one team, but the larger team is all the people with whom we interface. We can start helping build our own team by letting them know that our style is *cooperation*, not competition. We start early by seeing that our people respect the jobs and the goals of others and offer help to meet those goals. All of this sounds easier than it really is. The philosophy is simple; the implementation is difficult. We have one advantage: *we don't have any history*. That can work for us as well as against us. We haven't made any enemies; we don't have any sacred cows to worry about. We haven't crossed anyone or stepped on any toes. Others before us may have, and we'll have to live with some of that, but we can come in with a relatively clean slate—and write our own history of cooperation.

CONCLUSION

Our ability to get along with the people we work with is one test of our maturity. After all, we're all working for the same organization with the same long-range goals. The advantages of having a peaceful environment to work in are obvious. We need to be careful in building loyalties, to see that they are built around the organization as a whole, rather than just around us or our small group. When we work with others under the same boss, we need to realize that in the long run, cooperation is the key to getting the job done satisfactorily. Cutting throats or ignoring others in our work and planning may seem the quickest way, but it is far from the surest way. The best way is to learn to communicate—not by telling, but by being sure that our fellow workers get a memo or a note from us letting them in on what we're doing and suggesting ways in which getting together might help both of us. These aren't the only times we need to communicate with them, of course. We need to talk to them about possible conflicts or problems that arise among our subordinates. But getting together should be pleasant, not an effort to build our prestige among our own people. They may think we're great, but that probably won't help the organization in the long run. What's most likely to help is for us to develop a good working relationship with our coordinates so that the situation will be conducive to productive work.

EXERCISES

1. Group discussion: In almost any organization, there is competition among the various groups working for the same department head or even for the same boss. Come up with a list of reasons why this happens in an organization and why it seems to be common in any type of work area. Record this list for discussion in the next two exercises.

2. Group discussion: Using the group's findings from exercise 1, come up with a group consensus as to whether the effect of this competitiveness is good or bad. In other words, if it did not exist, would the organization be better off or worse off?

3. Individual assignment: Let each person look at the list and think of ways in which he or she could avoid having each one of the instances of competition arise in his or her sphere of influence. This is a long assignment, and each person should consider each item. When all have, the group should discuss each item to find the simplest way to avoid the competition in cases in which the members feel the competition should be eliminated.

4. Subgroup activity: In small groups, come up with a policy statement that could be put into effect in the organization to deal with the problem of poor communication. This ought to

be explicit enough to describe what any supervisor should do and what he or she should tell subordinates. (This is a *team-building* exercise and very important. Each person should think in terms of *what* he or she would like to know, *when* he or she should know it, and how often there should be a *review process* for looking at communication. The statement should also deal with the accountability for the communications effort—that is, who should be responsible for seeing that the communications effort is made and what the consequences should be for failure to do it.)

Chapter 5

MONITORING AND MANAGING STRESS

The job of supervising was difficult even years ago, when the major worry was how to get the job done. The workforce was reasonably stable and most workers were willing to accept poor, unskilled, autocratic supervision. In today's workplace things are different and more difficult. The workforce is more mobile and less willing to accept poor supervision. Regulations have been imposed on hiring, firing, and treatment (and mistreatment) of employees, and specific organizations monitor such factors as safety, discrimination, harassment, and so on. Yet, the new supervisor still has the responsibility for getting the job done. Although it is a difficult task for anyone, getting the job done in today's workplace is especially hard for the new supervisor. Just as production schedules and budget restrictions apply from the first day as a new supervisor, so do all the safety and other regulations. *It is clear that with all these changes stress has become much greater.*

This chapter deals more with recognizing its causes and learning to cope with stress than with eliminating it altogether. It describes the obvious causes of stress and tries to overcome the idea that "real people don't have stress!" This is the one chapter that takes the supervisor outside the workplace to illustrate the catch-22 that job stress causes home stress, which causes job stress, and so on. It presents everyday cases and everyday solutions, with an emphasis on monitoring as well as managing stress.

DEFINITION OF STRESS

A complex definition of stress goes something like "the reaction to change: biologically, physiologically, and psychologically." Perhaps a more usable definition is simply "how we react to things that put pressure on us." If we get in the car to go to work and the car doesn't start because the battery is dead, we are in a stressful situation. If we have an important meeting with the boss, which is now in jeopardy, there is more stress. If we're supposed to pick up others for this same meeting and can't get in touch with them, there is even more stress. If we've recently paid a good sum of money to replace our old, undependable car with this new car, more stress. If a member of our family left the headlights on overnight, which ran the battery down, more stress. If, when we finally get to work, we find our parking place has been taken by an unknown person, more stress. By this time we've worked up a good case for considerable stress.

Although this scenario is more an illustration of the causes of stress than a definition of it, we can all recognize from this extreme example both the cause and the feeling of stress. As with pain, we don't have to have an official definition of stress to know what it is! Our job in this chapter is to examine stress from several standpoints, such as:

- Cause of stress
- Results of stress
- Recognizing stress
- Predicting stress
- Monitoring stress
- Easing stress
- Coping with stress

STRESS IS ALL-INVASIVE

Although we use the skills presented in this book, such as motivation and communication, outside the job nothing else discussed here affects our lives as stress does. It is impossible to separate job stress from home stress or driving stress or financial stress or personal relationships that cause stress. If we have a stressful day at the office, we tend to take it home with us, and problems arise. If we have a stressful situation at home, we tend to bring it to work with us. If we have an argument at the bank at lunchtime, our employees may suffer from that stress in the afternoon. By the same token, if we resolve outside-the-job stress, we often relieve job stress considerably.

In the chapter on counseling we point out that the supervisor often has to deal with employees' family problems that cause jobs to suffer. Employees may come to work late, be irritable, or even be careless on the job. Although as a supervisor we aren't in the counseling business, nor are we trained to be counselors, nonetheless someone has to talk with the unsatisfactory employee. It's easy enough to say, "You have to quit bringing your family problems to work," but that's like saying, "You'll have to leave your left foot at home!" The same thing works in reverse. People who work long hours find their stress building and often see that stress increasing when they get home—because they haven't been home. They have been neglecting children, spouse, appliances that need repairs, lawns that need mowing, or PTA meetings. Because they haven't learned to anticipate and manage the stress, they find themselves in a downward spiral. Their job suffers and their family relationships suffer, which cause more stress, and so on down into the abyss. The point of all of this is to show that we can't ignore outside stress and talk only about things that happen at work. Of course, the things that help us anticipate, manage, and cope with stress outside the job work equally well on the job. We'll see what those things are in this chapter.

IS STRESS A PROBLEM FOR SUPERVISORS?

Let's try this little "Agree–Disagree" quiz:

Real (macho) people don't have stress. Agree_____
                                         Disagree_____

Does a world-class tennis player experience stress right before a championship match? Are the quarterbacks of the two teams playing in the Superbowl under any stress? Does a champion sprinter feel any stress right before the final heat of the one-hundred-meter race in the Olympics? Now ask ourselves—new supervisors—as we go in to hold that first meeting of the whole department, with our boss present, if there is any stress. Ask ourselves, when the department is running behind schedule on an order that will be canceled if it isn't out today and the production line is down because of a burned-out generator, if there is any stress.

Some people feel admitting to stress is a sign that they can't handle their jobs. These same people often solve their problems by taking things into their own hands. They storm around, scream at workers, push people out of the way so they can get in and do the work themselves. Everyone walks around on eggshells trying to keep out of the way of these supervisors. This is the result of stress, caused by unforeseen circumstances over which people have some, but not total, control. The process used by these people to handle stress seemingly solves the problem but does not relieve the stress—of the supervisor or of the people under him or her. The point of all of this is that although some people feel it is a weakness to admit that they have any stress, stress is a part of life. It is not always bad, and it is not always good, but it is always there.

Stress can be a serious problem. It affects our lives in many ways: at home, at work, even getting to work on the highway. ("Road rage" is a new expression in our vocabulary, referring to how people deal with traffic delays or actions of others that interfere with them on the highways.) Remember, "It's how we react to the stress that is the problem, not the stress itself." When we come on the job as a new supervisor, that very fact is stressful. A new job—even if it is a lateral move—causes stress. Moving from a nonsupervisory job to supervising others can be the most stressful.

In our previous job, our evaluations were based on how well we did the job itself. Now our success is measured on how well we can get others to do the job—the same job we could do so well before we were promoted! To make matters worse, the people on whom our success depends may be the same ones we ate lunch with every day last month, went fishing with last weekend, and bad-mouthed the boss with during breaks for the last year.

There's more to it, though, than just being a new supervisor. We don't yet have the supervisory skills to get the job done through others, yet the job has to get done. And not just the first day or the first week, but next week and next month too. We can't learn the necessary skills that quickly, so stress builds. The more we do wrong—as a supervisor—the more our people are less likely to help out, hence we're in more of a bind. More stress. The chances are we're not very good at this point at handling stress, so we begin to react improperly (like the supervisor we described earlier). Our reactions make things worse, and more stress builds. It becomes a downward spiral, if we're not careful.

In all the examples we've used, we've seen the results of stress, the signs that stress is taking its toll. One key to managing stress is to recognize its symptoms before the downward spiral sets in. If we can learn to predict a stress-producing situation, even if we can't eliminate it, we may be able to diminish our harmful reaction to it. If we can reduce our improper reaction to the stress, we automatically reduce the negative consequences of that reaction.

EFFECTS OF STRESS

Next we'll look at the effects of stress on our minds and bodies. Then we'll begin to examine some solutions to the stress problem. Without quoting studies or extensive statistics, we can make the following statements about the effects of stress:

- Every year, millions of people experience heart disease, heart attacks, high blood pressure, ulcers, or become alcoholics.

- Every year, billions of prescriptions are written for tran-quilizers, amphetamines, and barbiturates.

- Every year, billions of dollars are spent because of premature death, alcoholism, absenteeism, and tardiness of employees.

- Every year, up to 90 percent of illnesses are estimated to be psychologically related.

These are frightening facts, which we recognize as true, for even if we aren't directly affected, we know people who are. We've had friends and acquaintances who have had serious heart problems, directly related to their job stress. We've seen people develop ulcers from stress and could have predicted it would happen to them. Stress affects our body in a manner to protect us. The blood flows to the surface, the adrenaline level rises, body temperature increases, and the body prepares for battle. Eyesight improves, and hearing becomes more acute. All these physiological changes give our muscles great strength. That's fantastic—when we're trying to lift a heavy weight off someone or get a person out of a burning building fast.

Suppose There's No Battle

What happens when there's no real battle that needs all this readiness? What if, for instance, our boss throws a report on our desk, mistakenly thinking it's ours, and let's us know in no uncertain terms, in front of everyone else, that we did a lousy job? If we overreact to this false accusation with screaming, anger, even threatening fisticuffs, our body has risen to the occasion. If we make accusatory statements about our boss, including counter-remarks of ignorance, we are accelerating the deteriorating situation toward chaos. But what have we accomplished? There was really no war—just a skirmish that could have been avoided with some calm words. Of such are ulcers made and heart attacks born. Our body hasn't really vented itself of the stress; in fact, the stress will stay with us for some time, renewed whenever we see our boss. Chances are that we'll take it out on some unsuspecting driver on the highway on the way home or on pets, children, or spouse once we get there.

To Vent or Not to Vent?

Some see venting as a solution to their stress problem. "I feel so good when I've told that person off!" Yet the situation will still be there in one form or another. If we unload on someone at work, we'll have to live with our remarks when we deal with that person from day to day. Taking the stress home presents the same diffi-culty. Sooner or later, we'll need to apologize and make it right. In the meantime we are not helping our mental state any. When we let our actions get out of hand because of our feelings, our judg-ment suffers, we make bad decisions, we become preoccupied, and we lose a degree of our reasoning. If we get angry and upset because someone has cut in front of us in the cafeteria line, start to grumble and make loud, snide remarks to our friends, and try to figure out how to get even, we're enlarging the problem and making our friends uncomfortable. We certainly aren't doing much to aid our digestion at the meal!

Where Does the Solution Lie?

Beyond a doubt, the solution lies within us. Only we can decide how bad the stress is going to be, how long it will last, and what actions we will take as a result of the stress. This means we have to do several things that are difficult to do, and that will take some willpower. First, we have to overcome the inclination to get even. Harder yet, we have to overcome it while we're in the middle of the cause of the feelings. We have to go against ever fiber of our being that's saying, "Get 'em, get 'em, get 'em!" This is the time to call on the "take-a-deep-breath" solution. Our body—mental and physical—needs time, time to calm down and to become rational again (or to stay rational). Our mind needs time to get back to a degree of normalcy, free of the anger that causes mental blindness. We'll deal with this later on.

HOME STRESS VERSUS WORK STRESS

We saw earlier that stress is nonselective. It invades all facets of our life. How are home stress and work stress related? There are many similarities and some pointed differences between the two. Although the situations are different, the circumstances are similar. At home, perhaps the car won't start; this is the same circumstance as the line's being shut down. In either case, we can't reach our objective because something over which we don't have full control is in the way. We may accept an invitation from the boss for a dinner meeting with the staff, only to find out when we call home that there's a surprise for our daughter scheduled for the same night. At first glance this appears to us to be a lose–lose situation. We will have to live with whatever action we take, and whatever we do, we are likely to experience stress. Reacting incorrectly to either circumstance can cause problems. Yet there are solutions that don't entail lasting casualties.

There are some differences between the two stresses that have to be taken into consideration. First, we can have some pretty pointed differences in our inner feelings about home and work. If we're already at odds with our home relationships, our reaction to the stress is going to be much more severe than it might be if we had a comfortable relationship. The same is true with the work environment. Yet *work* is different from *home*, and we have different emotions about each. Although we spend about the same amount of time at each place, our parent-child and spouse-spouse relationships are most often much deeper than are our peer-peer or boss-subordinate relationships. There are also distinct external influences at home and at work. Our neighbors, in-laws, and friends affect us differently than do our fellow workers. Although our commitment to both home and work is strong, it is a different kind of commitment. We don't get promoted at home; we do at work. We don't get fired at home; we do at work. We don't get transferred at home; we do at work. Conversely, we don't get affection and physical and emotional satisfaction at work; we do at home. We don't project ourselves into another's Little League successes and failures at work; we do at home. We don't have financial responsibility for our own money at work; we do at home. We don't have responsibility for mowing the grass at work; we do at home. The list goes on, underlining the importance of knowing ourselves and our commitments and influences as we deal with our stress. Most important, these examples *point out the need for us to establish our priorities with clarity!*

Can We Separate Home and Work Stresses?

Is it possible to identify a stress as either a home stress or a work stress? In major situations we can, but in most situations, it's not that easy. Our home stresses may cause us to create stress at work and vice versa. When our boss screams and threatens to fire us, and we go home and kick the dog, we create a new stress (for us and for the dog). We need to begin to think of how we are reacting to stress now and to change those things in our actions that are adding to the stress or prolonging it.

One of the offshoots of stress is *moodiness*. If we've had a bad morning at home, we may come to work in a bad mood. This is unfair to the organization, and certainly unfair to our subordinates. Because of our bad morning our workers can't get their job done; they dread talking to us in the mood we're in. They suffer, the organization suffers, and in the long run we suffer the most. Any time an action on our part reduces the level of communication, serious damage has been done to the success of our work arrangement. The reverse is true as well. If we miss a shipment, lose a customer, lose a valuable employee, or have a run-in with our boss, we may take it out on our family, resulting in serious damage to our home relationships.

It doesn't have to be this way. We should determine to resolve the conflicts or problems or whatever causes the stress where it occurs. We may have to put the issue on hold for a few hours or even for a day or two. If so, we should spend the time thinking of solutions, not reveling in stress-induced depression. Success will come from our ability to recognize the stressful situation and be wary of our actions and reactions. Now let's look at some basic rules that will help us in dealing with any kind of stress, home or work.

BASIC RULES FOR DEALING WITH STRESS

1. **Don't let surprises surprise us.**   If we get to know ourselves well enough, we can predict our reactions to certain situations. We can also train ourselves not to act improperly by letting stress take over. When we get hit with the unexpected, we need to think, "Time, time, time. How can I get some time?"

It's not unprofessional to take a moment to reply, to get up from the table and walk around without speaking, even to take a restroom break while we cogitate a suitable answer to a surprising question. These are good times to count to ten, take a deep breath, count to ten again, if the situation is very stressful. In most cases, people won't object if we say, "Wow, I'm going to have to think about this," and *then think about it!*

2. **Give up always being right or first.**   One of the lessons we need to learn early is that there are most often right answers other than ours. Other people have good ideas, too. Most successful supervisors got where they are by using other people's ideas or suggestions as much as possible. The secret is that people are much more likely to make their own ideas work than they are to try to make an idea work that is forced down their throats. We should let others have their say, or even their way. We need to stand for principles and policies, but be flexible with opinions or alternatives. This approach is a subtle way of shifting some of the stress, by the way. If it's another person's idea, that person has a claim on it and a need to make it work. We will work hard to support the idea, but the person who originated it will have the majority of the stress until the project is finished.

3. **Win wars, not battles.**   Getting even is the downfall of many wars. Somebody does something horrendous to us at work, makes us look bad, gets us into trouble, and we spend the next year trying to get back at that person. That grudge we're holding is costing us some health, some peace, and some effectiveness at work. We are picking small battles and putting all our effort into them, instead of directing our energies toward the war of meeting production quotas under budget and over quality, while keeping a professional workforce intact. Worse yet, we may need the very person we're doing battle with. Someday he or she may be just the friend we need to get a project done on time, to get information for a report, or clearance for a new specification. If we don't let the stress get us in trouble by leading us to get even with the person, if we try to make friends and smooth over differences, perhaps even apologize for our apparent mistakes, we might find ourselves sailing easily through otherwise trou-

bled waters. Keeping our calm, in the long run, is a sign of strength, not weakness.

4. **Don't let stresses pile up.**   Deadlines can be dangerous in a backwards kind of way. Having a deadline of next week for a project means we don't have to finish it this week. Not having to finish it this week means we have some time to spare. Having some time to spare lulls us into slowing up on the project or taking on another, less important project. The next week comes and we're hurried—and harried—on two projects rather than one, when we could have finished the more important one ahead of time, or at least on time with ease, and avoided the accompanying stress. Waiting until the last minute or hour or day to finish a project entails the risk that something of greater importance will come up, and then we won't have that other minute, hour, or day! Many successful supervisors and managers force an earlier deadline on themselves, knowing that missing a deadline is much more stressful than the pressure of meeting the deadline. Since it's pretty well accepted that people do about 80 percent of most jobs in the last 20 percent of the time available, imposing the earlier date on ourselves simply moves that last 20 percent up some.

5. **Planning is the enemy of stress.**   Proper planning gives us a look at the bigger picture. When we start our day with the first phone call we receive or the first person who walks into our office, we are in for a stressful day. A workable to-do list will give us some opportunity to weed out some stressful but unimportant items. A list will allow us to concentrate on the bigger, more important items and to do away with some of the time wasters—or at least find out which are the time consumers. An obvious caution here is to avoid sweeping something under the rug that will come back and haunt us later. If it has to be done, even if it's trivial or unpleasant, not doing it will create subconscious stress until it is handled.

6. **Better health handles stress better.**   We think better, sleep better, work better when we're in better health. This has two implications with regard to stress. First, if we do all these things better, we'll have less stress. Second, if we are in better health, we will handle the stress that does come our way

better. The important thing is to give our health serious consideration. Excessive vices, poor eating and sleeping habits, and lack of exercise are extremely detrimental to our health. Regular physicals, watching our weight, blood pressure, and cholesterol, and following a good exercise program will maintain our good health and thus reduce the amount and duration of the stress. "Being too busy" is a poor excuse for not exercising and eating properly. Simple steps such as taking a parking space farther from our workplace or walking up a few flights of stairs rather than taking the elevator will go a long way to improving our exercise routine. Ordering a vegetable or fruit salad occasionally will do wonders for our food problems. There are lots of good books on nutrition, exercise, and maintaining good health. It's worth reading them!

MANAGING STRESS-RELATED PROBLEMS AT WORK

Unfortunately, we can't eliminate stress by following a step-by-step formula. Stress—and stress management—is an individualized matter. One situation may cause one individual a great deal of stress, but simply roll off someone else. One individual may react differently to the same stressors at different times. Solutions to stress function the same way. What may work very well for us on Monday may fail completely on Thursday. Because so many factors affect our managing stress it's hard to determine what will and won't bother us. Our diet, our exercise, our natural tendencies, our sleep habits, our general health, our outside activities, even our friends and associates influence how we react to stressful situations. Although it may seem as though there is little hope for us, there is actually much we can do to manage, avoid, control, and influence the duration and severity of stress. Let's talk about those things we can predict and see how we can manage them.

Obviously, we can predict some stress. If we commute to work, we can be certain that there will be some traffic, and perhaps some daily trouble spots. If we leave late, we can expect each traffic light or stop sign to bother us more than it would if we had plenty of time. In both these cases we can predict a degree of stress. If each day we travel to work on the expressway causes us some stress because of the danger or slowness or drivers' impoliteness, we need to examine that situation. If we're stressed out by the time we get to work every day, we should either change our route or find ways of reducing its effect on us. We can plan to avoid the problem by using surface streets or leaving earlier, before the traffic becomes too bad, or we can plan to listen to soothing music during our commute. This is one way of managing stress: predicting it from past experience, then trying to remove the cause. This is a form of avoidance, which is fine if it works and is possible. But sometimes it's not as easy as that.

Imagine that we are working on a project that has a deadline. It is an important project, and people are coming in from other cities to hear the results. We've assured our boss that there won't be any glitches, so our boss has told everyone to go ahead and plan the trip. We know we are in good shape, pressured some, but not really stressed. As we approach the deadline, we call for some information we asked to be put together by someone who works in another department. We aren't worried because that person has always been helpful and dependable and produced quality work. Also, when we've checked along the way, he or she has been on or ahead of schedule. Today when we ask the status of the information gathering, we hear, "Oh, I was just about to call you. I had gotten it all together on my computer, but one of our apprentices was working at my desk last night and dumped the whole thing. Unfortunately, I hadn't saved the file and don't have a backup. Looks like I'm going to have to pretty much start over. The boss understands the situation and will give me the time to work on it, but I may miss the deadline you gave me by a few days. Hope that isn't going to cause you a problem. I'm sorry it happened. It was a really stupid mistake!"

Now where are we? When we hear this, we very likely come close to panicking.

> *The deadline will be missed!*
> *There goes my bonus!*
> *Can I hide?*
> *People will think I'm incompetent!*
> *The boss will wonder why I gave the work to somebody else!*
> *I must tell the boss right away.*
> *The boss will be mad!*

It's not my fault!
The boss will look bad!
People have their plans made, their reservations made!
My credibility is shattered!
I will look pretty foolish!
I may never work again!

STRESS SETS IN BIG TIME

It's too late to play past tense. Finding out why and how it happened isn't important. There are a number of things we can do to solve the problem, but we're talking stress management here, not problem solving. There is no way to avoid all stress. We face that up front. Blaming others, getting angry, making excuses that will come back to haunt us later—none of these measures reduces stress. But to think and function properly, we need to reduce the amount of stress we have or are going to have as this incident begins to be processed through the organization. In this case, again, we can predict what will cause us stress, and, we hope, relieve some of it, just by expecting it.

Sometimes counting to ten will reduce stress. This probably isn't one of those times. That approach works best when we are trying to avoid getting angry or jumping into a situation without proper planning. Now, however, is a time for action. We need to consider all the things that we predicted will cause us stress, to figure out which to address to gain the biggest payoff. First, though, we need some facts. When will the results be available? Can we do anything to get them quicker? Have the people planning to attend the meeting already made their reservations? Armed with this and any other pertinent data, we notify our boss as soon as possible. When we meet with our boss, we should have a solution, or at least some options, to offer. We can suggest using partial data. We may offer to write a letter to the people concerned accepting the blame and providing the solution. We don't want to blame the problem on the other department. We will undoubtedly need help again, so there's no point in alienating others to get ourselves out of a hole. Our best alternative is to solve the problem and spend as much time as possible working on solutions. We shouldn't worry about looking bad ourselves. If we can come up with a reasonably good alternative, we'll get our credit, in due time. We will gradually work down our stress-causing list and put each item in proper perspective.

Our plan, then, is:

1. Identify and prioritize our stress causers.
2. Get facts quickly.
3. Start action immediately.
4. Inform higher management of the difficulties.
5. Offer solutions, not problems.
6. Accept blame, but don't dwell on it.
7. Work hard to make it work!

The good thing about acting immediately is that activity has a tendency to reduce our stress level, the more so as we begin to see a solution developing. Action takes our mind off our own embarrassment and failure (which we will soon reverse anyway). Is this a foolproof plan? Certainly not, but it's better than living with panic and letting stress get hold of us so we can't function. Naturally, the action we take should be well thought out so we don't get into a more stressful situation. This might be a time for the count-to-ten process. In this case, counting to ten means pausing in what we're getting ready to do and asking ourselves, "Is this really the way to go?" We think of the consequences and of alternatives. When we're satisfied that we're making good sense, we pick back up and start the action.

DEALING WITH CAUSES IN THE WORKPLACE

It's an obvious oversimplification, but there are really only three things that give us stress at work:

1. People: who are contrary to our direction and have to be dealt with (or lived with)

2. Things: that break, often at critical times, and have to be fixed

3. Situations: that may or may not be changed

Things

People are the biggest stress causers, so we'll deal with them last. Things are often out of our control, but still give us grief. Just as we are ready to duplicate a document we've worked on for hours, the copy machine runs out of toner and there isn't any more in the supply cabinet. We have some important work on the computer, which we haven't saved, and the computer crashes. We run out of staples as we are putting together the handouts for a meeting, or we end up with a stack of handouts with holes punched on the wrong side, without time to get more made.

Cursing a piece of equipment may seem to ease our stress, but it doesn't solve the problem. There's a solution to prevent the problem next time: move the deadline up a little, if we're depending on equipment to help us meet it, and know where back-up equipment is. Don't put off the equipment-dependent part of a project until just before the deadline. When we finish a part of an assignment, we should get it stapled, punched, or printed immediately. At least we'll have less to worry about, and if there's a mistake it won't affect everything.

Of course, this is not going to relieve our stress at this point. Since this isn't a chapter on problem solving, we won't discuss how the problem is solved. But we will discuss the stress relief. The basic rule is, "If I can't fix it, worrying about it won't solve the problem." A corollary is that we should always ask, "How can I cut my losses?"

If the house is on fire, we run in and grab the items that are most valuable to us. They may be photographs, instead of sterling silver. Cutting our losses means picking out the most immediate and serious problem and dealing with that. If the copy is worth more than the embarrassment of holes on the wrong side, forget about the holes, as long as we have the copies. There's a point of value in being sure that we don't get into these kinds of situations all the time. Even on unimportant things, we should always try to be ahead of schedule and to take care of equipment-dependent tasks well in advance—and to get to be known as that kind of person. Then it will be more likely for others to forgive us when things do go wrong.

Situations

Situations may involve things or people or both. They have a way of developing differently than we would like. Say we're planning a safety meeting or computer training or a planning session with a few other supervisors. We've reserved the one meeting room in our facility and have duplicated our materials ahead of time. We have doughnuts and coffee scheduled to be delivered. It's a pretty simple operation, and there's nothing to get excited about. An hour before the meeting, we call the person who schedules the room to see if we can get in and check it out.

SUPERVISOR: *Hey, Sandy, when can I get into the room? The meeting starts at nine, and I'd like to put some papers out.*

SANDY: *Are you with Al's group?*

SUPERVISOR: *I beg your pardon? Al who?*

SANDY: *Al Simmons. They've got the room reserved all day. I thought they had already put their stuff in there.*

SUPERVISOR: *But I had the room reserved for three hours this morning. I made the reservation with Marge last week.*

SANDY: *Yeah, well, you know she's not with us anymore. At least, she'll be out on maternity leave for a while. Her baby is due in a couple of weeks. They're expecting a little girl. She said . . .*

SUPERVISOR: *Hey, let's talk about the room! I've got five people coming in at nine.*

SANDY: *Are you with Al's group, then?*

SUPERVISOR: *No! I'm with my group. I don't even know what group Al has got. What happened to my reservation?*

SANDY: *Unh, I'm not sure. Things have gotten pretty hectic around here since Marge left. We've had this problem before. Yesterday two groups showed up at the same time. Some people from accounting started showing up about the time the planning groups showed up. It was really confusing. I don't know how they worked that out. It seems to me that . . .*

SUPERVISOR: *So you're telling me that I don't have the room?*

SANDY: *Not unless you're with Al's group. You aren't, are you?*

SUPERVISOR: *Look, I'm not with Al's group! I've got my own meeting and I'm really frustrated! How in the world could you people be so poorly organized?*

SANDY: *Hey, wait a minute! Don't start screaming at me! You're*

*the one who doesn't have a reservation, not me! I don't have to
take yelling from anyone!*
SUPERVISOR: *Well, you're supposed to be the service group and you
sure don't sound like one to me. Let me talk to your boss. I'll tell
her a thing or two. (click) Hello! Hello! Don't you hang up on
me!!*

So now we have some stress over a situation. How did it happen?
Somebody, somewhere messed up, forgot to write something
down, overlooked our reservation, whatever. The situation is that
people are coming to a meeting, but there is no place for them to
meet. Time is short. We know of no other room. Our office isn't big
enough. Our stress builds. Also, a typical thing happened when
we got stressed out: we made it worse! We violated a cardinal rule:
"Don't bite the hand that may feed us someday." (Or may be able
to feed us right now.) Let's see how this might have come out
better:

SUPERVISOR: *Hey, Sandy, when can I get into the room? The meeting starts at nine, and I'd like to put some papers out.*
SANDY: *Are you with Al's group?*
SUPERVISOR: *I beg your pardon? Al who?*
SANDY: *Al Simmons. They've got the room reserved all day. I
thought they had already put their stuff in there.*
SUPERVISOR: *I made the reservation with Marge last week. I had the
room reserved for three hours this morning.*
SANDY: *Yeah, well, you know she's not with us anymore. At
least, she'll be out on maternity leave for a while. Her baby is
due in a couple of weeks. They're expecting a little girl. She
said . . .*
SUPERVISOR: *That's nice, Sandy. I'll bet they're happy, but I'm
concerned about the room. I've got five people coming in at nine.*
SANDY: *Are you with Al's group, then?*
SUPERVISOR: *No, this is my group. And it looks like we don't have a
reservation.*
SANDY: *Unh, I'm not sure. Things have gotten pretty hectic around
here since Marge left. We've had this problem before. Yesterday
two groups showed up at the same time. Some people from
accounting started showing up about the time the planning*

group showed up. It was really confusing. I don't know how they worked that out. It seems to me that . . .

SUPERVISOR: *So you're telling me we've got a problem.*

SANDY: *Unless you're with Al's group. You aren't, are you?*

SUPERVISOR: *No, I'm not. Since you've had this problem before, maybe you can help me. Can you give me some help in finding a room?*

SANDY: *Let's see. There aren't any more meeting rooms. How many people do you have coming in?*

SUPERVISOR: *Five coming in. Six, counting me.*

SANDY: *That's not so many. Can they use your office?*

SUPERVISOR: *'Fraid not, Sandy. Unless somebody sits on the floor and on my desk. It's awfully small.*

SANDY: *Yeah, I know what you mean. I don't even have an office. My boss has a pretty big one. Hey, that's an idea! She's out today; gone to a funeral . . . an uncle, I think. Died suddenly.*

SUPERVISOR: *Could we use it?*

SANDY: *Her room, you mean?*

SUPERVISOR: *Yeah.*

SANDY: *Well, I don't see why not. If it's not all day. We've done that before, for small groups, when things got messed up. She may be back this afternoon. Now, when was it you wanted the room?*

SUPERVISOR: *At nine o'clock. Six people. For three hours—till noon. That'd be great if we could. I can bring a couple of chairs.*

SANDY: *Sure, you can use it for that time. We've even got that many extra chairs. We can even use Marge's chair. She's out on leave, you know. Having a little girl . . .*

We may not always get the happy ending we'd like, but we have a much better chance of it if we use a little better approach to the situation than we did the first time. We'll have Sandy on our side the next time we need help, even if this situation doesn't work out. What did we do differently? We controlled our stress. We didn't let it control us. We decided whether it was going to bother us and how much and for how long it was going to control us. We also kept Sandy from having to deal with our stress and from developing some of her own. It took some patience on our part. We had to keep focused on our problem. We even involved Sandy in our dilemma by calling it "our" problem (hers and ours). Further, we asked for her help, since she'd had the same thing happen before, implying that she could solve the problem. Again, we're not trying to show how to solve the problem in this chapter, but to show how keeping our cool will reduce the stress level and get us out of trouble more easily.

People

People consistently cause us the most stress. Without trying to solve all the people problems, we'll consider some basic, helpful steps in handling people stress.

We have a boss who is inconsiderate, unyielding, bad-tempered, and generally hard to get along with. He or she makes life miserable for us. We have constant stress as we try to do our job.

Much has been written about how to get along with a bad boss. How do we handle the stress, though? We know that every time we deal with our boss, we're going to end up with stress caused by something he or she does or says. This knowledge itself causes stress, too.

SUPERVISOR: *Here's the report you asked for.*

BOSS: *Well, it's about time. I hope it's what I'm looking for.*

SUPERVISOR: *I hope so, too. I did the best I could on the short notice you gave me.*

BOSS: *So you're going to blame me if it's wrong?*

SUPERVISOR: *No. I just mean I'm doing the best I can with the workload I have.*

BOSS: *Have you ever thought about working harder, or maybe smarter?*

SUPERVISOR: *I don't know how I can do any more than I'm doing. I don't think I'm wasting any time.*

BOSS: *You still take breaks, I notice.*

SUPERVISOR: *Yes, but I only stay for ten minutes. And I cut my lunch time down to thirty minutes.*

BOSS: *One thing you might learn is that you won't starve to death if you miss a lunch or two every once in a while. Of course, the fact that I rarely ever go out to lunch has not come to your attention.*

SUPERVISOR: *I have noticed that, but I don't stay very long.*

BOSS: *I hope you realize that while you're out to lunch — and break — with your friends, I'm in here correcting the mistakes you all made before you went.*

SUPERVISOR: *I'm sorry for the mistakes. I didn't realize the work was so bad. I'll try to do better. I won't take any more breaks until I get caught up.*

BOSS: *If you get caught up — which isn't likely — then I'm not doing my job.*

SUPERVISOR: *I beg your pardon?*

BOSS: *My job is to see that you don't ever get caught up. That's what they're paying me for — to get as much work out of you people as possible.*

We could go on, but the pattern is clear: no matter what we say, the boss is going to make it wrong and drive us deeper into despair. Admittedly, not many bosses are quite this bad, but the scenario is exaggerated to make a point. The same scene could be played out with a peer or even with a subordinate.

The word that will help us in this situation is *cope.* Coping means deciding just what we will stand and where to draw the line. We did two things here that caused us more stress. First, we didn't stop and ask for a specific definition of our job and exactly what we were doing wrong. Second, we prolonged the agony by trying to win an argument with our boss. Even with no chance of winning, we kept introducing subjects. We started with the short time frame for completing the job, then we talked about breaks and lunch and getting caught up. In a way, we got suckered into that. We should have dealt with the job at hand only. Let's try again:

SUPERVISOR: *Here's the report you asked for.*

BOSS: *Well, it's about time. I hope it's what I'm looking for.*

SUPERVISOR: *I hope so, too. You'll let me know if there's a problem?*

BOSS: *You bet I will. I'll probably find a lot to correct.*

SUPERVISOR: *Yes, Uh-huh. Is that all?*

BOSS: *Yeah, till I find all the mistakes you made.*

SUPERVISOR: *Call me if you need me.* (And leave.)

What was the difference? We didn't give the boss a chance to change the subject or go into our faults. We decided not to let our boss do this, and we kept the conversation focused on the subject of *this job.* We started to *cope,* rather than succumbing to stress. In this case, we knew what to expect and we did not give the boss room to go beyond what we were there for. When we are called back because the boss is unhappy with something, we continue along the same lines. We should hear ourselves saying, "Yes, now, just how did you want that?" instead of trying to justify our actions. This takes practice, of course, whether we're dealing with things, situations, or people.

CONCLUSION

So, where are we? Have we made it possible to avoid all stress? Is all stress bad? Let's go back to the opening of the chapter, where we referred to the quarterbacks, the sprinter, and the tennis player. Obviously, these people have a lot of stress. They will say that's how they win. Their adrenaline flows because of the stress of the task ahead of them. We aren't Olympic athletes, but if we didn't have some stress to keep us going, life would be pretty boring. We need to know that stress exists, that it can do us harm, and that we can determine its strength, its duration, and our reaction to it. We can learn to see ourselves reacting, then learn from our reaction to improve our response to stress. Our best defense is to recognize potentially stressful situations and adjust our lives to alleviate as much stress as possible. Most important, we need to put things in proper perspective and prioritize. It may help to remember the saying, "Don't sweat the little stuff; it's all little stuff!"

EXERCISES

1. Individual assignment: Have each person make a list of the things that create the most stress in his or her life. Suggest a long list, since many things are potentially stressful. When the lists are done, have people rate the items using the following codes:

   C—Things they pretty much can control
   NC—Things over which they have very little control
   OS—Stressors that have been a part of their lives for many years

NS—Stressors that were new in the last year
T3—Top three items that cause the most stress

Now have them pretend the top three no longer exist or are no longer stressors. Would three other items become more stressful? Would they be better off? The point of this exercise is to confront stressors and determine which ones need to be addressed in order to reduce stress overall.

2. Question for discussion: In this chapter we learned that we can determine what will cause us stress, how much stress it will cause, and how long it will continue to give us stress. Have the class give examples from in and outside work.

3. Ask for a show of hands of how many will try for a week to ignore the car that pulls in front of them or the person with too many items in the express line at the supermarket. Have the class make a list of items they will laugh at, rather than get stressed out about, for the next week.

Chapter 6

THE IMPORTANCE OF GOOD COMMUNICATIONS

COMMUNICATING—GOOD OR BAD?

It's easy to tell people they should be good communicators; it's much harder to tell them *how* to be good communicators. One problem is that we aren't always sure just what we mean by "good communications." The preacher who presents a great sermon gets rousing support (orally) from the congregation, but when asked what the sermon was about, very few people may be able to answer correctly. A politician may hold an audience spellbound, but if those people go out and vote for someone else, the politician may have failed to communicate. As a supervisor, we are most often transmitting messages that should produce some action, change something, or speak to the action that has already been carried out—if only to say that it was right or wrong. What is good communicating in this kind of situation?

We might define good communicating as getting the right message to the right target in an efficient manner. Notice that we said "in an *efficient* manner," not necessarily in the cheapest, quickest, or easiest manner. Efficient means *correct*, also. The reason for saying it this way is that so often we take the easy way out and just *tell* somebody something. But since memory is not very reliable, this isn't a very efficient method. Pretty soon we will find that the person we told will have to be told again, or that he or she is doing it wrong, or that he or she has somehow got the message all fouled up. Perhaps another word we could use is *effective*. *Effective* carries yet another implication—that the message got through and the correct results have come from the action taken. When we send a message, we should think to ourselves, "It isn't enough to be sure that it *can* be understood; I must be sure that it will be very difficult to *misunderstand* it."

FOUR BASIC ELEMENTS IN COMMUNICATING

We can understand communicating better if we break it down and look at the parts or elements that make up any communication effort. In essence, there are four basic elements—namely, the *sender*; the *receiver*; the *message*; and the *environment*, or conditions under which the message is sent. Each of these things affects the results, and the effectiveness of our communication depends on how well we take each one into consideration. For example, the most powerful speaker we know will have trouble when the room is hot or the audience is uncomfortable in some way. This doesn't mean that this speaker can't do a better job than someone else; it means that he or she could be even more effective under better circumstances. On the other hand, when the person we're talking to really wants the information we're presenting, and is eager to hang on our every word, our presentation can be pretty poor and still get across. *But it could get across better if we were doing a better job.* When a person brags to the car pool about his or her success at fishing, we doubt seriously that very much is getting through, especially if traffic happens to be bad; but if the person is talking to the parent of a child he or she has just seen in a distant city, we expect the message to get across much better. When our child wants to be picked up rather than walking home, he or she is likely to go into much detail and even repeat the message so there will be no misunderstanding.

Note that different elements influence the effectiveness of the communication in these examples. With the fishing story, neither the subject matter nor the environment is conducive to successful transmission. In talking to the parent about the child, because the message is very important to the receiver (parent), he or she is ready to hang on every word. When our child talks to us about giving him or her a ride, we may not be very interested in the message, but to our child it is all-important. And it is important to the child as the sender to see that we (as the receiver) get the message. There are several things to notice here about effective communication. First, different conditions exist when we transmit information. Next, the sender and the receiver have different degrees of interest in the subject matter. The simple truth is that it is rare for the sender to have the same feeling toward the message that the receiver has. But if we fail to take this into consideration when we try to communicate to someone, our message may get lost.

One problem we have is that as senders we always want to put the responsibility for successful communication on the receiver rather than accept it ourselves. We always react the same way when someone fails to get what we were saying. We think (or say), "But I *told* him . . ." The first thing we tend to do is to rationalize that if the receiver had listened, he or she would have gotten the message. And that's what it is—*rationalization*. We are failing to accept responsibility for taking all the elements into consideration. Did we realize that the receiver wasn't getting the message? Did we realize that he or she may not have been interested and we should have done something to stir up that interest? Did we consider that the environment might not have been the best for good communicating? Were the doors open and others listening in? Was the phone ringing? Was the receiver waiting to see the boss? Were there other distractions either in the office or in his or her mind? Was the receiver really just tolerating our conversation, waiting for the chance to begin his or her own monologue? Did we choose the right time and the right place to discuss the subject? Did we prepare the receiver for the discussion by making it clear what it was we were going to discuss?

These are all important considerations, each one of which can help or hurt the effectiveness of our communications. We can't choose to pay attention to them or ignore them; if we ignore them, they will still tend to disrupt our communicating efforts. What usually happens is that we use about the same approach each time, except in very critical situations. We say things the same way to different people, regardless of the circumstances or whether the person we're talking to is interested. We wouldn't dare approach the boss for a raise and promotion in the same manner as we would ask for a sandwich in a restaurant, but what about the times between those extremes when we probably should take a little more care in the way we choose our words and our approach? Unfortunately, the *natural* approach is to put things in *our own* frame of reference, on the basis of our interests, our vocabulary, our need for telling. What we *should* do, of course, is to put all our conversation and other types of communication in the *receiver's* frame of reference, but this is a lot easier said than done. *We just don't think that way.*

THE RECEIVER HAS A DIFFERENT FREQUENCY

We think in terms of *our* goals, *our* interests, *our* needs, *our* problems—not in terms of the *receiver's* goals, interests, needs, problems. When we communicate successfully, we do so by either tuning in on the receiver's frequency or getting the receiver to tune in on ours. The chances are pretty good that both the sender and the receiver would like the other to make the change. But the sender generally has the message that needs to be transmitted and so should accept the responsibility of seeing that both are on the same frequency.

Perhaps one of the best things we can do before we try communicating is ask ourselves what frequency the receiver is on. In other words: "What is there about this message that would make Fred think he wants to get it? It's important to me, but why should it be important to him? *I* know he needs it, but does *he* know it?" When we've decided what the receiver's frequency is, then we must decide whether, if we were the receiver, we would get the message from the communication we're preparing. To put it another way, we must ask: "Is this the best way to get the message across to Ruth? Will she really read this memo or this bulletin? Will she read it carefully enough to see that it was meant for her or that it is a completely new policy, different from the one she is familiar with?" There are plenty of cases on record in which important new policy changes have been put into letters and lost completely by the time they got down to the people who were supposed to act on them.

BARRIERS TO EFFECTIVE COMMUNICATING

This brings us to the important point of looking at some of the barriers to good communicating. Take the case of losing a new policy by putting it into a letter and sending it down through the organization. To an outsider reading the letter for the first time it may appear that the policy is perfectly clear and there is no reason for a communications breakdown. A closer examination, however, may show that many letters go up and down through the organization every day, carrying insignificant details. Those who receive them have learned through experience that rarely does anything important come to them this way, and when it does, a big announcement will also be made by someone else at the same time. This means to them, "If it's really important, somebody will tell us without our spending a lot of time reading useless material." (This ought also to be a lesson for first-line supervisors: be alert enough to catch important messages without having to be told by some other source.) The first barrier, then, is hiding important messages among those that the receiver has learned aren't very significant.

The second barrier is the other side of the coin—sending unimportant messages. It just doesn't make good business sense to send messages about which we can think, "Oh, well, nobody ever reads these things anyway." It doesn't take us long to get into some sloppy writing habits with this thought in mind. Equally senseless is the idea of writing just to shift the responsibility to someone else's shoulders: "I did my part; I wrote a letter covering it." This becomes an unnecessary message or perhaps even a much more damaging communication than none at all. This is a third barrier, if we consider that our motives weren't very honest in the first place. We aren't likely to work very hard at making a message clear if we have ulterior motives in sending it. After all, what we're really trying to do in such a case is hide the truth, so what better way to do it than in garbled communication?

And even when we have the best of intentions, we run into

another barrier: overkill. It's so vital that everyone get the message that we go into too much detail or give too many facts. As a result, the real message gets smothered by a lot of background information that belongs right there—in the background. The problem comes when we start to *sell* the idea instead of just giving out the necessary information. When we start selling, we almost always go too far, often raising questions in the receiver's mind about things that aren't really important to the subject we are discussing. Contrary to what may seem logical, it is usually better to give too little information than too much. Too much not only raises questions, but may start the receiver thinking about something to which he or she is particularly opposed or about which he or she has already made some kind of judgment. When the receiver starts thinking about such things, the real message is bound to suffer and probably get lost. Trying to get it across the second time is going to be much harder, too.

This suggests yet another barrier to good communication— the matter of organizing the message. If we hide the message among unnecessary information, it can't help but get lost. By the same token, if we organize it so poorly that the receiver gets confused trying to figure out what we're really trying to say, we might as well not have sent the message in the first place. Let's do a little thinking about how to organize. It stands to reason that the more time we spend leading up to an important point, the easier it will be for the receiver to get lost or lose interest. So one of the ways to organize profitably is to get the important part of the message out as quickly as possible. We start off by saying what it is we are trying to get across. "This is to recommend that we proceed with the project outlined below," or, "Starting tomorrow the salary structure is being changed." If nothing else happens, at least we will get the person's attention!

We remember longest the first and last things we hear or read. This means that the closing shot at the receiver should also contain either a summary or a conclusion. In another chapter we'll deal specifically with writing; for now, let's consider one of the ways this barrier works against most letter writers. When we write a letter, we say what we want to say, offer answers to problems, give out the necessary information—but then, we don't know how to close the letter. Instead of just stopping, we look for some way to end it. Almost without exception, we use some kind of trite phrase that is impersonal and stuffy sounding: "If we can be of any further assistance to you in this or any other matter, please do not hesitate to call on us." If it's true that we remember the first and last things we read, then what will the reader remember about us? Not that we are willing to help, but that we are very unfriendly and use form letters to convey our messages! If there's nothing at all friendly and helpful by the time we get to the end of the letter, the reader isn't likely to believe it just because we use some worn-out phrase.

One more barrier we want to talk about is the matter of trying to communicate with people who have different viewpoints or different kinds of information. A difference in viewpoint can cause the message to be lost or confused before it does its job for us. For example, when we talk to the nonsupervisory people who work for us about something the company wants, we have to remember that their views of the company are quite different from ours. Even their loyalties are different from ours. So we have to realize that they will likely receive the message as meaning something else if we put it in terms of "the company." Of course, education, experience, and other background factors play a big part in our ability to communicate and are a part of this same barrier. The employee who is struggling to make ends meet or who is worried about making the next house payment while adding a new bathroom to accommodate the relative who has just moved in isn't likely to get the message that the company's new long-range savings plan is a good investment even if it means doing without for the time being.

APPLICATION

Now let's see how some of these barriers work in real life. Take the matter of hiding the important messages among the less important ones. Consider the supervisor who has a large number of people working for him or her and sometimes finds it necessary to get important messages to them—but is unable to call large-group meetings because of the nature of the job. A particularly important policy change has come up, and it is necessary to get it to the people as soon as possible. The choices are: (a) meet with the people in smaller groups until all of them have been covered,

(b) pass around a memorandum to all of them, (c) appoint several people to come in and get the message and then take it to the rest of the people, or (d) post the message on the bulletin board. Which is the wisest choice?

First, let's make sure that we understand that in supervision there is often no clear-cut right or wrong way. There are advantages and disadvantages to any method, and the decision really depends on which approach has the fewest drawbacks. So how do we communicate the policy matter to the employees? Let's see what is likely to happen if we choose (d), putting the message on the bulletin board. If the board is like many, there will be all kinds of insignificant notices posted there, from lost dogs to cars for sale. But even if it is reasonably clean, the bulletin board offers several drawbacks. It gives us no assurance that all employees will see the notice unless we contact them individually and remind them to look at it. But if we could do this, we could have called them about the policy message in the first place.

How about (b), passing a memorandum around to all the employees? This has the advantage of seeing that everyone gets the message at the same time and in the same words. But this isn't a very good approach if there are likely to be questions, because people will ask their peers, who got their information from the same memorandum. Maybe the best thing to do is to choose (c), brief a group of employees and have them take the message back to everyone else. There are some real advantages to this idea, even though it sounds as though it would take the same amount of time as calling in all the people in small groups, since that's what we will be expecting the group leaders to do. The advantage of (c) is that we will have a chance to sell the idea to the leaders; then they will be doing the selling of the new policy change to the rest of the employees. In the long run, this may work out best. But here again there is the danger of having the employees get the wrong story, since it will be coming from several people instead of one. This can be corrected by having the memorandum discussed earlier sent out with a note indicating that there will be group meetings later in which employees can ask questions. If we do a good job of briefing the leaders, our work is reduced considerably. The final choice is (a), do all the briefing ourselves. If we think there will be any problems about the work group's accepting the policy change from one of their own members, then we shouldn't hesitate to call the small-group meetings and get the policy change across as best we can.

Let's look at the idea of overkilling the message. We have decided that a certain idea suggested by one of our employees is a great one, and we want to pass it on up the line to higher management. In an effort to prove what a good idea it is, we decide it would be well to give some background information on both the employee who came up with the idea and the need for the idea itself. We want to do a fair job of presenting both the employee and the idea, so we lay it on pretty thick. Of course, the results are inevitable—we oversell, and by the time the people who might be interested finish wading through all the nonessentials, they have lost interest, and we have lost a chance to sell a good idea and do a favor for a deserving employee.

HOW CAN WE IMPROVE COMMUNICATION?

So far we have talked about the barriers that might hinder us from getting the message across. What are some things we can do to really communicate effectively? First and foremost, we must get the message straight ourselves! After all, it was only an idea in our mind when it all started. It wasn't full grown, nor was it in any shape to be transmitted to someone else. But if we rush right ahead and start to explain it without first getting the whole picture straight in our own thinking, we're in for trouble. The next thing we can do is try to *sell* the idea. The fact that we think it is a great idea or plan doesn't necessarily mean others will, especially since they probably have a few ideas of their own. Just trying to force our ideas down someone's throat isn't likely to get us very far. Another thing to do is to get the message out in the open. We sometimes try to sneak an unpleasant idea or change by someone by hiding it between two pleasant things. The end result may be success—at least in hiding the idea. There's nothing better than tact when it comes to handling unpleasant messages—we should use it and whatever other human-relations tools we can—but in the end we must make sure the real message stands out and gets recognized. If we want to correct tardiness, sloppy work, poor writing, bad attitudes, or anything else, we'd better be sure that the employees know these are the things we are talking about. The situation may be unpleasant, but at least the message won't get lost!

Next, we should make certain the message gets there. It's not enough that we know what we plan to say or that we say it. It's only successful communication *when the message gets to the receiver*. How will we know that? Not just because we can say, "Don't you remember, I told you . . ." We will only know for sure when we hear our people tell us what's been said. We want to know how they hear the message, what it meant to them, how they have interpreted our remarks. Successful communicators have different ways of getting this feedback. Some simply ask the person they're talking to what that person has heard. This tends to put the responsibility on the hearer, but is effective. Others may ask the person to give them some feedback because they aren't sure they're communicating the message as well as they ought to. This keeps some of the blame for the misunderstanding (if there is any) on the communicator. Still others try to get their feedback in the form of results from the message sent. They'll ask the hearers what action is planned as a result of the message they've heard. As action plans are described, the sender will know just what the receivers heard and how it was understood. However we get feedback, we must be sure that we don't rely only on our own confidence in ourselves as communicators. We may be good, but we can be better, and we aren't as good at one time as we are at another. Also, we aren't as good with certain people and with certain messages as we are with others.

The third part of good communicating is the *ability to listen*. Listening is a skill; it must be learned, and it can be forgotten even after we've learned it! Of all the skills of communicating, listening is the hardest to learn and the hardest to practice with any kind of consistency. As a matter of fact, the more we communicate, the more we are likely to forget to use this skill. We get so used to hearing our own voice and so used to saying things in ways that sound good *to us* that we forget that everyone isn't always tuned in to our voice or our message. Listening is more than just being quiet. We listen for content. We listen for meanings. We listen to see if our message has gotten through. We try not to get into the habit of hearing what we want to hear instead of what is really being said. When we are doing a good job of listening, we don't interrupt people, nor do we jump right in at the end of their remarks with a quick response because we can't stand silence. We pause, if necessary, until we've processed the information we've just received. We repeat the statements or facts if we've any doubt about whether we heard right. We ask for clarification if there's any chance of our misunderstanding something. We learn to effectively use such phrases as, "Do I hear you saying . . ." and "Let me see if I have this straight . . ." Of course, we don't do this all the time. But we don't hesitate to do it if there's room for doubt. We aren't afraid of admitting that we may not be getting everything that's being sent.

These skills have been classified as the skills of good communicators. We can summarize them like this:

1. Knowing the message
2. Knowing that the message got there
3. Listening

Remember, these are skills. They have to be learned, and as we move up in the organization, we tend to fall back on the first one: *know the message*. We see ourselves as well-informed. Because we've communicated a lot in our lives, we naturally consider ourselves pretty good at it. So we stop listening, and that means we've lost any chance for good feedback. In the absence of feedback, we have only our knowledge of the subject to fall back on, and we may not be as good as we think we are. The key: *we can always be better at communicating*.

USING REFLECTIVE LISTENING

We've seen the three skills of good communicators and the four basic elements in effective communicating. Let's now consider a *special kind of listening* that will make us successful in our listening efforts. We'll call it "reflective listening." It implies that while we listen, we are actually doing something *actively*. We generally have the idea that on our part, listening is what we do while we're waiting for our turn to talk. As it happens, we can actually help the other person to be a better communicator by what we do when we listen! Remember the time we went into someone's office to talk and found him or her reading or working on something? We waited, only to hear, "Go ahead, I'm listening," but the person continued to work on something else. Not only is this rude, but it is bad listening. Remember how we felt? Frustrated, angry, wishing we could come back some other time, or maybe just say, "Either listen to me or call me when you've got time to give me your undivided attention!"

Again, effective listening has three parts. First, there is *eye contact*. People are more likely to be organized when we are looking them in the eye. If we're looking at our desk or at our watch or at a book or even at the ceiling, they lose their train of thought more easily. It's *not* a matter of staring at them. We look at them to show that they have our attention. The next part is *body language*. We send a lot of messages with our bodies. As we look at other people, we nod, lean forward, maybe even take a note or two. That lets them know that we're paying attention. It lets them know that somebody is home! If we lean back, arms folded, staring unconcernedly at them, with a look that says, "Hurry up and get out of here," the eye contact will do more harm than good. Finally, *reflective listening* is what we do when we give feedback by mirroring what other people have said: "I hear you saying . . ." or "Do you mean that . . ." or "So you feel that it would be . . ." We aren't agreeing or disagreeing with them. We aren't being defensive. We are simply letting them know that we've heard their message by mirroring their words. When we do that, we not only guarantee that they are saying what they mean to say, but we have helped them be organized and have encouraged them to say what they had on their minds. After we've done that, then we can weigh what they've said and deal with it in whatever way we see fit.

CONCLUSION

Much has been said about communicating. In fact, it's the "much saying" that has made communicating so hard to do. There's a lot more talking going on than there is listening, and there's a lot more talking going on than there is understanding. To make things worse, most people who are poor communicators don't know it and even blame others for not understanding what they say. Because there are always at least two people involved in any communicating effort, a problem arises—namely, each can blame the other, with neither accepting any blame. Good communicating is neither simple nor something that can be learned overnight. There are skills involved, and these skills are often difficult to learn. The best solution is for supervisors to develop some ways of checking how we communicate, so that at least one party in the communicating effort will be aware of the problem. The steps to effective communication are: knowing the message, knowing that the message got there, and listening. Listening is the most difficult to learn, but it is the most valuable step of the three. It is through listening that we receive the feedback that tells us whether the message arrived. If we aren't very good at getting the message there initially, the knowledge that it didn't make it at least gives us a chance to try again. Somewhere down the line we'll start to become good at getting the message there!

EXERCISES

1. Group activity: Have one person write down the following information: when and where he or she was born, when he or she came to work with the organization, when he or she made supervisor, and the name of one person working for him or her. Then have the writer *whisper* that information to another person, who whispers it to a third, and so on until the message gets around the room. Have the last person to receive it write the message down. The initiator should then read his or her information, and the last receiver should read the information he or she received.

2. Individual activity: The activity in exercise 1 is often used at parties to show how messages get messed up, but in this case it's meant to help people find out how to communicate more effectively. To get this information, perform the following activities: Individually, each person should write down what his or her *feelings* were before, during, and after the exercise. Next, these feelings should be discussed in small groups. The findings should be presented and recorded for the whole group to discuss.

3. Group discussion: Have the whole group decide whether any of the feelings listed in exercise 2 affect communications

efforts within the organization. Look for such phrases as "I wasn't interested," "I didn't care," "I thought it wasn't very important," "I couldn't remember." Have the group discuss these feelings and decide whether they hinder communications within the real world where they work.

4. Subgroup activity (workshop): In every organization there are communications problems, most of which could be eliminated or at least improved. Have each subgroup look at the real world in which each of its members works and decide what are the most serious communications problems within each person's part of the organization. Spell out each problem in enough detail so that it can be addressed. Be sure not to offer the solution, just the problem. (Of course, sometimes the problem suggests the solution. For example, "The boss doesn't tell me anything" implies that the solution is to have the boss tell more. It doesn't really spell out the exact problem, though. Why doesn't the boss tell me more? And how much more? What kinds of things? When should I be told? All of these need to be addressed.) The solutions will come in the next exercise. *Note:* When problems are finally defined to the satisfaction of the subgroup, they should be put in priority order. Which of these problems are the most critical? Which should be dealt with first? Which would have the greatest payoff? And so on. Taking all of these things into consideration, rank the findings in order of importance.

5. Group exercise: Combine the problems from the subgroups and see if there is any similarity among the top-ranked communications problems. Look at those at (or near) the top of most lists and decide how best to tackle them. Before ending this discussion, a decision should be made to take some kind of action or to recommend to the organization what action to take. Consider only one problem at a time during the discussion, and don't try to solve them all. At a later time others can be considered.

Chapter 7

SETTING UP THE WORK (PLANNING AND ORGANIZING)

As we have already seen, our job as a supervisor is to get work done through other people. We are doing our best work when we deal with the problems of getting the job accomplished rather than do the work ourselves. While we have the direct responsibility for the workers and how they do their work, we still are not supposed to do the work ourselves. (Of course, emergencies arise, but we're talking about the normal activities of a supervisor.)

SUPERVISORS AS MANAGERS

Some people make a distinction between supervisor and manager. For our purposes in this and the next chapter, we will talk about the supervisor's job of *managing*. Since the usual definition of a manager is "one who gets the job done through people," we won't do any harm if we use the terms interchangeably. Any supervisor has certain managing responsibilities. We will want to see what that means to us, the new supervisor.

Everyone above the worker or specialist level has some managing to do. The only difference between the first-line supervisor and the head of the organization is the scope and responsibility of their managing assignments. Basically, every manager, whether the top executive or a foreman, has four managing functions to perform:

- Planning
- Organizing
- Directing
- Controlling

The first two we'll discuss in this chapter, the last two in the next. While all supervisors perform all of these functions, the extent to which they do each of them usually depends on their level in the organization. For instance, top executives would probably spend most of their time planning and organizing, while first-line supervisors should devote most of their time to directing and controlling the activities of people. Now, since all supervisors perform all these functions, let's see what they *really* mean to the new supervisor.

PLANNING

First, let's be sure we understand something about *all* these functions. Each is done along with, and as a part of, the job. Although we should learn each as a skill and be aware of the fact that we are doing it, we shouldn't be scared off because it has a fancy name. The chances are pretty good we'll do some of each one, whether on purpose or by accident. So when we talk about planning, we're talking about the everyday job—how it's done, what will be done tomorrow, where we hope to go from there.

Planning is by far the most important of all the activities we've listed because everything else results from it. It is simply the means by which supervisors decide in what direction they want their group to go. The process can be carefully done, or it can be haphazard. The interesting thing is that even *doing nothing* will produce some kind of result! The organization will still exist; tomorrow will still come; and the employees will do something, right or wrong. The organization will not stop just because we fail to plan. It may well get off the track or head in the wrong direction, but it will still struggle along, because one supervisor cannot stop the entire organization.

Another reason for the importance of planning is that it's much harder to correct the results of poor planning than it is to do it right in the first place. The results of poor planning can be pretty disastrous, and, unfortunately for the new supervisor, they usually show up more quickly for him or her than for higher management. When top management makes a mistake in planning, it sometimes takes many months or even years for it to come to light. When the first-line supervisor makes poor plans, it is sometimes only a matter of *hours* before the results are known. If an executive decides to spend more money on advertising to boost sales of a certain product, it may take a year to see whether the campaign was a success. If a supervisor manages his or her workforce incorrectly, so that too many people are off during a peak period, the resulting slowdown in production will be known before the day is over.

How and What to Plan

How do we, as a supervisor, plan our work? Obviously, we want to consider whatever alternatives are available to us and select the best one, all things considered. Too often supervisors think of planning as deciding to do—or not to do—*one certain thing*. Good planning always takes into consideration all the possible alternatives, weighs them carefully, then selects the one with the most merit. There is a caution here, though: *don't* try to find the perfect solution or the one that has no drawbacks. *There seldom is such a plan.* We may have to settle for the plan with the fewest drawbacks because none of the plans is completely satisfactory.

We form our plans by making four basic decisions:

1. What is to be done?
2. Who is to do it?
3. How is it to be done?
4. When is it to be done?

Now let's take these one at a time and see how they fit into the day-to-day job.

1. **What is to be done?**   We should have this answer definitely in mind before we go on to any of the other questions. For example, it isn't enough to decide that we are going to give our people more training, then go out and find someone to do the training. We must first decide exactly what training is needed, how much we can do ourselves, how much can be done by someone else, and how much can be left undone. If we aren't careful, we'll find ourselves trying to carry out plans that weren't very definite in the first place, resulting in a lot of muddling around trying to make something work that didn't have a very good start. So the rule here is to be sure that we know exactly where it is we're going before we begin our trip. It isn't necessary to write all our plans down, but it sometimes helps us understand what we are going to do if we record on a notepad a positive statement of precisely what we plan. The plan may change as we go along, but at least we have *something to change*. Otherwise, we'll end up making our plans as we proceed, changing those, repeating our errors, and in general botching it all up.

2. **Who is to do it?**   Part of planning is to determine whether this is a project for the whole workforce, for just a few people, or for one individual. If it is a onetime job, there is a great advantage in having only one or a few people work on the project. It's easier to keep up with a special project if only a few people are involved, and less training time will be required. On the other hand, if the work is the kind that will continue to be a part of the responsibility of our work group, then our planning should include deciding how soon we want everyone to learn the new work.

    There is an important training note here: if we aren't careful, we may let a job just gradually slip into being. No one is ever really trained for it, but finally everyone is doing it—and probably not very well. We may have it in mind that *one of these days* we'll do the training, but we keep putting it off until a more convenient time—which never comes. A basic fact to remember about training is that—like everything else on the job—it must be *planned for*. Left alone, it will not happen. The good supervisor plans for it to happen!

3. **How is it to be done?**   Once a goal or objective has been decided (and agreed) on, we still have to decide how it's going to be met. This decision has to be considered at every level, but especially at the first level. *Policies* about the work will be set at a higher level. Decisions about the *actual work* are usually made at that point in the organization where the work is to be carried on—hence, the first-level supervision. (The decisions may not always be made here because some supervisors *give up* some authority to their bosses. Then they complain because they don't have enough authority to carry out their jobs, when in reality they didn't use it when they had it.)

Policy setting is sometimes done unconsciously because we can set policy by *doing nothing*. If we don't come up with firm policies on matters such as overtime, safety, time off, promotions, or appraisals, precedents will begin to set the policies for us. If we intend to do a job without adding employees, we may be setting a policy for more overtime toward the end of the job!

4. **When is it to be done?**   The final question to be decided has to do with one of the most important ingredients in successful planning: time. While the obvious conclusion is that when it comes to time, the completion date is the most important consideration, this is only part of the story. No deadline is missed *all of a sudden*. Long-range plans usually fall through because of poor *short-range* planning. As first-level supervisors, we are seldom directly involved in the long-range objectives of the organization, but we are often very much involved in the short-range plans. So meeting these short-range objectives is the most important time aspect of our role in planning.

A Word about a To-Do List

One of the simplest things we can do in our planning is keep a basic to-do list. Time-management studies indicate that even a list jotted on the back of an envelope will save time in the long run. There are many kinds of planners and methods of keeping to-do lists, and just as many arguments over which is best. The answer is easy: the best method is the one that works for us. By works, we mean that it tells us what to do and in what order of priority, and furnishes us with some information about the task, for example, a telephone number, a name, or an address. The list can be as elaborate as necessary, but it is dangerous to create a list that is too complex to use easily. Ideally, we should start off with a list that notes that a certain job or meeting or purchase must be taken care of. There should be an order of priority (A, B, C, or 1, 2, 3 will suffice). If a person is involved, there should be a name; if a phone call is required, there should be a number; if a place is to be visited, there should be an address; if a deadline or meeting is involved, there should be a time.

When we successfully use to-do lists, we learn to depend on them to keep from missing meetings, forgetting to make calls, and so on. We also use them to make on-the-spot decisions when something unexpected comes up. If our boss calls and announces a meeting, we can quickly see what's on the docket and what changes need to be made to accommodate him or her. We can make a quick phone call to change an appointment, since we have the number handy. As the day goes on, we may have to add to, subtract from, or reorder the list, but at least we have it. We can change our list to reset the priorities as other more or less important things come up.

The to-do list is useless if we don't use it. Ideally, we will pick a time each day to look over yesterday's list, develop today's list, and check off things that have been accomplished. Sometimes we are amazed that something that was a very hot item yesterday— that didn't get done—is not nearly as hot today. That's not reason enough not to do it, but it may say something about our perception of what is hot and what's not. People who don't use a to-do list say that their day is too hectic to try to plan it. The truth is, the more hectic the day, the more need there is for serious planning. We shouldn't have the idea that planning is simply a matter of making a list of things we need to do and assigning a time to do them. Nobody can be successful at doing that. Unexpected interruptions occur, other assignments come up, and priorities change, sometimes drastically. People walk into our office at the wrong times, our people have problems that need our attention, and we are slower or faster to finish a task than we expected. The single most important thing about a to-do list is that it's there, it's current, and it's real. The things on it need to be done; some are more important than others; some may not get done at all. The list can be added to or deleted from. *But there is a list!* If we spend fifteen to twenty minutes in the morning working on the list, that organizing will save us much more time later. At the end of the day, we can easily review the day and our accomplishments. As time goes on, we'll probably become more sophisticated and want a planner that is a little more complete. By that time, we will be pretty dependent on some kind of daily help, so we'll be ready to move to a higher plain of planning.

Understanding the Plan

It's almost too obvious to mention, but no plan is very good if it isn't understood by those affected by it. The reason for mentioning this is that we tend to blame someone else when a plan begins to go awry. The first thing we should investigate is whether the planning included safeguards against misunderstanding. Were the employees informed? How were they informed? Were they just told, or did they have an opportunity to ask questions, seek additional information, and generally become familiar with what was expected of them?

This sounds like something pretty big that would only be done when some major operation is undertaken. Not so! Employees need to know what's expected of them even for a small, one-hour assignment. Remember, our people are more interested in day-to-day activity than in long-range operations, so it's the smaller things that are important at this level.

Who's Watching the Clock?

Something that should concern all supervisors is the fact that since higher management is interested in the "big picture" (i.e., the long-range objectives), executives usually aren't watching the short-range objectives nearly as much. This means they may do no more than read an occasional progress report, always keeping an eye on the final completion date. If we first-line supervisors aren't careful, we may be the only ones watching the short-range dates. We can be sure a lot of people will be looking, though, when it's too late to do anything about it.

Sometimes at the first level we may get the delusion that everybody is watching everything and that we're just insignificant little cogs in a giant wheel. But once we've been trapped by this thinking, we're heading for trouble, especially with short-range plans. Even though everyone seems to be watching over our shoulder, they still expect us to watch the day-by-day progress of the work. For example, if the long-range objective is to reduce absenteeism, higher management will be concerned with quarterly or perhaps monthly reports, but we—and the other first-line supervisors—must worry about who shows up and who doesn't *every day*.

Objectives and Policy

Planning, then, is a function of management in which we are concerned with the future of the organization in those operations for which we are responsible. In the process of planning, we decide where we are going and how we intend to get there. Usually, we call "where we are going" the *objective* and "how to get there" the *policy*. Some have compared this to a ship taking a trip. The objective is the ship's destination, while policy is the course the ship must take to get there. In a sense, planning is the rudder steering the ship. The supervisor doing the planning controls the ship, and without planning the ship has no rudder.

While it won't be dealt with in detail in this chapter, we should learn quickly that the more we take our people into the planning effort, the better our chances of reaching the objective. Since we are more likely to be involved in short-term planning, we are setting short-term objectives, often with short-term policies. These may well involve day-to-day operations about which our people know as much as we do. Getting them to assist in setting deadlines is a good way to get their commitment to these deadlines as well. Getting them to participate in laying the ground rules is a good way to motivate them to work according to these ground rules.

A Brief Word about Controlling

In the next chapter we'll talk in detail about the function of controlling. We need to mention it here because planning and controlling are very closely associated with each other. As a supervisor, we control according to the planning that has been done. For example, budgeting is a type of planning, but the budget itself is a control. While it is being prepared, the budget is part of the planning function. Once the operation is begun, it becomes part of the controlling function.

Other examples might be quality control or service standards. Determining the organization's policies on quality or service is a basic part of *planning*. When those policies go into operation, they are actually *controls*. The importance of all this is that we should be glad that budgets, standards, and controls exist, because it is through them that the desired end result is reached. They not only direct our actions and tell us when we've reached the objective, but they give us a standard to measure against all along the way.

TIME MANAGEMENT

It wouldn't be appropriate to discuss planning without dealing with one of the things that needs the most planning—*our time*. One reason for planning is to help us make better use of our time. For the most part, we don't do a very good job of making use of our time, primarily because we don't plan for its use. We waste our time doing things that we shouldn't do, and we don't have a good way to prevent others from using our time to get their work done. If we look at some of the problems around us that are related to time, we'll see that good planning can eliminate some of these problems.

As we spend more time in supervision, we see more and more things that waste our time. They seem endless, as we can see from this abbreviated list:

No time deadlines set	Procrastination
Cluttered desk	Daydreaming
Pet personal projects	Poor mail routing

Poor self-discipline	Poor mail handling
No clearly defined objectives	No priorities
Inability to say no	Poor priority setting
Failure to delegate	Poor work organization
Snap decisions that have to be changed	Leaving tasks partially done
No real planning	Underestimating others
Attempting too much	Overestimating others

The list could go on and on, but we can see that many things use up our time—most of them our own fault. A brief look at the items listed shows us that these are all things that *we* could and should control. Other time wasters, which aren't on this list, have to do with outside forces over which we have little control. We'll talk about these external forces later. The internal forces, as we'll call them, are things that we usually have the opportunity to control. The failure to control them may be due to a lack of knowledge as to how to do it, a lack of skill in doing it, or simply a failure to realize that they are wasting our time.

For example, if we fail to delegate, then we wind up doing things that others could, and perhaps should, be doing. We may not feel it's necessary to delegate that particular thing because we can do it quicker and thereby save time. As we'll see in another chapter, this is a pitfall for many supervisors, both new and old. We'll see that when we do something others should be doing, it always costs us time in the long run. But we may not know how to delegate and get the results we want. Our problem may be not knowing what or to whom to delegate. The end result is that we do it ourselves and waste time. We could come up with similar examples for any one of the items we listed.

Internal Time Wasters

Instead of looking at all the time wasters—something we all should do as we read this—let's look at some of the things that researchers have found to be the primary causes of poor time management. A major problem is that we attempt too much. In the following subsections, we'll consider a number of causes for this problem.

Can't-Say-No Syndrome. We may not know how to say no when somebody asks us to do something. The person comes to us with a pitiful story, a pleading tone, or maybe a demanding approach, and we fall into the trap of agreeing to do the job ourselves. How do we avoid this trap? There are several ways. First, we may have to take a more assertive approach in dealing with people. We should remember that every time we take on a project that someone else gives us, we're saying that what we would otherwise be doing isn't as important as what these people have given us. We're saying, too, that we aren't as busy as they are. The obvious result is that they will keep giving us things to do instead of doing them themselves.

Another thing we can do to get out of the can't-say-no syndrome is to get in the habit of offering alternatives to the person who asks us to do something. We can suggest some better ways, some other people, some shortcuts, maybe even some ways of eliminating the work or cutting down on it. We can apologize for not doing it, but only if we feel some obligation to do it. We have no reason to feel guilty for not doing something that isn't ours to do in the first place. If we don't want to do the assignment, if we aren't supposed to do it, or if the person asking us could do it just as well, perhaps the best thing for us to do is simply say no. It is important to establish the fact that we're busy, that we already have something to do, and that it is a serious thing for us to take on another project. We must demonstrate that we have things to do and that we have our work planned so that we *know* whether or not we can take on another assignment. It may be satisfying to our ego when we take on a job that is giving somebody else a tough time, but if it messes up our work schedule, means we do less well on something else, and overloads us, then we may have to forgo some of that ego reward by saying no.

Ambition. Another cause of our attempting too much is that we're overly ambitious. This may be a part of the ego problem we just mentioned, or it may be that we don't have a very realistic view of what we can and can't do in the time allotted. Whatever the case, we need to realize that most projects take longer than we first think they will because of interferences that distract our attention and because others may fail to do their part. If we're going to continue to improve our ability to perform up to our level of ambition, we must get time estimating down to a science. There's nothing wrong with being ambitious, by the way. The problem is that if, in our ambition, we take on so much work that we either fail to do the job well or don't have time to learn from the jobs we're doing, our ambition is getting in our way rather than helping us.

Disorganization.   Another cause of poor time management is being *disorganized*. The old cartoon that shows a couple of people sitting around a desk piled high in disarray, with the caption "Tomorrow we've got to get organized," is not as funny as it might appear on the surface, especially if the picture mirrors our own work habits. No matter what we may think, we can't work effectively in the midst of confusion, with things piled high on the desk, stuff on the floor, files poorly kept, unfinished projects cluttering our work space, and the general air of our office or workplace resembling the dumping ground for the local garbage-disposal plant.

There are those who argue that since they work on more than one project at a time, they have to have more than one thing on their desk at a time. This is no doubt true, but if we are organized at least we have the several things in some kind of order. The argument, "I can find anything on the desk I need without any trouble," doesn't hold much water, because the mere fact that we feel the need to defend the condition of our workplace proves that it is more disorganized than it ought to be. Even if we are working on several projects and can find anything in the chaos, we need a place to work that isn't confusing or distracting. The appearance of things out of place and disorganized isn't very healthy and won't help our thought processes very much. So, how can we get rid of this problem of poor organization? Let's look at some of the answers.

First, a cardinal rule: never let more than one pile of material accumulate on our desk at one time. This doesn't mean that we let the pile get higher and higher. If we find that we need two or three stacks of things on or around our place of work, we know that we're taking on too much or not finishing enough. We should take time to finish some of the projects before we take on more. We may be having a problem with procrastination, getting something almost finished and taking on something else before we take the last steps on the first job.

Another cause of personal disorganization is failure to file things very well. We may have a good filing system that we don't use, or we may have a poor system. Whatever the reason, having a place for something, putting it there, and *being able to find it* when we need it are essential to being organized. The essence of a good filing system is the ease with which things can be found when we want them. Most of the time *simplicity* is the key word. As we've said, though, if we have a system, we must use it. This means that as soon as we decide that something should be filed, we decide where it should be filed and see that it gets there. There is no reason for it to stay on our desk or in our outgoing-mail box after we've decided that we're through with it for now.

We also have to learn to throw out material that is no longer needed, so that our files do not become cluttered and bulky. A good rule to follow on filing is to set a time limit—two or three years—then go through and find all those things we haven't used in that period of time. Unless there is some legal requirement to keep these things, or unless we have positive proof that we are going to need them shortly, we should *throw them away*. The time we save in finding things in uncluttered files will offset the occasional absence of things we'd like to use that have been discarded.

One very good way to get and stay disorganized is just to let our day happen. A phenomenon called the overcoat syndrome describes how many people get into their day. They come in with their coat on, the phone rings or someone meets them in the hall or someone is waiting for them in their office, and whatever that person wants or asks for gets the day started. At some point they may take off their overcoat. To start each day in this manner means that we will never be in control of our work lives—others get control before we can even remove our overcoats. The solution to this problem is much simpler than we think. *It takes a little planning.*

A Good Starting Point.   Those who have studied time management tell us that the simplest approach to managing our time—an absolutely essential approach, in fact—is to have some kind of that daily to-do list we talked about earlier. Some prepare such a list on the back of an envelope (good, but inefficient); others prepare it in a very complicated notebook (good, but time-consuming); some prepare it in a small notebook (probably the easiest to start with). Different people do it in different ways.

This to-do list very soon becomes a reminder, a calendar, a contract with ourselves, a way of prioritizing our efforts. After a few days or a few weeks of using the list well, it becomes natural, as wearing a seat belt does over time. It *is* our seat belt in a way. It protects us from procrastination, for we have to live with a certain item's still being on our list when we know we wasted time doing something less important. It protects us from having to say, "Oh, I forgot about that." It is there to remind us of our goals for the day. We can revise it—delete or add things—but it is still there. If we keep a pretty neat sheet, it can also become a dated record of our achievements. It is that tangible thing we were looking for in Chapter 2, which gives us a satisfying sense of accomplishment!

External Time Wasters

So far we've looked at time wasters over which we have some control—such things as attempting too much and poor personal organization. Now let's think about things over which we have less control—external time wasters. The most obvious one is the unscheduled interruption that comes either by phone or in the form of a drop-in visitor who wants only to chat. Of course, not all unscheduled interruptions come from people who are just passing the time of day. Visitors may have legitimate reasons for wanting to see or talk to us. It's just that their interruptions can't be sched-uled; hence, they interfere with our planned day. (It would be a great planning asset if we had the power or imagination to sched-ule unplanned interruptions at specific times!) Let's look at these problems and see what we can do to get a little control over our lives, even when the problem is caused by someone else.

First, there is the matter of the *drop-in visitor*. We're working away at something we've scheduled, which we may need to get out on a tight deadline, and along comes someone who decides to honor us with his or her presence. It may be a friend who just wants to visit; it may be someone looking for a place to hide from work; it may be someone who has a legitimate reason to see us but didn't see fit to call ahead to let us know he or she was coming; it may even be the boss, with or without a good reason for interrupting us. Whoever it is, and for whatever reason, the person is here in our office. What do we do?

Before we look at some solutions to the problem of what to do after such people get here, let's see if there's something we can do to prevent their being here in the first place. We need to see if there is something about our workplace that is particularly inviting to people looking for a place to light. We may have our workstation turned toward the door in such a way that everyone can see in and glimpse a vacant chair, which is a temptation to drop in. We may be sitting in such a way that we look right at people as if we're inviting them in. Further, even if we aren't situated in an open-invitation mode, there may be something about our behavior that keeps people coming back. Maybe we're *too friendly*. Maybe, in our effort not to hurt anyone's feelings, we've given the impression that we don't have much to do and we welcome visitors. We may be so helpful when they're with us that we prompt them to come back for more help. It's not that we don't want to be helpful, but we should be helpful only in those things that pertain to our job. If someone comes in and wants something that we don't usually do, and we go out of our way to find an answer for him or her, we are actually encouraging that person to come back. We must remember that when people are looking for help to get their job done, they aren't particular about who helps them. Even if it isn't our job to do it, they will keep coming back as long as they get the help they need. It may be time for us to direct them to the right person or place so they'll quit coming back.

We have to admit that most of us enjoy a certain amount of socializing, so if we've done it in the past, we can't expect people to stop coming to see us just because we've decided to get busy for a change. But if we've come to the conclusion that these visits are costing us valuable time, we need to start somewhere. We start by being busy, letting people know we're busy, and doing things in a businesslike manner. We will have to give the impression that we're doing something important, something we've planned to do, and that we, in fact, *are* busy. That's the rule for dealing with *anyone*, including the boss, who drops in to see us unannounced. Let visitors know not only that we're busy, but that we're on a schedule. This doesn't mean that we don't also give the impression that we want to help, but the offer to help comes *after* we've established these other ideas. When the visitor says, "How's it going?" we answer, "Fine. I'm trying to get this project out on schedule by eleven o'clock. What can I do for you?" It's that simple.

Suppose the visitor doesn't leave even after we've established that we have a busy work schedule? Then we don't have to worry as much about hurting his or her feelings. We don't have to be rude. If, after we've explained about our workload, he or she doesn't catch on that we don't have time to socialize, then that person isn't likely to be so sensitive that his or her feelings will be hurt easily. We may have to get up and move toward the door. It will be hard for our visitor to stay seated when we stand. When the visitor gets up, we simply say, "It's good to see you. Let's have lunch someday." With some people we may do well not to sit down in the first place. When they come in, we meet them at the door, sort of block the way while we talk to them, make some idle conversation, establish that we have a busy schedule, and then bid them farewell. The problem is that all of this sounds as if we're playing games—and really, we are. By far the best thing we can do is come right out and tell people we're busy, we can't talk right now, and we'll try to get back to them later. The reason we don't do this is that we worry about hurting people's feelings, or we're embarrassed to be that bold, or we're afraid of how they will react. To some extent, these are all good reasons, but they lead us to playing games. We must decide whether we want to play games or learn how to be more direct.

Another external time waster is the unexpected *telephone interruption*. The telephone is perhaps the thing that wastes the most time, but it is also the most easily overlooked. It doesn't take much to have a couple of fifteen-minute telephone conversations, but when we do, we've shot one-sixteenth of our eight-hour day! The important thing to remember about a telephone interruption is that it is the single most impolite event in our workday. Even the rudest and most insensitive person would not come into our office when we were talking to someone, come between us (physically), and start talking, expecting the other person to have no feelings about the interruption. Every time we answer a phone when someone is in our office, we're allowing the caller to do just that. We need some strong habits to deal with this type of interruption.

The rule here is the same as for the drop-in visitor: establish that we're busy doing something important on a planned schedule. We establish this early and then let the caller take it from there. If he or she doesn't choose to respect our time, at least we've made it clear that we do have other things to do, which gives us grounds to end the conversation if we need to. We establish our schedule by making that the first thing we say in the conversation. When the person says, "Hello, how's it going?" we answer with our busy-important-scheduled answer. "Pretty good, . . . trying to get some stuff out for the production people before lunch like I said I would. What can I do for you?" We've said it all; now it's up to the caller to decide whether he or she has something more important to talk about. If we have somebody in the office (and it's not someone we'd like to get rid of), we say, "Just having a little meeting with Pat about the overtime schedule. We should be through in a few minutes. Can I do something for you right quick, or would you like me to call you back when I have a little more time?" The politeness is there, and we've made it clear that we want to help, but we've gotten the message across that we've got something important going on.

Telephone conversations have a way of dragging on, long after all the messages have gotten across. Take the following conversation between people in engineering and shipping:

ENG: *Hey, Ed. This is Sue.*

SHPG: *Hi, Sue, how's it going?*

ENG: *Fine. Just wanted to check to see if you got that order for supplies we sent yesterday . . . the one we marked "RUSH."*

SHPG: *Sure did! Got it out to you this morning.*

ENG: *Hey, that's great! We really are hurting for that stuff.*

SHPG: *I figured you were. That's why I had the people move fast on it. You don't usually mark things "RUSH."*

ENG: *Well, that's right. I sure do appreciate it.*

SHPG: *Hey, no problem. You folks are always considerate. Glad to deal with a friendly group every once in a while.*

ENG: *Thanks. We try. I'm glad the stuff was in stock.*

SHPG: Well, it was here all right, and we got it out first thing this morning. You should have it in the noon shipment.

ENG: Good, we can start using it right after lunch.

SHPG: Just remember we're here to help. At least we try to.

ENG: You do more than try. I'll let you know if it doesn't show up.

SHPG: It'll show up all right, but you let me know if it doesn't. We'll get to the bottom of the problem if there's any mix-up.

ENG: I'm sure there won't be any problem. We'll get it.

SHPG: I know you will. It would be too bad if you didn't, after we got on it so fast. We started to do it last night, but we just had too many commitments.

ENG: There's no problem with today. I didn't even expect it that quick.

SHPG: Most people don't, but we try to move fast when somebody marks it "RUSH" and we feel they really are rushed.

ENG: That's fine. Well, I just wanted to check to see where things stood. Thanks a lot.

SHPG: You're welcome. We want to get things out as soon as possible. After all, that's our job.

ENG: I appreciate it, too. Maybe we can return the favor sometime.

SHPG: Hey, no need to think like that. We don't deserve anything for doing our job.

ENG: No, but a lot of people aren't doing their job. It's just good that somebody cares.

SHPG: Well, we sure do. We try . . .

This could go on forever, and usually does! How does it happen? It's simple. Nobody is working hard at getting out of the conversation. It takes two to have a conversation; as long as each is taking a turn, the conversation will go on forever. Somebody has got to quit taking a turn and just stop talking. The long pause will set the stage for hanging up. Then it's just a matter of saying good-bye and hanging up.

In all we've said about time management, we've tried to say that our goal is to let others know we're busy and that we're doing something important on a schedule. This will save us time only if we actually are busy, if we do spend our time on important things, and if we do plan some kind of usable schedule. It's not enough to get more time and protect the time we have. *We have to use the time well once we get it!* This means we need a plan, we need to follow that plan, and we need to check at the end of the day to see if we accomplished what we set out to do. We also need to be sure that we're more than just busy. We need to ask if we are doing what *we* ought to be doing or if someone else should be doing it. We'll talk more about delegation in another chapter. For now we'll say that more people waste valuable time by doing what others should be doing rather than by doing their own stuff poorly.

ORGANIZING

So far we've talked about only a part of what is necessary to set up the work. Another function, called *organizing*, plays a big role in getting us to the final objective we have set. *Organizing* is a pretty broad term and generally includes two things: the *structure* of the organization we have set up to do the job and the *people* in this organization. Since higher management usually handles the structure of the organization, we'll look mostly at that part of organizing concerned with people. First, though, let's note that we aren't talking about something big and complicated when we use the word *organization*. We're simply talking about any group of people who have joined together to get something done that they couldn't get done by themselves. This fits the *small work group* in one location as well as it does an entire organization of thousands of people scattered across many states or countries. And the same principles apply.

In Chapter 11 we will talk in detail about interviewing prospective employees, so we won't go into that here. However, since part of organizing includes staffing the organization, we should realize that when it comes time to fill a vacancy in our group, we will be expected to do interviews. Also, since one of the prospective employees will be working in our organization, we should look forward to meeting and finding out as much as possible about him or her. Most new supervisors, however, dread this particular phase of the job. A little knowledge of how to conduct the interview—and a little experience—should cause these fears to diminish considerably.

Right Person—Right Job

The whole object of the staffing phase of organizing is to try to match up the potential of the employee with the requirements of the job. Unfortunately, we often find that through poor staffing we end up making ourselves and our employees miserable. Frequently, we do a poor job of matching an employee's skills and interests with the job, then blame the employee for poor performance. We should really blame ourselves for poor judgment!

Getting the right people to do the right job makes a lot of sense from a lot of standpoints. Obviously, employees who are doing jobs for which they are well suited have fewer frustrations, see that they are useful to the organization, and feel that they have a chance to be recognized. As a result, they are most likely to be motivated to do their best and will be reasonably satisfied employees. From our standpoint as a supervisor, this solves a lot of our problems, because the employees' motivation should reduce absenteeism and turnover and increase productivity. We will then have more time to handle other aspects of our job. From the organization's standpoint, it is not only getting value for wages paid—it is also getting a good impression of *us* in the process. When our people perform well, it naturally reflects favorably on us. Note, too, that a mismatch between employee and job can make all of these things come out unfavorably.

There is another phase of organizing that we will deal with in detail in Chapter 12: *training*. It isn't enough to try to get employees and their jobs matched as well as possible. We must still make up the difference between the employees' present skills and the job requirements. This can best be done by training. Given enough time and patience, of course, employees will learn on their own. Many do. But this is rarely the most efficient way or the most practical approach from the organization's standpoint. Not only do we need our employees to know how to do their job, we need to *know* they know how to do their work. Training gives us this assurance because it gives our employees the opportunity to learn needed skills. If it's good training, we will see them demonstrating their proficiency. Then if they do not do their job properly, we look for some cause other than lack of training.

CONCLUSION

We have often defined the supervisor's job as getting the work done through other people. However, a portion of the supervisor's job includes some functions that are usually classified as managerial rather than as supervisory. They have many different names, but we'll divide them into four functions: planning, organizing, directing, controlling. Two of these, planning and organizing, have to do with setting the work up; the other two have to do with getting the work done. The world is full of proverbs about having a goal, but "If you don't know where you're going, any road will get you there," best describes the problem of planning. Many organizations never get anywhere because they don't really know where they want to go. Supervisors should always think in terms of planning, planning, planning. As simple as this sounds, it isn't easy to do with all the other things that are going on around the work area and across the desk. Once we've decided what to do, it's equally important to see that the right people are doing it. This comes under the heading of organizing. It's not enough just to plan: we must act on that plan. In simple terms, it's a matter of the right people doing the right thing at the right time. Anytime the supervisor has control over this function, it's important that attention be paid to it rather than allowing things to be done as they always have been done. When we coast along and neglect our responsibility, we are reminded of the old saying, "There's no special *reason* for doing it this way; we've just *always* done it this way!"

EXERCISES

1. Group discussion: Generate a list of things that the organization has to plan at least five years ahead. To how many of these do people make direct contributions, with specific inputs that help in the decision making? Should and could people contribute more than they do? Record the list for further discussion.

2. Group discussion: Generate a list of things the organization cannot plan more than a month in advance. To how many of

these do people contribute specific inputs that help in the decision making? Should and could people contribute more than they do? Record this list for further discussion.

3. Half-group discussion: Let half the group take the long-range-planning list and the other half the short-range-planning list. In small subgroups within these halves, decide what information is needed for each of the things planned. Go into as much detail as possible, even down to listing forms or reports that would be required, if applicable. When the subgroups are through, let each half compile its findings.

4. Group discussion: With the lists from exercise 3, see how much the long-range planning is dependent on the short-range results by comparing the two lists. Also, see if there is similarity or overlapping in the lists. (This exercise will do much to show the relationship between short- and long-range planning.)

5. Individual activity: Each person should look at his or her own organization and decide how it could be best organized if it were just now being created. The idea is to decide how many people would be required, what their qualifications would be, who would report to whom, etc. In other words, simply make up an organization to do what is now being done.

6. Group activity: Take one of the organizations worked on in exercise 5 and let the whole group decide how it would be organized if it were done from scratch. This means selecting an organization with which the whole group is familiar or creating an organization to do one of the tasks the organization now does. Note that one of the requirements is to find out what the goals, plans, and services for that operation are. (It shouldn't be an *expansion* of the work. The end product or service ought to be the same as it is now—or less—so that people can see that if they were starting over, they'd probably do things differently. As it is, tradition, custom, and the existing workforce have been used to reach the organization's goals.)

Chapter 8

GETTING THE WORK DONE (DIRECTING AND CONTROLLING)

All supervisors, no matter how many or how few people they supervise, can view their job as that of getting the work done through other people. Planning and organizing—discussed in Chapter 7—set the stage for the next two functions, *directing* and *controlling*. The best of plans and the best organization won't do the work. Only those under us can do it, and we must direct them in doing it and control the efforts they put forth *while* doing it. In most cases, planning and organizing are done at higher levels in the organization, while directing and controlling are done at the lower levels—usually at the first levels. So as a new supervisor we must be doubly conscious of the functions of directing and controlling.

DIRECTING

Of all the functions supervisors perform, by far the hardest is directing. Directing involves people, and people are complex, differing from one another and even themselves changing from one day to the next. People's needs vary, as do their ambitions, and as these things change, so do the ways in which people react in given situations. This means that just about when we think we have figured out how certain people will react to certain things, something we may not even be aware of (at home, at church, at the Little League field, etc.) causes a change so that they now react completely differently.

But the situation isn't hopeless. There are some common grounds on which people react pretty much the same way all the time, and even different people react the same way to certain things. This means that there are some things we can do that will give us a predictable result, even though we do them to people who are otherwise quite different from one another. Once we have found out these things, we can build our management philosophy around them. Let's look at some of these things and see if we can't find a basis on which to act and react with our people.

Facets of Directing

There are three facets of directing: leading, communicating, and motivating. Each is a skill, but each is hard to learn and even harder to define.

Leading.   What is leadership? If we ask a dozen people, we'll probably get a dozen different answers. It is an elusive quality, but recognizable in the people who have it. (More accurately, we can recognize the results of its presence, if not the quality itself.) Perhaps the easiest way to define leadership in this context is "a supervisor's ability to inspire the workers under him or her to work hard to achieve the goals of the organization." Although this is easy to measure in terms of results, it's hard to identify a specific action that a supervisor takes to get those results.

One thing we know: the idea that leaders are born, not made, is out of date. All of us can be better supervisors than we are. We can learn things that will produce better results. Leadership skills can be practiced, learned, and measured. There are some characteristics shared by people who have been rated as good leaders, and we can develop these as we get more experience and training.

For example, successful leaders usually have the ability to see other people's points of view. They don't necessarily agree with them or give in to them, but they at least have some *empathy* for those positions. They are sensitive to other people's problems and know why people feel the way they do. Successful leaders know how what they say will be taken—how it will affect other individuals. They probably know how those individuals will react to certain things that are done, and when the reaction is different from what they expect, they may even be able to analyze why it's different. Perhaps most important, successful leaders don't write off every undesirable behavior as just a "bad attitude."

Another characteristic good leaders have is the ability to see themselves as others see them. We generally speak of this as self-awareness. Here, again, is the ability to see how what we do will influence others. We should know how what we say will sound from another's perspective. Will the person resent it, miss the point altogether, or agree with it in principle? Good leaders can predict the answer pretty accurately. Good leaders even know their own weaknesses and faults and try to work around them. They don't let such flaws interfere with either their own performance or that of others under them. The important thing about seeing ourselves as others see us is that we are more likely to treat others fairly if we know they are reacting to something we have done or said, especially if we know why they are reacting that way.

Another characteristic of successful leaders that we can all learn is willingness to work. There are very few substitutes for hard work, and for leaders there is none. But the kind of hard work done by leaders is different from that done by those who are not leaders. Leaders are willing to put in long hours on tasks that are not exciting or rewarding—that may even be unpleasant—*just to get the job done.* This doesn't mean that they don't know how to delegate; it means that they don't shirk those tasks that have to be done sooner or later. When they see that a particular task has to be done, and that it's their job to do it, they tackle it without thinking about getting out of it or putting it off. Of all the characteristics of a successful leader, this may be the most difficult to learn.

Still another common characteristic of successful leaders is their ability to generate enthusiasm among their people. This enthusiasm is projected from the leaders and catches on with their people, so that they, too, seem to be caught up in the willingness to work just to get the task done. The ability to generate enthusiasm works differently in different leaders, but the results are the same. Their employees tackle their jobs with interest and excitement and may even give a cold shoulder to anyone who would make light of their job or try to change what they are doing. They get satisfaction from their jobs and don't think of their work as "that miserable interlude between weekends." As we said, leaders may differ in how they project this enthusiasm, but the results are there nevertheless. Most likely the leaders don't have what is popularly thought of as enthusiasm—the running-around-and-shouting kind. It isn't the back-slapping or hand-shaking style that sometimes passes for enthusiasm. It can best be described as an *intenseness that is contagious*.

A final common characteristic of good leaders is the willingness to accept responsibility. In fact, good leaders become very bored when there is little or no responsibility connected with what they are doing. They aren't afraid to accept the challenge of doing something that has risk to it. They are willing to take on a job at which they might fail, providing it also allows them the opportunity to succeed. They may go out and look for responsibility if they don't get it otherwise. Instead of waiting for someone to give them the authority to do something, they will probably be pushing the limits of their responsibility. If they get called on the carpet, it will be for taking on too much responsibility, not too little.

Communicating.   In Chapter 6 we discussed the subject of communication in great depth, so we suggest that the reader reread that material to get a refresher on the subject, keeping in mind that effective communication is an important characteristic of leadership. A few points need to be considered here, though, that were not mentioned earlier.

When we càn deliver a specific message to another person or a group *in just the way we want to get it across*, that's good communicating. Whether we are writing letters, speaking to groups or individuals, giving orders, or passing on policies, we haven't ended our responsibilities until the message is received *and under-*

stood. Whenever we hear ourselves saying, "Don't you remember, I told you . . . ," we can be sure we have just indicted ourselves as poor communicators. We have said to the receiver, "It's your problem, not mine!"

The best single measure of our ability to communicate is to see whether what we said produced the results we were trying to achieve. After all, that's the usual reason for communicating, anyway—to get some kind of action. The best sign that the message has gotten through successfully, then, is to see if the policy is being carried out, or if people are coming in on time, or if they are responding in a way that indicates that they really understand what has been said.

One final word about good communicating: it is not merely an asset, it's a *requirement* for the job. As a supervisor, we must accept responsibility for what we communicate. We cannot leave it up to those on the receiving end. We cannot blame our subordinates for not getting the message; rather, we must see that our subordinates get it even if it means doing the communicating all over again. Just as important, we must work equally hard to communicate up the line as down. Our boss and bosses higher up must manage as well as they can on the basis of the information they get from us.

Motivating.   Motivation is a little different from leadership in that leadership inspires people to work for external reasons—often for the leader—while motivation gets them to work for internal reasons—because they want to, regardless of how they feel about the boss or the organization. Motivation is probably the single most important aspect of our supervisory job. We can't *make* the employees work for very long and expect a good job from them. The desire to work must come from within the individual if it's going to last. But now we have a problem, because it's our specific responsibility as a supervisor to see that the workers feel this way about their job—that they *want to work*. This means that we can't just say, "Well, it's not my fault. They simply don't want to work." When we say that, we are openly admitting we're doing a bad job of supervising. This doesn't mean that we won't run into this problem; it only means that we have to accept responsibility for correcting it.

In order to motivate our employees, we have to understand

why people work in the first place and what it is that makes them work harder or keeps them from working as hard as they can. Of course, the basic needs are as they have always been: food, clothing, shelter, and safety. Once these needs have been satisfied, certain *social* needs must be met, and people are motivated when they see a chance to meet these needs. For instance, people want to be accepted by their fellow workers. They want to think that they are liked and that others want to have them around. They want to be an accepted part of the work group. We must recognize this need and make every effort to help the workers feel that they are a part of the organization and that the other workers respect their work. We can even do this purposely, by reflecting any favorable remarks we hear: "By the way, Charlie liked it very much because I gave you this assignment." Very few successful leaders have gotten that way by sowing discord and suspicion among their workers.

Another need workers have is for *self-esteem*. This relates somewhat to our previous discussion: people like to think that the job they are doing is important and they are good at it. It's hard for any of us to get motivated over a job that has been downgraded and doesn't appear to amount to much as far as the organization is concerned. That's why people worry about titles and having their name on the door or being in the official directory. They like their coworkers to know that they are important enough to the organization to be recognized for it. Such little things as putting nameplates on the desks often go a long way toward meeting these needs. Employees also want to feel that other workers respect them for their ability to do the job. They like to think that others look up to them just a little for their ability. When we come along and ridicule any employee in front of the other workers, we not only put that employee in an embarrassing position, we also destroy the self-esteem that is so important to him or her. That's the main reason we are always told to *correct in private, approve in public*.

In discussing these three points—leading, communicating, and motivating—we haven't meant to imply that we should baby employees. It is just common sense to recognize that certain things cause workers to work better and that we should take advantage of these things. This is simply a calculated effort to get the best results from the individuals who work for us. After all, we expect those individuals to give their machinery the proper care and maintenance; how could we possibly do less for them? It is our way of getting employees to work because they *want* to, not because they *have* to. In the end, the results are better for the organization, for us, and certainly for the employees themselves.

CONTROLLING

While directing is the most difficult function, controlling is perhaps the most *critical*. When we plan, organize, and direct, there is still the problem of controlling all of what we have planned, organized, and directed. Without the proper controls, all the effort may be wasted. Essentially, we control three things, or a combination of them—money, material, and people. The problem is that each is handled differently; each takes a different skill. We find it easier to budget money and materials because they are usually quite constant. Money will buy just so much, and we have just so much money; therefore, the decision is what to do with what we have. But people aren't that easy to budget; they aren't all alike, and even a single individual may show different qualities from one time to another. While a dollar is a dollar, a worker isn't a worker. Replace one secretary with another and things can be quite different. When we start to budget (control) people, we have to take into consideration that they work at a different speed in the morning than in the afternoon and that their attitudes and behavior may not be the same on Monday as on Friday.

Controlling is most closely related to planning, which simply means that we must have something to control. Often we may try to control when we actually haven't got a plan to follow. The plan serves as the *standard* against which we control, so without the plan we are doing some guesswork with our controlling. For example, when we decide in the middle of an operation that the cost is getting out of hand and then start to control, we really aren't measuring against a preset standard (or plan), so it isn't completely correct to say we are practicing the function of control. If we had planned correctly and started our controlling as soon as the plan went into effect, things wouldn't have gotten out of hand in the first place. A rule of thumb (which is not really a rule but a guide) says that when we find ourselves in a drastic predicament with people, materials, or money, either the planning or the controlling stage broke down somewhere.

Steps in Controlling

We generally think of controlling as consisting of three steps:

1. Determining standards
2. Measuring results against standards
3. Taking remedial action as necessary

As we have said, the plan is the standard, but here we are talking about something more specific. We are looking for the answers to certain basic questions. We need to know who sets the standards and how we will know that they are the standards. The plan may or may not have specified how far off the standards we can get without being in trouble. That is information we must have; we cannot hope to control without it. Another thing we need to know about the standards is who will measure the results of our work and who will see the results of those measurements. Is there a quality-control person who reports to headquarters, or do we have someone on our staff who has the partial responsibility for watching quality?

Of utmost importance is the question of what will be measured. Why is this particular thing being measured? Are we getting valid information, or are we watching a meaningless figure? For example, do we fill out forms to track the number of magazine subscriptions held by the office while we disregard the cost of rearranging walls and partitions? The point is that we must control the right things or the controlling effort will go for naught. Along the same lines, we may end up controlling something to death. If we have two people assigned full-time to watch for flaws or rejects that aren't really that costly, we are in fact driving a tack with a sledgehammer. We may *over*react to situations. The boss says to watch out for certain problems or expenditures, and we set up a control system much more complicated than is really needed. Long after the crisis is past, forms are still being filled out and reports are being sent up the line. Once forms and reports come into existence, it's very difficult to get rid of them. *Start them only when there is a truly pressing need!*

What are some of the items that may be measured? Obviously, we want to measure output of goods or services. How long did it take to provide the service or turn out the product? How much money did it take? What was the final quality, and how many units did we actually produce? Then we need to look at expenses closely. When we measure expenses, we must measure *all* of them. Are we taking into account everything that is being charged to the particular job? Are we considering staff help, hidden costs, load factors, and other costs that will eventually have to be accounted for?

Another thing we must account for is the use of resources. Again, we're talking about people, time, and money—but this time in a little different light. Here the question of measurement is one of efficient use. Are we doing a good job of matching people and jobs? Remember, it isn't necessarily proof of good supervision if the job gets done well. We must consider who's doing the job. If our people are capable of doing much more because of experience, education, or natural talent, we can't be too proud of the fact that the job is done well. The trick is to match ability and job requirements as closely as possible, then let the people grow out of their jobs as they develop. As a supervisor we must constantly measure—at least in our mind—how well each employee fits the job, as well as whether he or she has outgrown it.

All of this is true for the other resources we have. Are we really getting the most out of our overtime? Are we doing some jobs that could be left undone or eliminated altogether, then spending time and money on overtime to do essential things? We get trapped sometimes by saying that we have to go into overtime to do a very important job, failing to realize that we got into this situation simply because we failed to control our time properly. We spent valuable time doing unimportant things, thereby forcing ourselves into overtime. The same objection applies to using people to handle nonessential details when they could be doing things that *must* be done sooner or later. It's all right for everyone to pitch in and help, but if pitching in means that we must neglect other work that will get us behind schedule or cost us time and money later on, then we've made a bad decision.

Using the Budget to Control

Perhaps the oldest and best control mechanism we have is the budget. We complain about it and even wish we didn't have it, but we should be glad that there is something as rigid as the budget to guide us in our controlling. Few organizations could run very smoothly without a budget, because it provides one of the best standards we could want. It gives us not only something to measure our progress by but also something to aim at. As we constantly compare ourselves with the budget, we are also getting feedback on where we can expect to be at the end of the budget period. Here is a means of measuring even the small parts of the job, because budgets are made up of parts. Good budgets are made up of *accurate* parts; bad budgets are made up of *padded* parts. This isn't the place to go into detail on the budget, but let's notice a thing or two about it. First of all, it is put together to let the organization know just how much money there is and where the best places to spend it are. Good budget planning takes into account local needs, and those preparing the budget will solicit help from all levels in determining the best use of all the money. The trouble comes when each level starts to be unrealistic about its needs. When each group, department, or division adds just a little, by the time the total budget is drawn up, there is either too big a demand or the organization is looking for more money than it really needs. When this happens, the fate of most budgets is that someone at the top starts to whittle down the figure and everyone suffers. "But if I don't raise my figure, I'll get hurt, because they will probably make an across-the-board cut!" Even if this is so, that's a management decision, and we don't have the right to pad our figures just because everyone else does. We shouldn't include anything we can't substantiate, because sooner or later we will have to account for what we have requested. If our figures won't stand the test, not only will the budget be cut, but our reputation as a supervisor will suffer. The wisest thing to do is to make a realistic budget, back it up with a good set of facts and figures, then let management wrestle with the problem of cutting the budget if it has to. Later on, if the work can't be done because of budget problems (lack of money), we can show that we put in a legitimate request that got cut by someone else.

Measuring Results

Once we have determined the standards by which we are to control, we have to measure the results *against these standards.* Sometimes this measurement is routine—just a matter of seeing how many units were produced, how many pages were typed, how many sales were made, and so forth, then reporting the obvious results in whatever manner is expected. But not all of our evaluating is that clear-cut or that easy. In some situations there are so many contributing factors that we aren't quite sure just what the results mean. It may be that the operation is too large, like a long assembly line with many feed-ins, or it may be that there are many people making different contributions to the end product—or the output may be a service, and that means there is the customer to consider. How can we measure in circumstances like these?

One of the best avenues open to us is the process known as *sampling.* There isn't anything complicated about it. It's just a means of looking at large or complicated operations and getting reliable results without having to measure every detail and assess the output of every person working on the project. We simply look at a small, average sample and take the results to represent the entire operation. Another way to accomplish the same thing is to take one complete operation out of several, assuming that all the rest are like this one. Actually, with a little help, we can do a pretty good job of sampling and obtain very reliable results. Once we get in the habit of doing this, we will be on the lookout for useful sampling techniques all the time. We check the absentee list on random occasions and see if particular individuals or a particular number of people are absent. We spot-check three or four days in a row to see just how much time our workers are taking for break or when they are coming in from lunch. We look at customer complaints once a week for several weeks to see if any one thing is beginning to give trouble. Such assessments will provide good indicators of just how well we are doing and are effective means of controlling.

When sampling doesn't seem to be a very good way of measuring the results, and it seems too difficult to measure the whole operation, there is another way that may help: finding a *substitute* measurement. For example, we can look at such things as absenteeism or tardiness and get a good idea of what the morale is in the group. If turnover is high, this fact may be a good substitute measurement of how much job enrichment is going on. A look at previous production records may be a good measure of the group's motivation or morale, providing other things are equal. The substitute may be a tangible means of measuring very intangible things, such as attitudes, job satisfaction, and morale.

Of course, when we are measuring one thing to assess something else, as with any of our measurements, we'd better be sure the measure is accurate. Even measuring a seemingly simple thing, such as how well one typist is doing compared to the others in the office, can be tricky. If one typist is doing simple items and the others are doing more complex ones, counting the *number of pages* is a poor way of looking at results. On the other hand, one usually accurate typist who is doing the same simple job day in and day out may begin to show a high error rate because the job *doesn't* have some variety in it. The errors may indicate that the typist is getting less satisfaction than previously. It might be the same for a salesperson. We need to be careful in evaluating one salesperson's results against another's until we are sure the territories are comparable. It's all right to measure sales as a means of determining how good a salesperson is, providing we know what other salespeople in the same or similar territories have done. If a salesperson isn't doing as well as he or she should, what is the potential in that territory? Is the competition getting stronger? Does the salesperson really know the new line? Has he or she had the proper training—the same kind of training as the other salespeople? In other words, is our measurement really accurate in all respects? If so, then it becomes a good control device; if not, it becomes a dangerous tool to use in making decisions.

Remedial Action

Controlling would be useless if it didn't include the final facet of control—taking remedial action when it is required. While controlling shouldn't be thought of only in terms of remedial action, it certainly includes this aspect. When things are shown by our measuring processes to be running along smoothly, then we should be good enough supervisors to recognize this and leave things alone. But when the results show that the situation is getting out of hand or that we really should be doing better, then we need to know enough to step in and take some action. Although we may not be the ones who should take the action, we may be the ones to instigate it. As obvious as it seems, just knowing that something is wrong isn't enough; reporting it to the right people is important. If we have found that a problem exists somewhere in the group, we should ask ourselves, "Who really needs to know this?" The answer should be someone who can do something about it. Whether it's an overtime problem, a union grievance, or what have you, telling the right person as soon as possible may head off a much more serious problem later on. When it comes to determining who the right person is, perhaps the worst thing we can do is say, "It's not my problem." Remember, it's our problem as soon as we hear or know about it, and it's our problem until something is done about it or someone else assumes responsibility for the problem. When our boss says, "Okay, I'll take over now," then we have done all we can, even if we don't like what our boss is doing.

Another important part of notifying the right person at the right time is doing it in the right way. And that doesn't mean giving him or her a telephone call at quitting time and reporting the bare details. If that person doesn't grasp the importance of the problem, or misses some of the details, we've got to accept responsibility for the poor results that come from improper control. The best approach is to put the problem in writing, which not only captures the information in permanent form, but also provides a record that we spotted the weakness and made an effort to get it controlled. But this latter reason is secondary to the first one. There is no justification to report something merely to protect ourselves. If this becomes our prime reason for acting, we aren't likely to do a very thorough job of reporting the facts; neither will we work at organizing our material, making sure what we say is clear, readable, etc.

Finally, let's repeat what was said earlier: it's a lot better to solve the problem ourselves than to pass it on to someone else. This means we must have the authority to take the necessary remedial action. It also means we may have to go through the entire planning, organizing, and directing process all over again. If that's what the remedial action requires, being a good supervisor means doing it that way rather than just closing our eyes to reality and continuing down our present path toward eventual poor results.

Discipline

Part of getting work done through others, and part of directing others, is using properly administered discipline to correct behavior or to prevent poor performance. For several obvious reasons, discipline is at times unpleasant, and it is certainly something that neither we nor the employees look forward to. But when it is necessary, it should be done properly.

Let's back up and see how we got to discipline in the first place. In many cases we discipline people because we didn't do our part when behaviors started to get unsatisfactory. If we considered our day-to-day supervision as important as it really is, we would have taken care of the problem before we needed to take more severe action. Ideally, use of *positive reinforcement*—praising people when they do a good job, thanking them for helping out, etc.—alone would preclude any problems. Unfortunately, we don't supervise in an ideal world. People mess up. They miss the standards. They come in late to work or from break. Employees leave messy workstations, miss deadlines, and upset customers. They are insubordinate, get cross with other employees, and use incorrect tools. They let poor-quality work get out and fail to report breakdowns. What do we do then?

Constructive Feedback.   For onetime violations of rules or missing standards, or for minor infractions such as coming in a few minutes late once or twice, we talk to employees about the expectations and use *constructive feedback*. We make certain they know the starting time; we tell them what we've noticed about their behavior, with dates and times, and see whether they have any problems meeting the standards. It's important for us point out two things:

1. "This isn't like you."
2. "This meeting isn't a big deal."

First, we provide encouragement when we say we know this behavior isn't like them. We are saying that they normally meet standards and do satisfactory work, that we're talking to them because their present behavior is unlike them and we want to make sure there isn't a problem of some kind. Second, employees need to know that we haven't jumped into formal discipline. This meeting is more a matter of counseling than of discipline. We're not writing them up or counting this as a verbal warning. The *coming in late* is a big deal, but this conversation isn't. Finally, we leave them on a positive note by saying something like, "I know you'll take care of this; thank you for your time," and getting their agreement as they leave.

So, when do we get to formal discipline? Here, again, there are a couple of things to remember. We consider formal discipline when (1) the frequency of the problem continues or increases and (2) it starts to affect others. If an employee continues coming in late and others have to take up the slack—do the person's work—then the problem is more serious and corrective action must be taken. Discipline becomes formal discipline when (1) we tell the employee it's formal and (2) we explain the consequences of formal discipline—the progressive steps of severity.

Trying to Change Behavior.   The hardest thing for us to remember at this stage is that we aren't trying to punish the employee for infractions; we're trying to change his or her behavior for the better. *We want the employee to perform up to standard.* We can think of the difference between punishment and discipline in this way: The purpose of punishment is to get the employee to pay a debt for the wrongs done in the past. The purpose of discipline is to get the employee's attention so he or she will perform correctly in the future. Many people call this positive progressive discipline: *positive* in that it ends up for the good of both the organization and the employee—the employee is performing to requirements and hence is still on the job; *progressive* in that the effort to get the employee's attention becomes progressively more severe if the behavior fails to change; *discipline* in that we aren't trying to punish, but to get the employee to change his or her behavior on the job. Incidentally, this is our focus from the beginning of our everyday supervision. Positive reinforcement is aimed at continuing the desired behavior. When this doesn't work, we try constructive feedback, which is a mild way to attempt to change the behavior back to the original satisfactory way of performing. If this doesn't work, then we institute formal discipline, which becomes increasingly severe as needed to get the behavior to revert to what it should be.

The first step in formal discipline is usually a *verbal warning*. As we've said, we give a verbal warning when the behavior starts to affect other employees and its frequency continues or increases. Discipline is formal discipline when we tell the employee so and when we explain the consequences of continuing the unsatisfactory behavior. The conversation may go something like this:

SUPERVISOR: *Al, I asked you to stop by because I noticed you were several minutes late again this morning. That's twice this week: ten minutes Monday and today. You know, we've talked about this before.*

AL: *Yeah, but what's five minutes? I more than make up for it when I get started.*

SUPERVISOR: *Yes, you work hard, but that's not the issue. The last time we talked, I made sure you knew that 7:00 A.M. is the time everyone is supposed to be at their workstations working.*

AL: *I remember, but I said then that I didn't see the big deal about a few minutes. Before the day is over, I'm having to make up the work of the others on the line. Why don't you talk to them about their work?*

SUPERVISOR: *Al, their work is not the subject of this discussion, is it? Is there some reason why you can't make it on time, or is it that you just don't think it's important? You could leave a few minutes earlier each day.*

AL: *Well, I've found that if I leave fifteen minutes earlier, I still barely make it. That's the time the school buses are rolling, so I don't gain much time.*

SUPERVISOR: *Then it sounds like you need to leave thirty minutes earlier, doesn't it?*

AL: *Aw, come on. Why should I leave in the middle of the night just to get here a few minutes earlier? Why don't you take into account my hard work?*

SUPERVISOR: *You should leave a little earlier to get here on time because that's the official starting time. I can't make an exception for you any more than I can make one for anyone else. For that*

reason, and for the excessive times you've been late — on the dates
I've shown you — I'm going to issue you a verbal warning. This
will go into your file. You realize the next step, if you don't start
coming in on time, is to issue you a written reprimand. I'm sure
you don't want that on your record, so I'm looking for you to start
coming in on time. How about it?

AL: *I'm sorry you feel that way. I still think you ought to do*
something about the other folks who aren't working as hard as I
am.

So, what did we accomplish with Al? Actually, we'll have to wait
and see. He never really committed to coming in on time. Remember, our goal is to change his behavior. Part of that new behavior is
to have him believe that coming in on time is important and
critical to the work operation. We don't have to defend our position on dealing with the other workers. That's between us and
them, not us and Al. We need to close this interview with a set time
for review of his behavior. We need to give ourselves enough time
to see what his pattern is going to be. If he is consistently on time
for that specified period, then we clear his slate of the verbal
warning. If he continues his present habits, then we get more
severe. Some organizations insert different kinds of discipline
between the steps we're talking about here, but all get to the same
three steps at one point or another:

1. Verbal warning
2. Written reprimand
3. Termination

Some organizations issue more than one verbal warning before
moving to the written reprimand; some try time off without pay
after the written reprimand. We should be familiar with these
rules, which are often a part of a union contract. *One of the quickest*
ways to foul up is not to follow the rules for dealing with poor performers.
In the conversation we had with Al we stated the observed behavior; we had specific dates and times documented; we asked if there
was a problem; we called it formal discipline; and we explained
the consequences for not following the stated standards. If Al
doesn't change his behavior, the next step will be to give him a
written reprimand and to let him know that the next consequence

is termination. Again, let's understand that our objective is to get him to change his behavior, not to punish him. If we give him the written reprimand and then he starts to come in on time, we should feel excited, not disappointed that we didn't get to fire him. We're not out to play "Gotcha!" If Al turns around and continues to meet the standards, it's a victory for us, it means the organization doesn't have to spend money hiring and training someone else, and it allows us to clear out our files of these reprimands.

There are certain rules to follow for successful discipline. Let's see what some of them are.

- *Rule 1: Be consistent.*   Nothing is completely fair in this world, but some things don't call for as much "fairness" as others. When we're handing out praise and give somebody too much, he or she seldom complains about the unfairness. But when we hand out a seemingly unfair amount of discipline, people resent it and are quick to let us know about it. This means we must strive to maintain some kind of consistency in our approach. If one person gets suspended for being tardy four times in a month, anybody/everybody should be suspended for being late four times in a month. The consistency must hold not only for our own employees, but also for employees across departments. It will quickly undermine our efforts if someone in another department metes out a different degree of discipline than we do, and we can undermine other supervisors if we don't strive to keep our own efforts in line with theirs.

- *Rule 2: Avoid being emotional.*   If we must discipline an employee who performs unsatisfactorily, we must not get emotionally involved when we discuss the situation with him or her. We can't get into a yes-you-did, no-I-didn't kind of exchange. If the employee has made us angry or if we are exasperated over the person's behavior, then we'd better postpone the action until we've had a chance to cool off. Even if the employee loses his or her temper and gets childish about the matter, we still must have the dignity and patience to behave maturely.

- *Rule 3: Match the discipline with the violation.*   It is a serious thing to invoke the power of the job to discipline someone. When one human being has the power to make another person lose pay, miss days at work, or have poor ratings noted in a personnel file, it is not to be taken lightly. In any society there must be order; this means that someone must have higher accountability than others, and hence the right to exercise control. If this control means that we have to discipline someone, we want the severity of the discipline to match the person's misbehavior insofar as possible. Not only are we being consistent this way, but we are also striving to be fair in the seriousness of the process.

- *Rule 4: Discipline for improved performance.* The problem with calling any form of discipline "punishment" is that it tends to make us look backward instead of forward. If we look back, we see only the poor performance, and we see the punishment as a way to get even with the employee for this misconduct. If we look ahead, we see the punishment as a means to correct the behavior and thus assure good performance in the future. Discipline serves two basic functions: (1) it keeps the employees from repeating the poor performance, and (2) it tends to keep others from committing the same violation of the workplace rules.

- *Rule 5: Provide an out for good behavior.* One problem we have in exercising a firm hand is that we fail to make provisions for employees to clean their records. When an employee violates the organization's rules to such an extent that some form of discipline must be administered, this goes on the employee's record. We also have to find a way to put something in the records when poor performance is corrected. If we use a demerit system, that system should have a positive counterpart—a merit system.

- *Rule 6: Don't delay discipline.* Even though we've said that we don't want to discipline when we're emotionally involved with the situation, neither do we want to delay action so long that the employee will fail to grasp the significance of the event and the action we're taking. If we are trying to see that the poor performance isn't repeated, the action we take should be as closely related to that poor performance as we can make it. We don't want to store up our discipline, like the mother who says, "Just wait until your dad gets home!"

- *Rule 7: Don't hold grudges.* When an employee does something wrong, remember that it is the performance we don't like, not the individual. If we make the mistake of holding the action against the person, then we're starting to become vindictive. We can't get into the habit of saying to ourselves, "She fouled up once, so she'll do it again," and then when it happens say, "I told you so!"

Obviously, there are more rules than these seven, but these will go a long way toward making us good disciplinarians. We won't deal here with the disciplinary interview, since that's covered in detail in the chapter on interviewing; but let's look at some questions we must ask if we're going to be successful at administering discipline, which includes some discussion and interviewing with the employee. First and foremost, we must be certain that the employee knows the standard on which his or her performance is evaluated. This means we have to ask ourselves, "Is there a standard?" If the answer is no, then we don't have to go any further; we can't discipline if there's no standard to go by. The standards need to be realistic, measurable, and certainly *doable*.

Next, we ask ourselves, "Does the employee know the standard?" If we haven't sat down and gone over our expectations with the employee, showing just what we expect and how we'll measure performance, again, we don't have to go any further. We can't hand out discipline to an employee who doesn't know what we expect. We might expand this question to include, "Has the employee been trained to meet the standard?" It is not enough that we have a standard and that we've told the employee what we expect. If we haven't trained our employees in how to do what we want them to do and haven't seen them do it correctly, we aren't on very safe ground when it comes to disciplining them.

The next question we ask is, "Have we told the employee how we feel about his or her performance?" Many supervisors will talk *about* their employees, but not *to* them. We'll tell all the other supervisors about the bad performance we're getting, but we never call the employee in to discuss this behavior. This is a pretty personal thing. We start off by saying, "Here's how I see your performance." Then we offer documentation, specific occasions when these things happened or when things either weren't done at all or weren't done a specific way. We compare this to the standard and show why we feel the employee has misperformed.

If we haven't been open and frank with the employee and don't have the documentation, we aren't ready to take disciplinary action.

We then ask ourselves, "Does the employee know the consequences for continued poor performance?" Most organizations practice progressive discipline, meaning that for each offense the discipline gets more and more severe, perhaps leading ultimately to dismissal. If we haven't explained this to the employee, we can't really proceed with further disciplinary steps. We might also add here that the employee ought to know the consequences for *improved performance,* too.

Now we ask, "Has a date been set for review of the employee's performance?" Failing to ask this question causes the downfall of many good supervisors. They do everything right up to this point, then say, "I want to see you straighten this out as quickly as possible," without setting a deadline for review. The review should be as soon as the employee has had a chance to perform the task a sufficient number of times or as soon as there is a chance to show that the problem has been corrected. If the employee has been late several times in a month, we should set a date for review in a month or six weeks, giving the employee an opportunity to make adjustments in his or her personal life.

As we've said, discipline isn't easy; but by following these rules and asking these questions, we'll be on much safer ground, especially if we remember one important thing: whenever we discipline, we should have specific documentation to back up the things we're talking about. This means dates, times, amounts, situations—even witnesses if necessary. We won't get very far if we go in and say, "I'm going to have to discipline you because you're late all the time."

Documentation.   We've spent some time talking about discipline, but we don't want it to sound as if all our emphasis should be on disciplining employees. Our goal is always to get the most out of our employees with the least effort on our part. The ideal is that all employees will perform at a high level, be interested in their job, and try to excel. We hope that there is considerable loyalty to the job and that each person is striving to improve his or her performance. Further, we are always looking for employees who need little or no correction, only an occasional training or coaching session. These are the things we shoot for, and hope for, but admittedly get only occasionally, perhaps never from all our employees at the same time. Hence, we do have to do some correction and take some disciplinary measures. The steps we've just discussed should aid us in doing the job more easily.

There is another phase of watching performance that we need to consider. As with discipline, it might sound as if we're watching the employees too closely and perhaps even as if we don't trust them. As we'll see, that's not the case. It is the matter of *documentation*. It is embarrassing when we confront an employee for some infraction and he or she discovers that we don't have accurate records of when and where the infraction took place. When we say to an employee, "You've been late a lot recently," and don't have the dates and times, it sounds pretty weak. If we say, "You're always negative about assignments," when we really mean that on several occasions the employee has given us some lip about doing a tough or dirty job, we are going to lose any argument that comes up. This means we must learn to keep better records. We make a note of dates, times, instances, situations, quotations, etc., so we can come back and document our discussion if and when we need to. Good supervisors make a habit of keeping records, even though they may not expect or plan to use the information. The rule to remember is that documentation after the fact doesn't hold much water. Simply trying to recall the days the employee got into an argument with another person on the same shift or failed to report that a piece of equipment was working improperly or came in ten minutes late isn't likely to give us solid information to go on when we have to confront the employee in a disciplinary situation. Remember, we aren't spying; we're simply keeping track of facts and situations as they happen—as they are *known to the employee* at the time they happen.

CONCLUSION

There are two parts to planning: planning the work and working the plan. We can't say which one is the more important. We can only say that unless each is done well, the results will suffer drastically. We've seen that getting the work done takes both directing and controlling. We have to emphasize that the task of *directing* the people under us is well named. In many ways, we're neither leading nor pushing; *we're pointing the way.* Since our job as a supervisor is to see that others do the work, we demonstrate our best directing not by our visibility out in front of the troops or by screaming orders from the throne, but by motivating, encouraging, and helping others do the work *because they want to.* Successful supervisors are the ones who direct by getting their people to believe in the job, not in the boss. (It's all right to believe in the boss, but that alone shouldn't be the reason they work.) If we really are looking to be a success at supervising, we have to give up the idea that only *born leaders* make good supervisors; we have to understand that supervision is simply a long list of well-done skills, each of which can be learned. Directing people is one of those important skills!

Controlling is the least exciting and perhaps the most critical of the skills required to get the job done. It's a matter of knowing what's going on and knowing it soon enough and well enough to do something about it before it's too late to change the direction in which things are headed. It takes attention to details. It takes looking at records. It means knowing for sure what we expect and seeing how close we come to those expectations. It means that we have to have a certain amount of flexibility and agility in order to move fast to rectify a bad situation. It's the last chance we have to correct poor planning and poor directing. If we're good enough at it, we can turn even a bad situation into one that gets the job done.

EXERCISES

1. Individual exercise: Individuals should think of a person who works for them now or has worked for them in the past whom they know is considered to have a bad attitude. They should think of a *specific* person. Then they should decide *why* they think the person has a bad attitude and make a list of the reasons.

2. Group activity: In front of the group, make a list of all the characteristics cited in exercise 1 that supposedly reflect a bad attitude. When the list gets fairly long, have the group decide how many of the characteristics listed are observable and how

many of them couldn't be seen by someone standing around watching the people being discussed. (The point is to show that what we consider a bad attitude is most often poor performance. If that's the case, we don't try to change the attitude but rather the performance.)

3. Individual activity: Let each person pick a manager whom he or she regards highly *as a manager* and write down the characteristics that caused that person to be selected. When this task is complete, list these characteristics in front of the group without specifying the names of the managers. See how many of the characteristics were the same. Begin to make an overall list of characteristics of good managers. Save this list.

4. Individual activity: Let each person think of a great leader he or she admires and knows a little about. These leaders may be historical figures, such as Napoleon or Lincoln, or they may be more contemporary, such as Golda Meir. After picking a *specific person*, individuals should list the characteristics of that person that made him or her a great leader. When the lists are complete, collect this data, and, without indicating the names of the leaders, come up with a list of characteristics that great leaders have in common. Save this list.

5. Group activity: Now compare the two lists from exercises 3 and 4. There's a good chance that the lists won't be very similar, though there will be some similarity, of course. From your comparison, decide whether we are looking for the same thing when we talk about a supervisor (or manager) and a leader. We might go a step further and ask how some of the leaders we picked would have made out as managers in our organization, especially at lower levels.

6. Group activity: Brainstorm all the ways the organization has of getting information that allows it to control the activities of the organization. Which information is supplied by the first-level supervisors? Could they do a better job of providing this information? Do people dread filling out or preparing any of these reports or forms? Why?

Chapter 9

DELEGATION

In the first chapter we define the supervisor's role as "getting the job done through others." Simply put, that's delegation. So, what is delegation? By any other name, it is still delegation. Over the years, changing vocabulary has given us such terms as empowerment, shared decision making, and creating entrepreneurial spirit. For the new supervisor, it's easier to say, simply, "I'm going to delegate this to you."

Delegation is a skill that doesn't necessarily come naturally. After all, we made it to the first-line supervisor's job because we were very good at *doing* something. Ironically, the thing we were good at—what got us this job—is usually something we should now be delegating to someone else. In this chapter we'll learn how to let go of something we've been good at, can probably do better and faster than can those who work for us, and probably get a lot of satisfaction out of doing. We'll learn what we can and can't delegate, should and shouldn't delegate, and how to deal with the risks involved in any kind of delegation.

IMPORTANCE OF DELEGATION IN THE ROLE OF THE SUPERVISOR

We know that a good supervisor gets the job done through others. But there's more to it than just getting others to do the job; there's the matter of getting them to *want* to do the job and to want to do it well. There's the matter of how much tracking and follow-up we have to do when we do delegate. There's the matter of how much training we have to do before and during the delegation process. There's the matter of knowing which person has both the skill to do the delegated tasks and the motivation to meet the necessary deadlines. (The matter of motivation is discussed in Chapter 10.) Good supervisors practice these things as a matter of course—when they have learned the skill sufficiently.

Why should we delegate tasks, when we can do them faster and better and are usually more motivated to do so ourselves? The easiest and most correct answer is that *it just isn't our job to do the work of our employees*. We have jobs to do that hourly employees shouldn't be doing, and we are appraised and evaluated on those things. When we spend our time doing other people's work, our work isn't getting done, and we should be appraised as not doing a very good job. Frequently, new supervisors compensate for doing other people's work during regular hours by catching up on their own work after hours. That makes for long days! The most important reason for delegation, though by far not the only good reason, is that delegation allows us time to do our own job. It allows us—the supervisor—to do the things that only the supervisor is supposed to do.

For example, it is our responsibility to do the *planning* for the work group we supervise. Workers should be involved in helping to set the goals, as they aren't likely to try very hard to meet someone else's goals, but the responsibility of seeing that the goals are set and are realistic rests with us. Likewise, the *scheduling* of who is going to do what each day or each work period is our responsibility. The hourly people are going to be *evaluated* on the work they do, and we are going to do that evaluating. The person's peers may have some input, but we must see that the evaluations are made and that they represent the truth about each employee's job performance. That takes time. Furthermore, we are the only one who should *discipline*, as we'll see shortly, as well as *praise and reward* employees. We have to do our own personal planning, too; keeping up with each day's to-do list and short-range plan is essential to being a good supervisor. These things shouldn't be done after hours. They demand good, alert thought time, and we should take the time during the scheduled work-day.

One of the things proper delegation does is define our role as supervisor. The grocery-store manager who consistently pushes in the carts from the parking lot or sacks groceries when high-school students are paid to do these things is failing to define his or her role, and all the employees will have a hard time identifying with his or her managerial role. (This also reduces the desire in many of the employees to become a store manager!) There's a pretty good chance that the reason there aren't enough eighteen-year-olds scheduled to work at the time the carts need to be brought in or the groceries sacked is that the manager spent too much time doing their work and not enough planning and scheduling the workers. A little time spent studying the customers-per-hour figures from previous weeks might reveal some meaningful numbers on how many workers to schedule on a given day.

In Chapter 8, we talked about directing and controlling as functions of managing (supervision). Delegation is one of the directing activities and one of the unique aspects of supervision; it means that we have the authority to tell another person to do something and to hold that person accountable for doing it. Another unique aspect of supervision is that we are held accountable for the completion of the task, even though we aren't the one actually doing the work. That's why we say that delegation is one of the skills that help define the supervisor's job. This process of assigning work to others and holding them accountable for it is part of the controlling function. Whenever we measure an employee's activity, set deadlines and standards, and hold him or her accountable for work, we are exercising the controlling function. When we become a supervisor, we take on a new role, which is the guiding, directing, evaluating, and controlling the work of others. Before we were made a supervisor, all we had to worry about was ourselves and our own job. Now we have to watch and look out for others and their jobs. That can get pretty frightening!

IMPORTANCE OF DELEGATION IN THE ROLE OF THE SUBORDINATE

Good delegation also defines the work of subordinates and the team they make up. As we will see in the chapter on motivation, delegation of real responsibility is a good motivating tool. The employees not only *feel* a part of the organization's real activity, they *are* a part of it! They get to make decisions, offer suggestions, and devise innovative ways of solving problems. Delegation allows for them to exercise these skills as well as to learn new jobs and new responsibilities and develop new skills. Watching subordinates as they accept or reject delegation is a great way to learn things about them as future supervisors. It is one of the best performance-evaluation tools available to us. The process of taking on these assignments broadens employees' view of the overall job function beyond their own activities. They learn more about what you do, thus more of what management is all about. They also learn more about why you do what you do and the importance of seeing things from management's point of view. This broadening effect gives employees a chance for a better look at possible future job opportunities. Finally, it makes for a finely tuned job flow when everyone does his or her job and develops into a better, more skilled employee as a result of the delegation.

CONSIDERATIONS IN DELEGATING: START SIMPLE

Where do we start with delegation? It's a good idea to start with a prediction of success. We want to pick cooperative employees, with steady work habits and a record of welcoming responsibilities and challenges. This step will give us some assurance of positive results, even if our skill in delegation isn't yet fully developed. Next, we choose tasks that are clearly defined, with specific standards. Later on, it will be easy to delegate things that are a little less well defined, but for the first entry into the world of delegation, it makes sense to choose a task that leaves few questions about what is to be done and how it will be measured. We set time limits, goals, and specific deadlines that are attainable. It's a good idea to get some input from the employee to whom we are delegating the task, but we must be sure not to leave any of these things up in the air, unspecified. Both we and the employee should know when the job is completed and how well it is done.

If possible, we should use what we already know about our employees. If we worked with an employee as a team member before becoming a supervisor, we can think about when that person was asked to do something new, meet a deadline, or produce work of exceptional quality. How did he or she respond to these challenges? Did he or she complain during break or lunch or show excitement about the new assignment? How has the employee responded to our minor delegation efforts since we became supervisor? Has the employee accepted our role easily or reluctantly? Assimilating and using this information are part of our new role as a supervisor.

It is essential that we always be the boss. Once we have begun the process of delegation, we shouldn't turn back or give in to nonimportant objections. There is room for flexibility and also for some changes, if we haven't done our work well up front or if something unforeseen develops, but if things are as we perceived them, we need to stay on the path we've started. This isn't a hard-nosed approach; it's not saying, "Do it because I said it." It's simply our way—as a supervisor—of getting the job done. Mostly, it's a matter of being confident and showing leadership. Most of our employees will want to do their job and to please us. For us to appear unsure or wavering in giving an assignment is frustrating to subordinates. It's all right to ask an employee, "What do you think?" This isn't a sign of weakness; it's a sign of respect. Remember, though, we aren't under an obligation to accept the ideas or suggestions if they don't conform to policies, procedures, or our view of the bigger picture. If this approach become second nature to us, the future will be much brighter and easier.

Finally, we must know the tasks. We have to find out what needs to be done. We may ask a subordinate or another supervisor who has experience with this particular task. We may study the manuals, but shouldn't expect to become an expert overnight. Our job is to figure out the best deadlines, the most doable goals, and so on. Remember, too, there is a balance between being an expert and allowing our subordinates to know more than we do about the tasks. There was a time when the best supervisor was the person who could do more of the task faster and better than anyone else (usually referred to the one who could outspit anyone else!). We know better than that now. The supervisor, especially at first level, needs to know a lot about the job. But in the long run, knowing people is more important for successful supervision. It may be more important for us to know more about the job in the beginning than it will be in the future, after the employees gain more respect for us. However, in the long run, it's still better to *ask* the employees to do the job than to *tell* them to do it.

USING AN APPROPRIATE DELEGATION STYLE

Most supervisors develop a specific style of delegation, which they use all the time. They give the assignment and then turn the person loose to do the job; or they give the assignment, then check on every little detail all along the way. But no one approach should be used exclusively. Each task being delegated and each person being delegated to requires a different style of delegation. The highly motivated person requires little tracking or monitoring. This person wants to get the job done and done properly. Given a clear task, deadline, and standard, he or she resents having every move checked. On the other hand, the poorly motivated employee requires frequent tracking if the job is to be completed. This person needs deadlines in smaller increments and needs to be checked at each one. Even if the person resents this approach, history tells us that he or she will procrastinate or avoid deadlines whenever possible. Tracking is the only way we can get the employee to meet the specified goals.

Then there is the matter of competence. The less competent person requires training. All the tracking in the world isn't going to get the job done if the person doesn't know how to do it, whether the person is highly motivated or not. Of course, highly motivated employees seek help when they find they lack a certain skill or bit of knowledge to complete the task, whereas less-motivated employees may fail to seek help and let the task slide. That's why it's important to know our people, their motivation, and their competencies.

To be successful in our delegation effort, we have to consider both motivation and competence in giving an assignment to our employees. For example, we tend to overlook the training needs of the highly motivated employee who has low competence, thinking that he or she will figure out how to do the job. That may be true, but it isn't efficient to let a person flounder when we know up front they don't know how to do the job. Such people are always looking for ways to learn more, so they won't resent being trained. They won't have to be told but once how to do the job, but they do have to be told at least once! On the other hand, the highly competent but poorly motivated employee requires tracking, not training. All the training we can give isn't going to substitute for motivation. As we've just seen, tracking this person is the only assurance we're going to have that things will get done.

How about the person who has both low competence and low motivation? We may hesitate to give this person any assignment beyond the bare minimum, but at times we may need to expand the capabilities of the work group by delegating even to this person. If we know for certain that the subordinate is poor in both skills and motivation, it becomes a matter of both training and tracking. This will take some time, and we have to determine if we have that time to spare. We also have to determine if that investment of time will pay off in an employee with increased skills. Although the training may provide some motivation, we are still going to have to do some tracking until we are positive the motivation is there to meet the deadlines and standards we are setting for the task.

Perhaps the biggest mistake supervisors make with delegation is using an inappropriate style when delegating to the person who is both highly competent and motivated. This employee needs neither tracking nor training. This is the person about whom we can confidently say, "Just leave 'em alone!"

It is possible to confuse the styles of delegation, as we've seen. Overtracking highly motivated employees will quickly cause the motivation to be lost. Checking them again and again may result in their saying, "Do you want me to do it, or do you want to do it? If you want me to do it, just leave me alone!" Not training highly motivated employees can result in low motivation, also. We don't have to belabor the training, but spending a few minutes in the beginning to give the benefit of our expertise, perhaps just a simple, "Here's something I've learned that's made it easier to do this task," can make all the difference. Overtraining highly competent employees will certainly demotivate them. Again, no matter how competent they are, if people aren't motivated, they need tracking. They may resent it, but we can take care of that by offering, "Hey, tell you what. You meet these next two short deadlines, and you can be on your own for a while. I'm glad you want to do this task by yourself!" Let them determine how much tracking they have to have by the way they handle the job in the beginning.

Finally, employees with both low competence and low motivation need both training and tracking. Sometimes they just aren't sure enough of themselves to branch out on their own. They may have had a previous supervisor who either let them get by with doing nothing or beat them down by hanging over them all the time. It may take some time to get these people ready to accept assignments without a lot of checking and hand-holding. Although this isn't our first challenge as a new supervisor, it is one we need to address fairly quickly. The best approach is to realize that once people have been trained, they've lost one of their excuses. They can no longer claim not to know how to do the job, providing the training has been done well.

AVOID REWARDING POOR PERFORMANCE

We should be careful in using delegation to try to motivate people. Giving a poorly motivated person an assignment outside his or her usual area may be a mistake. Above all, we should never delegate a plum assignment to a poor performer. Take the following situation.

June is not very motivated. She seems lazy and unconcerned about everything she does. Others make remarks about her getting away with things that they couldn't get away with. Doris, June's supervisor, decides to see if she can motivate June with a special assignment. There are others in the group who would like to have this assignment, but Doris decides to make one more effort at motivating June. She calls June in for a discussion.

DORIS: *Thank you for coming in, June. I thought we could have a little talk.*
JUNE: *So, what have I done now?*

DORIS: *Oh, nothing. I just wanted to talk to you about an assignment.*

JUNE: *Which one did I mess up on this time?*

DORIS: *No, you don't understand! It's something I want you to do.*

JUNE: *What is it now? Another dumb job that nobody wants?*

DORIS: *Well, uh, no. Actually, I think you might like it.*

JUNE: *That'll be a switch. Everybody else usually gets the good ones.*

DORIS: *I'm sorry you feel that way. Let me tell you about it.*

JUNE: *Sure, go ahead. What's to lose?*

DORIS: *There's a meeting Friday at the main office. There's a luncheon in the executive dining room, then a meeting of representatives from each work group Friday afternoon. I thought maybe you could represent our group.*

JUNE: *Doing what?*

DORIS: *Just taking a few notes. We'll get our bunch together Monday and you can tell them what you heard.*

JUNE: *How long will the meeting last Friday afternoon?*

DORIS: *About two hours, I guess; maybe a little longer. Why?*

JUNE: *Well, several of my friends were going to the beach Saturday and I'd hoped to take a couple of hours off Friday afternoon — vacation, of course — so I can get ready.*

DORIS: *You don't have to go; I just thought you'd enjoy the luncheon and a chance to meet some of the people from headquarters.*

JUNE: *How about if I just go to the luncheon, and you get somebody else to go to the meeting?*

DORIS: *Uh, well, that's not exactly what I had in mind. I can just get somebody else to go to the whole thing, if you feel you need to take off.*

JUNE: *Listen, I'll go to all of it if you tell me to. I'm not being insubordinate just because I want to go to the beach!*

DORIS: *I'm not saying you're insubordinate. I just thought you'd like to go. I can get somebody else. Several would like to go, I'm sure.*

JUNE: *Then let them go. Just don't write me up for refusing to do something. I said I'd go. Just tell me what you want me to do.*

So, how well did Doris do at motivating June with a plum assignment? Not very well. The good thing is that June didn't take the assignment. We can just imagine what the rest of the group would have said if June had gone to the luncheon and then come in Monday talking about it—possibly even telling them about the food, instead of about the meeting. It was a bad approach from the beginning. It's a pretty hard and fast rule that we never reward poor behavior with special assignments, certainly not ones that others, who are performing well, would like to have.

How should we handle this situation? It's not a problem to solve with delegation. It comes under discipline, or at least constructive feedback. We need to sit down with June, with our records of her performance in the past, and let her know the standards we expect from her. We show her what her performance looks like compared with the standards. We should do this along the way, as problems arise. We let her know not only our expectations, but the consequences for her if she doesn't change her behavior *for the better*.

WHAT CAN WE DELEGATE?

People sometimes disagree over what can be delegated and what we give up when we delegate. Let's clarify those issues. First of all, some say that *responsibility* cannot be delegated. This statement represents a misunderstanding and misuse of the word *responsibility*. Responsibility, often confused with accountability, is simply the area of the job a person is doing. When someone says that the area around the copy machine needs to be cleaned up, and a person responds, "That's not my job," that person means it's not his or her *responsibility*. He or she is probably right. If the task hasn't been assigned to the person, it's not really his or her responsibility. On the other hand, if a clerk has been told to keep the area clean, it becomes that clerk's responsibility to keep it clean. (Those who like to say that responsibility stops at the top make it sound better than it really is. Ask the poor clerk who got fired or demoted where it stopped!) We usually mean accountability when we're talking about who's to blame or who gets credit for the way a job is done. The truth is that nothing is given up when it is delegated to someone else. Even if we tell the clerk that he or she has responsibility and accountability for keeping the copy-machine area clean, we still have that responsibility under us, hence we have it ourselves. We also have to answer for the cleanliness, though we can say, "I told so-and-so to do it."

Another question is whether we delegate authority. Authority is the hardest thing to delegate, the thing that is least delegated, and the thing that is needed the most to make decisions concerning a task that has been delegated. It's easy for us to delegate tasks and blame, but we hate to give up our authority. The truth is, we don't give up authority when we delegate it. We still have the right to make any decisions we made before we delegated authority. We just fear giving the authority to someone else to make decisions without our having control. The key is that if we give work without the authority to do the work, all we've delegated is more work—which isn't really delegation in its purist sense! Many times our people fail because they still have to ask us for permission to do things because we feared giving up the authority for them to do the job.

Now, what is it we shouldn't delegate? Several things. First, we should never give over the disciplining of one of our employees to anyone else. We set the standards; we measure the standards. When they aren't met, we take the necessary steps to correct the action. The same is true for praising and rewarding our employees for outstanding performance. We should never get anyone else—unless it is someone higher in the organization—to share this good news with our employees. Nor should we turn over discussion of individual goals and career objectives. We know the employee; we should be the one to discuss his or her future. This means that we also do not delegate the evaluating of the employee's performance. That's our job, because it's our job to see that the employee performs up to or better than standard. We set the definition of good and bad performance, hence we should do the evaluating.

CONCLUSION

Giving up something that got us promoted is hard to do. We got the job because we were good at *doing*. Now we're in a situation that says our job is to get the job done through others. That's hard, because we're giving up something that's given us satisfaction for a long time. Now we have to get satisfaction from being a good supervisor. That takes some effort and skill on our part. It's also hard to tell former fellow workers to do things that we didn't like to do when we were working with them. It has to be done, and that's why it's called a skill. The worst thing that can happen to us, and what will guarantee our failure, is to try to stay a part of the gang, as we discussed in the very first chapter. We may decide it's easier for us to do a job and stay popular with the gang than it is to delegate it to someone else. We have to remember, the employees will let us do it all if we will take it on. In the end, they won't be happy, since they aren't learning or going anywhere. The advantages of delegation far outweigh the difficulties. It lets people grow; it lets the supervisor supervise; and, best of all, it lets the supervisor do what only the supervisor is supposed to do!

EXERCISES

1. Form subgroups and have them decide what style of delegation to use in each of these cases with regard to tracking and training. Discuss the reasons for each. (a) Bill has been in the department for a long time, is very quality conscious, and always finishes work on time. He has spent most of his time in one area of the department. You have an assignment only you know how to do, but you'd like to give it to Bill. (b) Alice came into this department a year ago and did well for a while; then her work started to slip. Now she rarely finishes on time and takes little pride in her performance. You have a job for her, but you're afraid it won't be finished on time. You want to make certain the job is done right and on time. (c) John came to work for you three months ago and drives you crazy. He always says he's not sure about what to do and finishes late. He doesn't seem to eager to complete his tasks on time. (d) Pat is the one bright light in your work life. She takes pride in everything she does and finishes on or ahead of schedule. She never does anything but quality work. You need to delegate a task that is very similar to one she did—on time—three months ago.

2. Form two subgroups. Have group one make a list of all the advantages of delegation; have group two make a list of all the reasons supervisors don't do more delegating. Record each list on a different easel, then discuss how to bring the lists closer together in supervisors' minds.

Chapter 10

MOTIVATING BY ENRICHING THE JOB

Motivation has long been a subject of discussion among supervisors and those who provide supervisory training. Obviously, we want our people to be motivated. If they are, then they will work harder, be more pleasant, and enjoy their jobs more—with the result that they will get more work done and make our job easier. A worthy goal, but one that puts a lot of emphasis on motivation and is difficult to reach *if we aren't sure how to motivate our people.*

WHY DO PEOPLE WORK?

In order to understand how to motivate people on the job, it's necessary to find out why people work in the first place. But the question goes deeper than that because what we really want to know is what gives people the most satisfaction. If we find this out, then we know what makes them work and even what will make them work harder.

Those who have studied the matter in great detail have found out some interesting things about why people work. At first, it would seem that everyone works to make money. "Stop paying me and you'll see why I'm working!" someone says, and we almost fall for it until we realize that if we made typists stand up and type all day, they'd probably quit pretty quick. By this line of reasoning, people work *so they can sit down*. We could follow the same line about benefit plans, treatment from the boss, etc. The point is, people do expect to get paid, they enjoy the things money can buy, and they like to make more money. But they don't work just for money.

Primarily, people do what they do to meet certain needs or to get satisfaction. People worry about their family's security, so they work to take care of this need. Food, clothing, and shelter are problems for any worker, so these are strong *motivating* factors. People also like to be liked. They like to have friends and loved ones who care about them and who show their feelings for them. Here again, the average worker doesn't come to the job to satisfy this need; it is met outside the job.

A Higher Need

But most of us have other needs that *can* be met on the job. In fact, they must be met before the employee is truly motivated. We all like to have our egos uplifted. We like to think we are useful. We like to contribute something for which we get the credit. This is a need that comes to the forefront time and again in all of us and is the one factor that supervisors can always depend on for use in motivation.

For a long time supervisors tried to motivate their people by making the work location a pleasant place. Often better lighting was installed, along with effective climate control by means of heating and air-conditioning. In many cases music and flowers and artistic decor were added. Supervisors were even trained in human relations, so they would know exactly how to handle the employees who worked for them. Supervisors practiced being pleasant to their people, and many tried to provide extras, like time off with pay and excused absences. Companies developed other benefits besides hospitalization and retirement plans. They offered tuition for employees who wanted to continue going to school and sometimes scholarships for the employees' families. Surely with all these benefits, in addition to attractive wages and vacation plans, the employees were motivated almost uncontrollably. *But they weren't.*

There is an interesting thing about the benefits mentioned here. If workers in one area have them, those who don't have them will be dissatisfied, perhaps even lack motivation. But the presence of such benefits seldom produces motivation over a prolonged period. There is no evidence to show that day in and day out any employees work hard because of a good hospitalization plan. Even when employees get an increase in wages, it rarely motivates them on a permanent basis. So do we do away with all of these things because they don't motivate employees? Obviously not, because their absence would do a great deal of harm, even if their presence doesn't serve to motivate greatly.

THE KEY TO MOTIVATION

If none of these things motivate people to work hard over a long period of time, what's left for the supervisor to do? Actually the solution is simple, although carrying it out is pretty hard. *The job itself* holds the key to motivation. The job is the one thing that can provide employees with the satisfaction they need to be motivated. They want a chance to succeed; they want recognition; they want to feel that they have an opportunity to advance; they want to feel that they are making a contribution to the organization. All the benefit plans in the world will not provide these satisfactions. Only the work can do it.

But there is a potential danger here: *the job can also prevent these needs from being met.* New supervisors may fall into the trap that many older ones are in now. We may fail to use the *job* as the best means of motivating our workers. In fact, when we take over our assignment from the last supervisor who had it, we may find that the motivating factors have been removed. If we just go along doing what the last person did, we may miss a great opportunity to provide motivation, get more work done, and look good in the process. Now let's see how it works.

Remember, we are looking for ways in which the employees' desire for recognition, achievement, a chance for advancement, etc. can be satisfied right on the job. We must look at the total assignment we have given our employees and see what there is about it that will meet these needs. There are several steps we can go through to analyze the job; let's take them one at a time.

First, are jobs clearly defined? Do the employees (and do we) know exactly what is expected of them? Have we taken the time to go over each detail with each individual to be sure that he or she understands what is and what isn't his or her responsibility? What about the interfaces between employees or departments? Does each employee know where his or her job stops and someone else's starts? Are there gaps or overlaps in the assignments? We're talking about more than just a brief job description; we're talking about a comprehensive look at the job duties of each individual. Some jobs are fairly clear-cut, of course, and don't require much effort to analyze. Others have some complexities about them that require a careful look to determine exactly where the boundaries are between responsibilities.

Next, we should see if there are any parts of the job that could be done at a lower level because they require less skill. Are we asking salespeople to type their own reports, secretaries to do miscellaneous filing that file clerks could do, or skilled lathe operators to sweep the aisles? Sometimes these tasks are best done by people with higher capabilities, but they rarely motivate those people or give them much of a feeling of accomplishment. The way to measure these kinds of tasks is to ask ourselves, "Does it really take that person's talent to do that part of the job?" Naturally there are some aspects of every job that are below the skills level of the employee doing it, but the important thing is to see just how much of the *total* time is spent on these activities and how much on those requiring more skill, judgment, experience, etc. If the less substantive tasks are using up very much of the time, then they should be removed or a different individual should be placed on the job, if possible.

The next step is to look at where an employee's work comes from and where it goes when he or she is through with it. Too often employees take work from some other person or department, perform some operation, then pass it on to someone else. Nowhere in the whole operation does anyone have any real responsibility or accountability. No one is a part of either the beginning or the end of the job.

THE SUPERVISOR'S RESPONSIBILITY

We need to look at our own actions, too, in trying to enrich the job. Are we still doing part of the job that should be done by those under us? There is a better-than-average chance that if we came to our job from the one below us, *we're still doing more of our old job than we should be doing.* Just because we're good at it doesn't justify not training someone else to do it. The real test of our supervisory skill is to see if we can quickly divorce ourselves from doing those things that others are paid to do and tackle those things that *we* are paid to do.

It doesn't come easily. We all look for satisfaction in and from our jobs. Since supervision is a hard job and the responsibilities sometimes aren't exactly clear, we tend to get frustrated early in our supervisory career. Trying to overcome this frustration often leads us to find satisfaction in working with *things* instead of *people.* This means we may start working on the machines every once in a while, stuffing envelopes, doing our own filing, anything to get a little satisfaction, a small sense of accomplishment. But we should remember that every time we do these things, we're admitting a bit of failure. We're trying to enrich our own jobs at the expense of those under us who should be doing these things.

"JOB ENRICHMENT" VERSUS "MORE WORK"

Supervisors have to look for ways to enrich the jobs under them, even if it means reorganizing the work or shifting responsibilities. They have to recognize that not every job can be enriched, nor can every employee accept an equal amount of responsibility. Each employee has to *earn* the right to whatever responsibility is added to his or her job. Too often, we get the process backward; we give the responsibility when employees haven't shown a willingness to accept it. We hope that in doing this we will motivate them. But under these circumstances they may see our action as increasing their *work* rather than their responsibility. We do better to reward the acceptance of responsibility. Note the difference between the following two approaches:

"John, up until now I've been handling this. From now on I'm making it your responsibility."

"John, since you've been making the decisions on this already—and I've just been signing it—from now on would you like to send it out directly without my looking at it?"

In the first case the assignment sounds like more work, even a little bit of a threat. In the second case it comes out as a reward for achievement, a recognition of acceptable performance, and an opportunity John doesn't have to take if he doesn't want to.

One of the reasons for rewarding acceptable performance is that when we begin to reorganize the work, we are likely to do it along the lines of each individual's capabilities rather than according to our own thoughts and ideas. The problem comes when we look at a job and say, "I need to give this person more responsibility," then assign more of the *same kind of work* he or she is already doing. What we have done is enlarge or expand the job, not enrich it. (Having to dig a *wider* or *longer* ditch rarely motivates! Selecting *where* to dig the ditch just might, however.)

PROTECT MOTIVATION

Strangely enough, if we try to motivate our people by giving them more responsibility, we may find that we have left ourselves wide open for criticism. Suppose, for example, that our secretary does a great job of answering certain types of inquiries. His knowledge of the subject is excellent, as is his judgment. We realize that he is checking with us only as a matter of routine. He makes the right decision, clears it with us, then handles the matter to completion. But when we are out of the office or otherwise tied up, action stops until we are able to give our approval.

Here is an excellent chance to enrich our secretary's job. We see he has earned the right to make his own decisions and handle matters without our being involved. So we offer him the recognition of doing the entire operation without our approval. If he agrees, all evidence points to his doing an even better job, because it really is *his* job now.

But a problem may arise. Unless those above us are in agreement with what we are doing, we could get into hot water. Everything goes fine as long as our secretary makes the *right* decision, but what happens when something goes out that is wrong or is contrary to policy? When we are called in by those above us to explain the action and reason for the error, we have a choice of blaming our secretary or accepting the blame ourselves. It may not be enough to say, "I was trying to motivate him," because the obvious question then is, "Why does he need motivating? I thought he was a good employee."

It's just as bad to say, "I've been letting him make those decisions because when I'm out of the office, there's no one to give the approval." The response to that could be, "Maybe you're falling down on *your* job by being away too much." The whole point of this is that there are some risks involved in giving recognition to those who have demonstrated their ability to achieve. It really cannot succeed unless those above us are aware of the principles involved and agree to go along with our efforts. The worst thing that could come out of this is for our boss to say, "This nearly got us into trouble, so from now on I want you to check everything that goes out." By the same reasoning, our boss could justify checking everything we do, and have his or her boss check everything he or she does, and so on up the line. Once such edicts are issued, they are difficult to remove.

Things That Motivate

We've talked about level of needs and the importance of letting the motivation come from the job itself. Perhaps it would be good to take a look at several things that are frequently used to motivate people and see just how each of them fits with the other as far as satisfying and dissatisfying people. Let's compare the more commonly used actions and areas.

Achievement.   This is simply the knowledge that we've done a good job and can step back and take a look at the finished product and know it's ours. Achievement is one of the highest satisfiers we have available to us, but there is a problem. It doesn't last very long. As soon as the employees start a new project, the achievement value of the last one is gone. Employees aren't terribly dissatisfied when they don't achieve, and won't complain about not finishing something worthwhile, but they will be happy to see (and hear) that they've carried something through to a satisfactory end.

Recognition/Status.   As we've seen, status or recognition for having qualities others don't have—qualities perceived as valuable—is a strong need in everyone. When we pat somebody on the back and recognize the person for doing a better job than others, we give him or her a good shot in the arm as far as motivation goes. On the other hand, the absence of recognition makes people unhappy. People frequently complain, "Nobody knows I exist around here." They also say things like, "I'm just part of the crowd—what I do isn't really all that important." But if we tell them they've done a good job, let them know they're important, or send them a letter about a well-done job, they'll bore people to death bragging about it and showing the letter around. We also have the problem that status is tricky and not very long lasting. If we give everybody status (his or her name on the desk, calling cards, his or her own telephone), it is no longer status, since status is having something others would like to have but don't. And the recognition lasts for only as long as the person is getting it. When everyone has seen the letter, it no longer serves as a motivator.

Responsibility.   Being responsible for something is important to most people, and, strangely enough, it is most often a *matter of perception*. We don't even have to change the job to make people feel they have responsibility. When someone comes in the shop or office to ask for some information, all we have to say is, "Ask Margie; she's responsible for that." When Margie hears that we think she's responsible for the activity, she'll be much more motivated than if we answered the question ourselves. As a motivator, responsibility lasts longer than most other things. (Later in the chapter, we'll take a closer look at perception of the job as a motivating factor.)

The Job Itself.   We've already talked about the importance of the nature of the work as far as motivation is concerned, but let's put it into perspective. More than anything else, the nature of the work, and the responsibility we have for that work, motivate us to continue to work well. If the work is satisfying, meaningful, and something over which the employees have some control, they will continue to be motivated over a long period of time. However, the absence of meaningful work and responsibility won't necessarily make them unhappy. We won't find employees setting up a picket line to demand more responsibility and more meaningful work, but in the absence of these things, they are much more likely to complain about the working conditions, wages, and supervision.

Advancement/Promotion.   Moving up to another job, or acquiring more duties in the present job, is a form of recognition, and to this extent it is a motivator. The promotion (or the prospect of getting it) is not something that motivates employees every day; but that's just as well, since we aren't in a position to give promotions to everyone every day. We can give some other forms of recognition and praise more frequently, so we depend on these more than we do on advancements. However, we shouldn't rule out promotions as motivation opportunities. The prospect of a higher-rated job or a promotion is real, and it serves to get more work from people as they see the prospect nearing reality.

Money/Security.   These, too, are tricky things. Since it is obvious that most people are working for money and some security, it is foolish to suppose that these aren't motivators. However, since we are never able to pay them as much as they'd like to have, they will always want more, spend more, and feel they deserve more. The most important thing for us to know is that when other important motivators, such as responsibility, recognition, achievement, and the opportunity to do meaningful work are absent, no amount of money will continue to motivate people indefinitely. Perhaps we can best understand the part these factors play by dividing them into two categories: the money and security we don't have; and the money and security we have just gotten. In the first, though we don't have them, anticipating them serves to motivate us if the prospects are real enough. If we don't have them and don't get them, if others get more than we do, or if we don't get as much as we think we should get, we're unhappy. When we do get them, we're happy for the moment. We're even happier if we get more than we expected or more than others got. In either case, whether we have money and security or not, we think about them every time we get a paycheck. If the amount is to our liking, we're motivated. If not, we're unhappy.

Working Conditions.   We hear a lot of complaints about poor working conditions. As we ride down the road, we're likely to see pickets carrying signs demanding more money and better working conditions. How good a motivator are improved working conditions? Over the years we've discovered that most often when employees are complaining about the working conditions, something is missing. Usually, we find that if they aren't getting much satisfaction out of their jobs, they notice the long hours or the dirt, heat, or cold. When we have employees doing a job they like and have a commitment to, they seldom mention the working conditions unless there's something about the conditions that prevents them from getting the job done.

What does all of this tell us? Mostly it says that people don't always know what makes them happy and unhappy. It tells us that there are things we can do to motivate people. We can give responsibility, since it is often only a matter of the employee's perception of the job. We can give recognition for employee achievement. We can make the job meaningful at least by letting the employees know why it's important and by letting them know that they have responsibility for the end results. Interestingly enough, none of these things costs money. The other things, which actually motivate less, do cost money; so we have within our power the chance to motivate employees without spending more money on higher salaries or wages and without spending a lot of money and time on improving working conditions.

PRODUCTION-MINDED MANAGEMENT

It really wouldn't be right to leave a chapter on motivation— where we've spent so much time talking about how we can enrich the job, how we can do things for the employees to motivate them, and how much responsibility we have as supervisors to enrich their jobs—without putting in something on *production*. When it comes right down to it, getting out the work or the service is what it's all about. It's why there are employees and why there are supervisors. Even charitable organizations don't exist just to keep the employees on the payroll, for the most part. Hospitals and service organizations have to give good service. They have to think about saving money. Any nonprofit organization can exist only so long as its directors feel that the service being given is reasonable in light of the amount of money it costs to offer that service. Profit-centered organizations understand this at management levels. It may not be understood at lower levels. Even first-line supervisors may be so closely tied to the working units that they miss the point that production is the reason there is any profit at all.

We have to understand that saving money and making a profit *aren't bad terms*. And they *aren't bad reasons* for working effectively. Whatever supervisory style we finally develop, it must take into account that if the employees don't produce (for whatever reason), something will have to be done. This is not to suggest that we aren't interested in the employees and that we don't try hard to motivate. In fact, it means just the opposite. We do all of these things because we've seen that they produce motivated workers and motivated workers produce more. It does suggest, though, that we must keep in mind that just making the employees happy on the job or making the organization a good place to work isn't the ultimate goal. The employees should understand this, too. The object of it all is to use the fewest people to produce the most and the best product or service that we can offer. In a profit-making organization, it also means making it better and/or cheaper than the competition.

What do we do as a result of knowing the need for production? We watch the results in terms of production, *not employee satisfaction alone*. If we are convinced that people are likely to respond with more production when they believe in the job, then we do whatever we can to enrich their jobs and make them meaningful and show how the jobs contribute to the overall scheme of things. We'll also watch production figures and job standards and see if we're on target. We'll see how many calls the sales force is making; we'll see how many cases are handled; we'll see how many customers are being served. We'll pass the information on to the employees as their *reason for being there*. We'll also show our dissatisfaction when we continually fall short of reasonable goals.

Finally, we have to understand that the first-line supervisor is closer than anyone else in the organization to the major causes—and the means of prevention—of inflation. To see this, we have only to recognize the typical inflationary pattern:

- Wages increase.
- Cost of materials increases.
- The time it takes to produce a product or service remains the same or increases.
- Production of a product or service increases slightly or not at all.

When these four elements exist—and it doesn't always take all four of them—we have inflation. That means we have to pay more for the same thing. And that means we go back to our employer and ask for a cost-of-living increase. And *that* means it's going to cost our employer *more* to provide the *same* service or product. So . . . prices will have to be raised, and the spiral will continue. It will always continue under these circumstances until one thing happens: *production goes up*—and far enough to offset the increased costs. If we get more production for the same amount, we can even *lower* the price, and the users of the service or product can get more for their money instead of less. This is the way to stop inflation. The new supervisor, especially at the first level, has to constantly think of ways to get more production from the same people or get the same production at lower cost—or both. An alternative would be to improve the product or service, so that when the customer pays more, he or she gets more for the money. But this may often prove a poor alternative to just holding down the cost of a product or service that has already proved satisfactory.

Employee Involvement

It goes without saying, perhaps, that we are all more likely to be committed to things we're involved in. Further, we're more likely to believe in and support things into which we've had some input. That's what we've been saying about motivating people by enriching the job to the extent that it is meaningful *to the employee*. In recent years we've found additional ways to increase employee involvement. We hear of systems with names like "quality circles" and "worker involvement programs." There are many variations on these, and over the years we've seen programs such as "management by objectives" (MBO, as it is most often called) installed to get employees involved in making some of the decisions about their jobs. With MBO, the idea is to have employees participate in setting goals in areas such as production and in determining ways to reach these goals. They are given the limitations and overall organizational targets and agree to develop goals for their own operation. This plan is passed up the line, with each level expanding it with additional goals. At the same time, there is an agreement as to how the results are to be measured. Each person involved in the program is then able to check his or her progress during the designated work period of a quarter, six months, or a year. Under this system, employees always know where they stand as far as production and performance are concerned.

One of the most popular employee-involvement plans in use today is a spin-off from the MBO system, which has been around for many years. Sometimes called "circles" because it involves a circle of employees, it operates on the principle that the people closest to the job probably know more about the actual operation than anyone else. These people are organized into groups, or circles, which, with support from wherever it is needed, examine various aspects of the job. They may look for ways to improve the work flow; they may see if they can increase production; they may try to find causes for delays or equipment breakdowns. They have access to whatever help they need from the engineering department, the maintenance people, the design or production experts, etc. They meet periodically, even once a week, and brainstorm. With some guidance, they make decisions about how best to spend their creative time and where they can offer the most improvement to the company.

Other systems do much the same things, working in similar ways. This brief discussion of these rather complex programs will give us an idea of how we can motivate employees by getting them involved. As always, the key is *involvement*. Because management has recognized that employees have something to contribute, and because management uses their ideas, the employees develop much more concern for production and for the overall goals of the organization.

But these are all formal, organized programs. What can individual supervisors do to get involvement? The answer is simple: we can use the same principles on an individual basis. We don't have to wait until the organization adopts a formal plan of employee involvement. All we have to do is get our employees together, individually or collectively, and ask them honestly what can be done to improve whatever it is that needs improving. Let the employees have some time to work on it, then try to use their findings and give them credit for it. We can reduce this to just one employee. It takes very little effort on our part to ask an employee what he or she thinks the problem is in a particular situation; we can even make it an interesting assignment. For example, "Frank, we're really having a problem getting these reports out on time, aren't we? Why don't you think about it for a couple of days, and then let's get back together and see what you think we can do. I'm sure you're closer to the problem than I am, so you'll probably have a better idea of how to solve it than I will. By the way, if you need any information or other help, feel free to ask around." In about thirty seconds of conversation, we've set the stage for some *work improvement*.

We can repeat this with any of our employees, for any problem we have. Just think how nice it would be if all our employees were working to make their jobs better, and all we had to do was sit back and wait for them to show up with their suggestions. Of course, it's not quite that simple, but the principle is! The worst thing that can happen is that they won't come up with any suggestions, and that is no different from where we were when we asked. At least they had a *chance* to contribute, and that should serve as some motivation in itself. The worst thing we can do is assume that our employees really aren't interested. If we decide for them that they don't know anything about improving, then we will make that prophecy come true.

"It's All in the Head"

One of the hardest things to convince new supervisors of is that for the most part, motivation is just a matter of perception. As mentioned earlier in the chapter, it's how we see our jobs, how we *perceive* them. We hear people talking about a job they hate or one they love, and we know that this is how they *feel* about their job. It's hard to get new supervisors to believe that it's possible to change that feeling by changing the person's perception of the job rather than changing the job itself. So far, we've talked about formal programs designed to enrich the job. Now let's see some things that we can do—without changing the job—to motivate the employees. Let's look at the following scenario:

The scene: You are Chad and are in your office. Your file clerk, Sue, is working at a four-drawer file nearby. A coworker, Ann, walks in.

CHAD: *Hey, Ann! What's going on?*
ANN: *Oh, a lot. I'm looking for a copy of the file on the Dunbar project. Can I get one from you?*
CHAD: *Sure. No problem. Sue, how about getting Ann the Dunbar project file . . . and while you're at it, make her a quick copy, okay?*
SUE: *Certainly. I'll do it right now.*

Sue opens the drawer, pulls out the file, crosses to the copy machine, and makes the desired copies, handing them to Ann. Ann thanks both of you and leaves. *End of scene.*

As we look at Sue, how do we suppose she *perceives* her job? No doubt she thinks of herself as a "gofer." Somebody needs a file, she gets it. Somebody needs a copy of something, she gets it. Somebody needs something put back into a drawer, she does it. She cannot help but think of her job as little more than what a well-trained monkey might be able to do. When we use the motivation techniques of positive reinforcement and try to give Sue recognition, it falls short of convincing her she has a motivating assignment. When we ask ourselves, "Would I like to get up in the morning knowing that would be my job all day?" the answer comes back, "Not particularly!" Certainly, we need to tell Sue that we appreciate her doing the work so well and being so cooperative, but what choice has she got? Somebody comes in and asks us for something, we still tell her to get it, and she does. How can she be uncooperative? Maybe she could frown or pout, but she would still get the file. Not only that, but if she didn't, we could do it ourselves in a matter of moments! So how do we change Sue's perception of the job? Can we do it just by telling her that she has an important job? That might work for a while, but not for long. Let's rewrite the script:

The scene: You, Chad, are in your office. Your file clerk, Sue, is working at a four-drawer file nearby. A coworker, Ann, walks in.

CHAD: *Hey, Ann! What's going on?*
ANN: *Oh, a lot. I'm looking for a copy of the file on the Dunbar project. Can I get one from you?*
CHAD: *Sure, but you need to see Sue about that. She's in charge of the files. She'll be glad to do what you need done if she's got the time.*
ANN: *Of course. How about it, Sue. Can you get the Dunbar project file for me, and have you got time to make me a copy?*
SUE: *Certainly. I'll do it right now!*

Sue opens the drawer, pulls out the file, crosses to the copy machine, and makes the desired copies, handing them to Ann. Ann thanks both of you and leaves. *End of scene.*

Now, how do we suppose Sue *perceives* her job? How does she feel in the morning about her job? We see that she doesn't think a trained monkey could be *in charge of the files.* She got to make the decision about getting the file and making the copy. She got to say whether or not she was busy. She heard the remark that meant, in essence, "From now on, see Sue if you want something done in connection with the files." The truth is, she didn't have much more choice than before; she couldn't say, "Sorry, not now." She didn't have to do it; she knew we could do it easily enough. *But* she was offered the option.

Let's notice something interesting about this. Suppose we had been a fly on the wall, with observation powers, but not understanding speech. Imagine we saw what was happening in both scenes. Physically, what did we see Sue doing in each case? *Sue opens the drawer, pulls out the file, crosses to the copy machine, and makes the desired copies, handing them to Ann.* What we would have seen is *exactly the same thing* in each case.

Sue's actions were precisely the same both times. We didn't restructure the job. What we did was *restructure Sue's perception* of her job. Indeed, we can be sure that Sue probably has some ideas on how to improve the filing system, perhaps even on the location of the cabinets and what goes into each drawer. With a little encouragement on our part, and by providing her with some direction, Sue can make more out of the filing job than it now is and offer valuable assistance to the organization in the process. We still have as much control over the job as we want and can always go back to the way it was before we "put Sue in charge."

We see from this example that changing the perception is simple, easy, and effective. We can repeat this process all day if we think about it. Somebody comes in and asks us what to do on a very simple job. If we are thinking "change perception," we ask, "Well, *what do you think* about how to do that?" We are about to make a decision on something, and we go by an employee and say, "By the way, Bob, I've been asked to make a recommendation on this operation—how we can speed it up, change it to be more efficient, etc. You got any ideas?" It only takes a few seconds, and we change the perception. It doesn't matter that Bob doesn't have any ideas. The important thing is, *we asked him!*

Team Building

One of the benefits that comes from having the employees try to improve things in the workplace is that in doing so, they often become an efficient and cohesive team. They work together, solve problems together, engage in some give-and-take activity, and gradually find themselves liking to work together. There are other things that help produce this result, most of which can be fostered by us, since they basically revolve around the *environment* where the work is taking place—though not necessarily the physical environment. Perhaps it would be better to describe it as the workplace atmosphere. For example, is it pleasant to work here, or is there a lot of bickering and bitterness? Is it a good idea to forget any suggestions, or is management receptive to new ideas? Is knowledge a source of power, or do people share their information freely; especially, do supervisors give information to their subordinates? Do people distrust each other (do the workers distrust the supervisors, do the supervisors distrust the workers), or is there a real trust among all the people?

The answers to these and many more questions are good indicators of just how much team building has been done in the organization. Having a good work atmosphere does not happen just because we have nice people around. It happens because we carefully and openly work at creating an atmosphere, or environment, where these positive things can develop to some depth. Some have suggested that examining the good and bad signs, like those we've just mentioned, is an effective way to measure the health of an organization. Let's take a mythical tour through an organization and look around for signs of good and bad health.

We begin the tour when the workers start their day. As we come in a few minutes before the starting time for the workers, we look to see if the people are already at their workstations (healthy) or if they are dashing in at the last minute, barely making it to their desks or workstations as the long hand points to the magic minute (unhealthy). As time for the start of work arrives, do people begin to work on their own (healthy), or do they wait for an assignment (unhealthy)? As they begin, do they spend a few minutes planning their day or reviewing the plan they made last night (healthy), or do they just take the first assignment that comes along, like answering the phone and doing whatever the caller suggests (unhealthy)? As they begin, is there a relaxed but serious approach to their job (healthy), or is there a replay of last night's ball game or TV show (unhealthy)? When the boss comes in, does the atmosphere stay the same, as the workers greet the boss or ask questions about the job (healthy), or do things suddenly get quiet while everybody tries to look busy (unhealthy)? As we watch the boss give an assignment, is there a respect for the task, with legitimate questions asked (healthy), or is there some bickering and complaining about the assignment, like, "Why me?" (unhealthy)?

When it's break time, is there an orderly approach to the rest period, with important jobs left in good shape before the break (healthy), or is there a mad dash for the door without regard to any project or activity (unhealthy)? Of course, the same questions can be asked at lunchtime. When the breaks or lunches are over, is there a respect for the allotted time (healthy), or do people straggle in late or start to work slowly (unhealthy)?

As we listen and watch, we see that a problem has come up— perhaps a serious one that may even affect a client. What happens first? Is the initial effort to get the problem solved (healthy), or are initial efforts expended in finding someone to blame (unhealthy)? When the problem is solved, is there a calm check to find ways of avoiding this type of problem in the future, including inputs from the "guilty" party (healthy), or are threats and edicts issued to "see that this never happens again" (unhealthy)?

As we progress through this tour, we see that the boss has a rather important assignment to make for a job that he or she would normally do but that can be delegated. How is it handled? Do we see the boss explaining the importance of the assignment, giving the guidelines of the responsibilities and the authority to go with them (healthy), or do we see the boss setting up numerous checkpoints, keeping most of the authority but delegating the work (unhealthy)? Drifting along, we see that one of the employees has done some original thinking. Do we hear the boss praising this in public (healthy), or do we see the boss either doing nothing or suggesting that the employee be careful about doing things differently?

Next, we see an employee making a mistake; it is not a serious one, but the employee did not perform according to the work standards. Do we see the boss taking the employee aside to do some careful counseling, pointing out the variance from the standards, perhaps with a statement about what continued poor performance can lead to (healthy), or do we see the employee being scolded in public, threatened with dire consequences if it happens again, but receiving no real coaching as to how the job should be done (unhealthy)?

We listen in on a meeting of middle managers. A change is going to be implemented—one that will affect many of the employees. Does the plan for introducing this change involve the employees, asking for their opinions and explaining why the change is necessary (healthy), or is the plan just to drop it on them without any explanation, perhaps waiting until they've heard rumors from other sources (unhealthy)?

Finally, we find that some of the employees are unhappy

about something. It may be something that's been going on for a while, and they feel it's serious enough to require some action. How does this get into the stream of things? Do we see the employees calmly asking for an audience, having information at hand but making no threats (healthy), or do we see some emotion building, with the employees demanding a hearing and starting a heated debate (unhealthy)?

We could continue, but there's a whole chapter devoted to team building. Perhaps each of us can see our own organization somewhere in all of this. Every organization handles each of the issues we've talked about in some way. How do we see them in our own supervisory efforts? Only we can make the team-building effort work. It's worth the energy!

POSITIVE REINFORCEMENT

We've used the expression *positive reinforcement* several times. Exactly what is it? For our purposes, we'll just say it means to receive something—a word of praise or a tangible item—that we want or like in return for something we have done or said. A pleasant experience. A rewarding experience—hence, positive. It is based on the established premise that people are more likely to repeat things for which they are reinforced or rewarded. We can think of it as somebody—usually the boss—giving us praise or making something pleasant for us as a result of something we accomplished. The idea is that we will be more likely to do it again the same way we did it before because it was a pleasant experience. We've already seen that recognition is a good motivator, but it doesn't last very long; it may last only as long as someone else is seeing or hearing it. We have to be careful in giving praise, for several reasons.

First, it needs to be genuine. We can't get much mileage out of going around and telling people they're doing a good job when even they know they aren't. We can reward people as often as we like, since they never seem to get tired of rewards, but we need to be sure that the people are being rewarded for doing what we want them to be doing. We also have to be certain that they realize just what is being reinforced. A simple "You're doing a good job" may not be much of a reinforcement if we don't specify the particular part of the job we like (especially if there are some things about the person's work we *don't* like!).

Next, not everybody gets it. If we go down the assembly line or through the office and tell everybody, one at a time, that he or she is doing great, it isn't much of an individual positive reinforcement. It might help to build a team, if we're saying the group is doing better than another shift or another department, but it doesn't do the individual much good to see that he or she is just a part of the pack. If the people are working on individual assignments, they ought to get individual reinforcement for doing their specific jobs well.

But positive reinforcement must be separated from negative reinforcement or criticism. To tell someone he or she is doing well, then add, "Better than the foul-up yesterday," doesn't put the emphasis on the good job. It puts it on the bad job and says, "We still remember how poorly you did yesterday!" We'll see how to handle negative feedback later in the chapter, but suffice it to say it takes several positive reinforcements to overcome a negative one, so just sandwiching them in isn't the solution. The solution is to handle both as they arise. If people are doing well, they need to know it. If they haven't met standards, they need to know that, too.

Ridicule, sarcasm, and humor should be avoided. We're dead serious about good performance, so we don't want to destroy our motivation effort by downplaying it or being sarcastic. Some supervisors find it hard to praise people, so they make light of it, using humor or even ridicule as a means of telling people they're doing well. When asked about it, their answer is something like, "Oh, well. They knew what I meant." Better to say what we mean rather than let the employees figure it out on their own!

Finally, it's no big deal. We don't have to announce the good behavior from the roof of the building. Most of the time, a firm handshake or a pat on the back, with a simple statement, "Hey, I really liked the way you handled that!" is reinforcement enough. It's personal, it's sincere, it shows we care and know about the person's performance. It makes for a very pleasant experience.

Now let's consider some good and bad examples of positive reinforcement. How about: "Well, congratulations! You're on time for a change!" One rule is that we should reinforce the thing we want repeated. The employee apparently has been coming in late too often. We have presumably discussed this as it happened. Now the employee is on time. We want to reinforce that, so we don't bring up the lateness. We base our recognition on what we want repeated. "You know, things really flow well when you're on time. Thanks."

Then there's, "You sure nobody's doing your work for you? It really is looking good." This is perhaps a try at humor, but a poor try. What do we want to reinforce? The fact that the work is looking good. So: "Nancy, your work is really looking good!" It's simple, true, sincere, and very personal. It deals with what we want to happen again—good work.

"This letter is well written—sure better than the others you've done." Again, we need to ask what behavior we want the employee to repeat. Obviously, we want the good letters to continue, so we need to reinforce that. If we see areas where there is improvement, we can deal with that, too, without bringing up the past. "This is a good letter. I particularly like this part where you answer the question of cost." If we've talked about the poor quality of the letters before, the employee will remember it without our mentioning it. The fact that we don't mention it is a form of reinforcement in itself.

"I really like your performance on the new machine. It's too bad the others can't pick it up as quickly as you have." Actually, this is positive in a way and certainly reinforces the behavior we want, but it never pays to compare people with people. The only standard we should ever use is the job standard. If the employee is doing a good job, then there's room enough for praise in that. If the employee is doing better than the others, then that's something for us to take up with the other employees, not the one who's doing better. We want the employees to succeed on the job, not just be better than the other people. If we had stopped this statement after the first sentence, it would have been much better: "I really like your performance on the new machine." If we want to praise the speed with which the employee is learning, then we add that: "It's good to see you pick it up so quickly." Remember, the employee knows who is learning it the fastest! We could cite other examples, but these serve to point out that we need to reinforce what we want to happen again—seriously, without ridicule or sarcasm. It's simple, and with a little practice, it becomes second nature.

CONSTRUCTIVE FEEDBACK

All of this positive reinforcement is fine when the employees are doing well, but what about when they mess up occasionally and don't meet standards? We can use negative reinforcement and be pretty sure the bad behavior will stop, but we're talking about motivation in this chapter. Criticism isn't very motivating. How do we deal with these situations? Note that we're only talking about occasional problems, not an employee who has reached the point of needing discipline—an occasional tardiness or dirty workstation or a sale muffed because of a needless oversight. How can we handle such a situation in a motivational way? The truth is, we worry more about keeping this from being demotivating than about how to make it motivational. But there *are* some steps we can take to resolve the problem in a positive way.

First, it should be noted that we don't have to deal with every infraction, but none should go too long without attention. If the employee is ignorant of how he or she is supposed to perform, then we're talking more about training than about correction. On the other hand, if the employee knows how to do the job right and slips into an error, then we need to employ some kind of *light* constructive feedback (or criticism). It's not something that goes on the record or counts as the beginning of progressive discipline. It's just a way to correct the employee and keep the problem from happening again, if possible. Let's see how it works.

- *State the standard.* "As you know, our starting time is 8:30 A.M.," or "You remember we said that the customer's opinion is critical to our customer-relations program." The idea is to start with the standard, so there'll be no doubt about what is right and wrong.

- *State the reason for the standard.* "8:30 is the time we have our staff meetings, so it's imperative that everyone be here then," or "The customers can give us good insight into their feelings about us and the products." We probably have been over the reasons before, but this will clear the air and make our observations of poor performance meaningful, without our having to explain it.

- *State the observed irregular behavior.*   "I noticed you got to your desk about 8:45 this morning; any problem?" or "When I passed by, you were cutting the customer off with a defense as to why we couldn't fill the order. How about it?" Here we show that the observed behavior and the standards are different. We aren't jumping down the employee's throat; we're just trying to get to the bottom of the problem.

- *Use reflective listening.*   In the chapter on communications, we stressed the need for listening *actively*, by paying attention, making eye contact, and leaning toward the person if necessary to let him or her know we're listening. Further, we saw that repeating or reflecting the things said gives a clear indication that we really are listening. "You felt you still had enough time to make it when you left?" or "In other words, the customer was being so negative you couldn't get in a good frame of mind?"

- *State the positive, changed, future behavior.*   "Notice how smoothly the job will go tomorrow when everyone is here on time for the staff meeting," or "You'll see that the customer will really come around when you are using the right techniques, even when you don't feel up to it." We don't leave any doubt that things are going to be changed for the better, with no further problems.

- *End on a positive note.*   "Time is important, and I know you'll overcome the personal problems without any further trouble," or "I know you care about our customers, and I'm sure I can depend on you to keep them coming back!" This says that the matter is dropped as far as we are concerned. The employee has been given constructive feedback, with our expectations being positive. The process should have been upbeat and painless.

The important thing about constructive feedback is that if we do it correctly, we don't have to get into formal discipline nearly as often. It also serves to motivate the employees by letting them know that we don't hold every infraction against them, nor are we standing around looking for things to put into their records.

CONCLUSION

As we suggested in the last chapter, when we were talking about directing people, leadership in the world of supervision is different from the rest of the world's idea of leadership. So is motivation. Many think that to motivate people means to stir them up to the point where they go charging out and work themselves into exhaustion just because their leader has inspired them so much. In supervision, the idea is to get employees involved in fulfilling enough of their own needs through the things the job offers that they get satisfaction from doing the job. When the job is challenging enough, meaningful enough, and provides enough recognition, supervisors don't have to offer *any* motivation. The supervisor's role is to make sure the job offers all those things. There's not much that will motivate a person more than having responsibility for some specific tasks that are well-defined and *recognized as necessary*. But not everyone deserves or can take responsibility. It should be given as a reward—and only when those it's offered to agree to take the consequences of failure as well as the rewards of success. This means the employees must have the *right to make mistakes*, to be wrong, as well as the right to be right. It means that when we give responsibility as a way of creating motivation, we can't check everything that goes out and correct the errors. If we check everything, we've only left the employee *the right to be right*. If we stop errors, the employee will never have to live with the mistakes—and the consequences of those mistakes. If the employee knows he or she will have to live with consequences, the end result is an employee who works much harder *at being right* and who is, in fact, motivated.

EXERCISES

1. Individual activity: Let all the participants think about themselves in their present jobs. Each should write down what makes a good day for him or her right now. Think of at least three situations in the last week where motivation has been high—so high that the person has thought about the activity before coming to work and was anxious to get to work and get

into it. After each has listed at least three situations, let him or her go back and analyze each one and see what there was about it that made the job exciting or motivating. Think of the characteristics of the job, not the actual activity. When all have finished, record the information for future use.

2. Group discussion: Looking at the list from exercise 1, decide how many of these motivating factors could be built into any job, even nonsupervisory ones. See how many of these factors were common with everyone. Is it possible to motivate their people with the same kinds of things?

3. Individual activity: Let each person think of one employee who is usually very motivated to do the job assigned. Carefully analyze the *job* that employee is doing and the way the assignment is made. See if the supervisor can figure out just what it is that motivates the employee on the job. See if it's possible that something about the job motivates the employee rather than his or her own attitude. (It's not enough just to say, "Anything I ask that person to do makes him or her excited." We also have to see how much responsibility we've given the person and how we make the assignment.) Record the results of the whole group and save the information for future use.

4. Group activity: Have the group analyze the motivation factors listed in the last exercise. Are there any common themes? Would any of these factors motivate them? Are they similar to the ones found in exercises 1 and 2? Now the critical question, would the same approach work for all employees?

5. Individual activity: Let each person think of one employee who usually is not in the least motivated. Carefully analyze the *job* the person is doing and the way he or she gives assignments to that employee. Try to figure out whether there is anything about the job that fails to motivate the person. Is it possible that the job itself isn't very motivating? Record the group's results and save them for future use.

6. Group activity: Analyze the characteristics listed in exercise 5. Throw out the ones that are not measurable, such as "The employee is just plain lazy," and deal only with those that

have to do with the nature of the job or the way the assignment is given. See whether there is anything about the job that
fails to motivate. If group members were working for this
supervisor and had this work to do and had this amount of
responsibility, would *they* be motivated?

Chapter 11

INTERVIEWING SKILLS

When we talk with people about specific things, such as telling them how they are doing on the job or correcting some fault in their work performance or trying to assist them in solving some personal problem they may have, we call this *interviewing*. This is one more technique we need to learn as a new supervisor, and the more we do it, the better we should get at it. The problem is, though, that we don't really do very much interviewing from day to day, so even experienced supervisors get rusty in the procedures. The best thing we can do is to look at the techniques required, practice them whenever we can, think about each interview we conduct, and bone up on the techniques each time we have another interview.

In this chapter we will talk about the general principles of conducting any kind of interview, then look at some specific types—namely, employment, counseling, disciplinary, appraisal, and exit. As we have said, interviewing is not an everyday occurrence for the supervisor, so we can't really expect to be experts on the subject, but since there are some basic points we can remember, it's good to look them over every once in a while. We categorize them so we can talk about them separately, but actually we find ourselves combining them at times, as we will see in the discussion.

GENERAL PRINCIPLES

Basically, there are three general purposes for an interview: to *predict behavior*, as in the case of an employment interview, when we want to know how well we think the employee or potential employee will do on a job; to *change behavior* that isn't meeting a standard, as with the disciplinary interview, for example, when the employee is tardy or below production standard or has an attitude that is affecting the behavior of others; and to *establish exactly what the behavior is*, as in the appraisal interview. When we are preparing for an interview—and let's hope we always do prepare before we have one—we need to decide which purpose we have in mind for it. Why are we having the interview, why are we having it now, and why are we having it with this particular person? We need to establish not only why we are doing this, but also *what we hope to accomplish* in the interview. If the purpose is to change behavior, do we know what the specific behavior is that we want, or do we just not like the way the person is performing now? It's pretty embarrassing to tell the person, "I don't like what you're doing now, but I can't tell you what I'd like you to be doing." Once we've decided what we don't like and what we would prefer, we need to know how we are going to get the person to change. And we should know whether we expect the total change to be made as a result of this interview or whether there will be more interviews later.

The best thing to do before an interview is write these points down on a piece of paper. We don't need to be elaborate, just write a note stating the purpose of the interview, where we're going, why we're going there, and how we expect to get there. This has the great advantage of making us organize our thoughts whether we like it or not. It may even convince us that this is not the time to have the interview, or that we need to talk to all our people, or that we need more information, or that we should have had the interview earlier. At least it will give us an opportunity to spend a few moments analyzing the situation before we get into it, which is always helpful.

Establishing the Proper Climate

Let's emphasize something we said earlier: interviewing is *talking with people*. We didn't say talking *to* people or talking *at* people. We said talking *with* them. There is a difference. Talking with people means that we listen as much as we talk. It means that the other person has something to say and a right to say it. When the interview is over, we can be sure it was a bad one if our reflections show us that we did most of the talking or if the interviewee got a lot of information from us. This tells us that we did the talking and he or she did the listening. On the other hand, we can probably say that it was a good interview if we got a lot of information and the interviewee did a lot of the talking. So *listening* is one of the things we must determine to do.

We must also determine to be *fair*. We must face up to the fact that each of us probably has prejudices that affect our thinking. Since we each see things from our own standpoint, we most probably don't see them alike. Part of deciding to be fair in our interviews is to admit that there is always the chance that the interviewee might be right. At least there is the possibility that he or she could be nearer right than we are. This doesn't mean that we are going against the established facts. It means that we are willing to admit that our employees have some right on their side and we are willing to hear them out. One good way to approach the interview is to try to put ourselves in the interviewee's position and view the situation from his or her perspective, even if we think the situation is an extreme one. Another part of determining to be fair is deciding how we will let the interviewee know we want to be that way. The best way to convince the person is by *showing*, not telling. When the person says something, we listen and accept what he or she says. We refer to it later, to show that we listened. We give the interviewee a chance to defend himself or herself or to state more facts or disagree with us, all in a threat-free climate.

We start our interview by letting the interviewee know that we want to talk under the best conditions. When the person comes in, we greet him or her in such a manner as to make it clear he or she was expected and we are planning to talk and listen. We don't say, "Wait a few minutes until I finish these important things and I'll talk to you." While we probably wouldn't say it just that way, we can easily leave that impression by continuing to work while the interviewee stands ill at ease. We greet the person and show that he or she comes first by making sure that our calls are taken by someone else and that no one will interrupt us. We seat our interviewee comfortably, where he or she will not have to turn to see us or look around some books or otherwise be uncomfortable. If we have room and it isn't too obvious that we don't usually do it, it's often a good idea to come out from behind our own desk and sit beside our interviewee. Of course, if we have papers we need to refer to, then sitting behind the desk is probably the best arrangement.

Anytime we are talking with people, it makes good sense to open the conversation on some light topic instead of jumping abruptly to the point. Our opening remarks, then, show an interest in our interviewee, his or her family, job, or hobbies. This conversation shouldn't be forced, though. It should be genuine interest. Most important, it shouldn't be too long. The interviewee knows we want to talk to him or her and maybe even what it is we want to talk about, so the sooner we get to the subject, the quicker the person will begin to relax. Some interviewers like to *sneak* into the subject, but that is a dangerous way to get to the point, because we really have nothing to hide. We wanted to talk to this person, so we have provided the opportunity for the interview. Even if the interviewee asked for the session, we still shouldn't wait for him or her to bring up the subject. We are the supervisor—the boss—and we are in our office. It's up to us to take the lead. All of this simply means that as soon as appropriate, we start talking about the subject of the interview, without beating around the bush. "Jim, I called you in so we could go over your question about . . ." This gets us started, and no one is surprised. This way Jim knows quickly what the interview is about and can get his thoughts in order. He knows why he's there and what we expect him to discuss, and he can give us information without guessing. After all, we want him to be free to speak and to give us as much good, usable information as possible. This can happen only if he knows what it is we're talking about.

As we have said, the interview is as much a listening process as a talking one for us. We give full attention to the answers to our questions. We listen when the interviewee talks. We consider the remarks and answer questions as best we can, but we keep the interview focused on the topic at hand. One of the errors most often committed is to let the interview get us off the subject and cause us to discuss things that we really hadn't prepared to talk about. When our time is up, we discover that we haven't covered the material we wanted to talk about and either have to schedule another interview or permit this one to run longer than we intended. But if we have directed the interview properly, we should close without letting it drag on. Once we've gotten the information we wanted, answered the interviewee's questions, or settled the problem, the wisest thing to do is to end the session as quickly and politely as possible. One good way for us to close and also to get a little feedback from the interviewee is to ask the individual to sum up the findings as he or she sees them. This way we can find out whether the interviewee has any misunderstandings about the things that have been discussed and also let him or her know that the interview is over. If there is any action to be taken, state that plainly, as well as who will do the action:

> "I'll call you Thursday."
> "We'll try it for a month, then talk again."
> "You call me when you've decided what you want to do about the job."

We should remember to let the interviewee leave on the same friendly note he or she came in on, regardless of the outcome of the interview. Even if there is a disagreement, there is no need to be disagreeable.

THE EMPLOYMENT INTERVIEW

Often interviewing new or prospective employees is not the job of the new supervisor, but it's good to know some of the techniques just the same. Even if the personnel department or someone over us makes the decision whom to hire, we still may have to interview the individual to decide exact job placement or to give our final approval. If there is a possibility that the individual will end up working for us, we should *want* to interview the person, not try to avoid it. Let's examine why this interview is so important to us, the individual, and the organization.

Anytime we add someone to our organization, we are trying to match a person and a job. Surely few things we do can affect the outcome of the job more than this. There is a good chance that we are starting someone on a career. We are saying that this person has the unique qualifications to fit the particular job or at least the potential to grow into it. In a real way the individual is relying on us to decide whether or not he or she is suited for the job. When we pose the typical questions, "Well, do you think you will fit into this job?" or "How do you think you will like this work?" we may be asking unfair questions. If we've done our interview correctly, we are in a better position to know the answers than the applicant is. We know the job, and we should know him or her pretty well by now. All of these are reasons that the interview is important from the applicant's standpoint. From the organization's standpoint, it's equally important. It's much easier to get an employee on the payroll than off of it. It's much more enjoyable, too! So we should do the hiring very carefully. Sometimes the organization may pass employees around from one job to another trying to find something they can do, all because they shouldn't have been hired in the first place. Whoever made the mistake in hiring them has cost the organization considerable money and wasted time. We need to be sure we do our job of interviewing carefully so this can't be said about us a few years from now. Finally, for a rather selfish reason, we need to do a good job of selecting the new employees who are going to work for us. They will be doing our work for us, or at least a part of it, and if they don't work out well, we aren't likely to be able to simply replace them. We will have to make do with them or let the job suffer.

When we conduct employment interviews, we should be certain of their purpose. Primarily, there are two things we want to accomplish: give information and get information. Perhaps getting information is the more important. What kind of information do we want to get? First, we want to get whatever past employment history we can. We need to find out what skills our prospective employees have *used*, not just which ones they have. How much growth have they shown? What kind of promotions or advancement did they have on their last job? How stable are they as employees? Does the applicant have a record of moving from one job to another, or has he or she been on one or two jobs for several years? Such questions as "What did you do to develop in your last assignment?" will tell us a lot if we listen carefully enough.

Asking questions is a good way to find out about the interviewee's attitude toward supervision, too. Is this person aggressive, not wanting to be supervised? Is he or she easily disgruntled? Adaptable? "What kind of bosses do you like best?" "Tell me about some of your good supervisors." "What bothers you the most about bosses?" These aren't trick questions; the answers should give us useful information. We aren't playing games, and we should let prospective employees know that. If an applicant says she likes bosses who leave her alone, let her make mistakes as well as get credit for what is good, then she may have the makings of an excellent employee. If another says he likes bosses to give him clear directions and keep him posted along the way, he may not be as aggressive as we would like, especially if the job requires independent thinking. And if still another person gives us a series of stories about supervisors who didn't understand him or who picked on him all the time, we may find that it won't be long before we fall into that same category—hearing complaints about how we pick on that person!

It's wise for us to delve into the interviewee's personal ambitions at this time. Where does he or she expect to go in the organization? (Not what job, since the applicant may not know our organization that well, but how high up might the person's capacity for responsibility and authority take him or her?) We need to know whether the person will be willing to learn the jobs one at a time or expect to move up very rapidly without really finding out what's going on. We should try to discover whether the applicant will be content to work satisfactorily on one job without a promise of promotion. But we don't find out these things just by asking about them. We don't say, "Do you want to learn the job before moving up?" We can ask the interviewee just how he or she envisions preparing for a career. We can ask the person what part experience plays in his or her development. Here again, we aren't likely to get explicit answers, but we will get some good indicators. Our ability to interpret the answers will grow as we get more experience, but it isn't as hard as it might sound. *The key is still our ability to listen.*

The second major purpose of the employment interview is to *give* information. Prospective employees need to know something about the organization, *but not everything.* They need to know about those policies, objectives, restrictions, and benefits that will most directly affect them and apply to them. Automatic increases, bonuses, and paid vacations probably mean much more to the young single person than do sickness benefits and retirement plans. Accomplishments of the organization, provisions for the family, and promotion opportunities mean much to the mature person looking for a career. But this isn't the time to oversell the organization. While we don't have to accentuate the weaknesses, we don't have to pretend the place is perfect, either. Above all, be honest, especially if the interviewee asks specific questions. It's better for the person to know about any restrictive policies now than to be surprised by them later on.

Part of the reason for giving out information is to let the interviewee know about the job he or she will be doing. Again, honesty is the rule. If there is likely to be much overtime, say so. If the job is routine at times, don't be afraid to mention it; at the same time point out the more exciting features as well. If the applicant isn't likely to understand the terminology, don't spend a lot of time going into great detail about the job. Let the person ask questions after you have given enough information to make those questions meaningful. It's even a good idea to help the applicant ask questions. "Do you have any questions about the operation?" "Is there something that I can give you more information about?" A key consideration here is to be sure not to hire a person based on the next job above the one he or she will be working on. To tell the interviewee, "After a little while you should be promoted to the next level, and on that job you will be doing . . ." is a bad way to go. If the person doesn't want the job we are offering, we don't promise another one as a bribe to take this one! Above all, let the person know what the salary and vacation schedule will be. Make it clear in exact terms. It is often good to give an applicant a rough breakdown of deductions so he or she won't be completely surprised if the paycheck is less than he or she expected. If the person won't be entitled to a full vacation with pay the first year, be sure to say so. Don't rationalize later by saying the person didn't ask about that. Don't leave it up to the interviewee to ask about such important considerations.

If the interviewee asks about the future, we answer to the best of our ability, but obviously we don't promise anything we aren't sure we can deliver. Perhaps the best thing to do is let the applicant see what others with similar backgrounds and experience have done. But since it's an interview, it's good to get the interviewee's views, ideas, and questions about the future. Find out where the person wants to go and how fast he or she plans to get there. "Where do you think your skills and talents will best direct you in our business?" This kind of question will always give us some insight into the interviewee's hopes and aspirations. The interviewee must realize that the future depends as much on the employees as on the organization, so questions that will let us know how the person is likely to relate to the organization and the people around him or her will give us more information. The questions should be worded correctly, though, or the answers won't give very meaningful information. It would be useless to ask, "How did you get along with your last boss?" Anybody would be foolish to answer anything but, "Fine!" If we ask, "What kind of boss did you like the most?" (as we have already suggested), then we get the prospective employee's views, not a baited answer. The same is true about asking, "Do you get along with people?" That's what we want to know, but we won't find out by asking a direct question. We'll get better information if we say something like, "Tell me about some of the people you didn't get along with very well in your last job." This is a leading question, but as we haven't supplied the interviewee with any clues as to the "right" answer, so the person must respond by expressing his or her own ideas and feelings.

The Civil Rights Act and the Employment Interview

Title VII of the 1964 Civil Rights Act prohibits discrimination in employment on the basis of race, religion, color, national origin, or sex. A 1972 amendment to this act gives any minority person, or any woman, the right to enter a complaint against any business or other organization based on discrimination in hiring, promotion, pay, and related factors. In 1973, the Rehabilitation Act was passed, making it unlawful to consider a person's handicap in making hiring decisions. The Equal Employment Opportunity Commission (EEOC) has the responsibility to administer the equal-opportunity program. The passage of these acts has led to many suits, charges, and judgments, which have resulted in the payment of millions of dollars in fines and adjustments. Also, many rulings that affect hiring and employment have been and still are being handed down. One area on which this has had the most telling effect has been the *employment interview*. Questions that have traditionally been asked and topics that were once routinely discussed have been used as evidence in cases where discrimination has been charged. Even where intentions and motives were beyond question or things were done innocently, rulings have gone against organizations because certain questions were asked that later could not be shown to have any direct bearing on the interviewee's ability to perform on the job.

The Problem.   The job of the employment interviewer is to select people for the organization who will fit into the jobs that are available and perhaps even move up in the organization's vertical structure. Historically, this has been a difficult job, because it places one in the position of being a prophet, a seer of the future, as well as part judge and part jury. Even at its best, employment interviewing has been something less than a science.

Over the years, a series of questions was developed to give interviewers a whole lot of information, with the idea that the more information, the better the chances of successfully predicting a potential employee's usefulness to an organization. These questions included criteria that in themselves weren't intended to be biased, but that when looked at in the light of equal-opportunity hiring standards became very hard to justify.

The most difficult issue was the absence of data supporting the relationship between the questions asked and the jobs to be done. Job descriptions and job-skills descriptions were not very good, and there was an almost total lack of information supporting the relationship between hiring standards and job standards. Organizations had requirements of high-school certificates, for example, but no information to show that the job required a high-school diploma before the worker could perform satisfactorily. It wasn't a matter of whether or not it *was* a necessary thing; there was just no proof to back it up. It was eventually called into question because such a requirement often screened out minorities, and no one could produce satisfactory data to *prove* that the requirement wasn't intended to be prejudicial.

There were other problems, also. Recruiters and employment interviewers were in the habit of giving tests to applicants. They administered standardized tests—which were valid in showing what was being tested for but which had never been matched up against the performance of someone actually doing the job being filled. The testing had been regarded as an acceptable way of screening people, with no thought of using it as a prejudicial tool against anyone, but the results were the same: it screened out many minorities, and no one could show that a certain test score was a guarantee of success at a certain job. In many cases, testing was discontinued as a screening device.

The Lack of Job Standards.   What was an even more serious problem, perhaps, was that the interviewers were never furnished an adequate breakdown of just what the jobs were that they were hiring people to fill. The job descriptions were almost always vague and full of generalities—often on purpose, for internal political reasons. In fact, in many if not most cases, the descriptions didn't exist—on paper, at least. The only descriptions were those used in such situations as union seniority cases or when there was a reason to separate one job from another for promotion reasons. The job title might have been all that existed by way of description. For example, there might be a title "staff assistant" and another, "technical assistant," of a higher or lower grade. Neither would be very clear, but one would be rated higher than the other, and if both were entry-level jobs, one would have a higher cutoff score than the other or perhaps require more education. When organizations were asked to justify these things in light of the number of minority applicants who were screened out, it was impossible to do so. Remember, for the most part, no bias was connected with the decisions to do it this way—it was just an expedient screening process that worked very well mechanically.

What was really needed, of course, was a good, written description of each job to be filled, listing the kinds of skills that had been demonstrated as being required to do the job satisfactorily. This takes time and requires knowledge both of the job and of how to write proper job descriptions. People with such knowledge often aren't available within the organization. Just as often, there is no one department that has been given this assignment or responsibility. In these cases, the descriptions just didn't get prepared. What happened many times was that as pressure mounted, job descriptions got written—*after the fact*. As organizations saw that they were going to have trouble because they had turned down so many minority applicants, they began to write descriptions. Such descriptions nearly always screened out the people *who had already been turned down*.

The Lack of Communication.   Another thing that compounded the problem was the fact that in large organizations, the recruiters or interviewers were far removed from the persons who needed the employees hired. The employment office was far removed—in reporting if not in location—from the operating people, and rarely did they ever communicate very well with each other. The operations people would simply turn in a request for a certain number of people to fill certain jobs, and once this was approved by operations management and personnel, and was checked against the list of available people from other parts of the organization, the employment people took over. They probably did a very good job with the information they had, but they actually had very little to go on. The end product was the hiring of people more or less blindly.

Later, when the question of discrimination came up, no one was able to explain just what it was the person hired was supposed to do. Since this was the case, neither was there anyone who could prove that the requirements set down for employment were really necessary for the job. In almost every case, somebody *felt* the requirements were just. Some said that, after all, we're really hiring for promotion later on. Some felt that it was their duty to hire the best person available. Some felt that they should continue to hire the "kind" of people who were already on the payroll, so that there would be a "compatibility" among the employees. Then, too, there were some who were just plain prejudiced against certain people because of their race or creed or sex or national origin. Since the law—like society—is unable to determine which people are actually prejudiced and which aren't, it was much easier to deal with the acts of discrimination than to try to decide about people's biases. Hence, the law stepped in and ruled against the various forms of discrimination. Later, of course, the law was expanded to forbid any discrimination against people with disabilities. There were those who predicted that all this would bring doom to the hiring process. But doom never did arrive. We'll see now how organizations have dealt with the law and what the law allows. It is not our purpose to show how to beat the law, but to show how to live within the law and still get the best employees available under the law's restrictions and limitations. We'll deal primarily with the employment interview, since that's where most of the violations—and the resulting suits and fines—occur.

The Employment Interview Itself.   It is far easier to state what we're *not* allowed to ask than to state clearly what *is* permitted. In many cases the jury is still out as far as clarity is concerned. Cases are pending, trials are in appeals courts, and investigations are under way to see if the laws have been violated. What is allowed one day might be disallowed the next. It sounds more confusing than it actually is, however. There are some rules of thumb that can keep most questions and questioners within the law and avoid discrimination.

The single most important thing to remember is that no question should be asked without good reason; there must be a direct relationship between the questions asked and the job to be filled. And the same question may be legitimate in one case and completely out of line in another. For instance, if the job requires that the employee use his or her own car, it certainly is necessary to ask, "Do you own your own car?" If it does not, then that question is not permissible. Likewise, if a job requires typing, then we obviously must ask the interviewee whether he or she can type. But if it does not, then we just as obviously must not ask that question.

Planning the Interview.   How can we avoid asking the wrong questions—or make sure that we do ask the right questions? Simply by doing a good job of planning. First, we never hire anybody without knowing the job he or she will be required to fill. Second, we make sure we have enough information about the job to do a good interview for it. We analyze the job until we're able to list all the duties and responsibilities of the person who will fill it.

We compare the responsibilities and duties of the job with the qualifications of the person who has applied for it and make sure that we're looking only at the minimum requirements. If these include some personal abilities or characteristics, such as the ability to meet people or answer the phone, then we make note of this, too. We look at people we've hired previously and see if we've hired below this qualification level before.

The next job of planning is for the interview itself. We decide on the type of questions we'll ask to get the kind of information we want. As much as possible, we even rehearse some of these questions to see how they appear to us and to make ourselves comfortable with them before we ask them of the applicant. We study the applicant's forms before the interview. We mark those things we want *and need* more information on, and we list other things that aren't dealt with on the application but that we want *and need* to know. As far as possible, we make a general outline covering the flow of questioning as we would like to see it go. (We can even reveal this to the applicant if we wish, so he or she will be able to understand just where we're headed with each question.) From here on, it's a matter of preparing for a normal good interview with regard to its key elements: place—comfortable and private; time—adequate, undisturbed; materials—available and familiar.

What We Can—and Can't—Ask. From here on, we'll talk about some of the things that can and can't be asked, bearing in mind that we've established the groundwork for determining the kind of information we need. (*NOTE:* The following is only a partial list and may change as various court cases are settled. Anytime a supervisor is planning to conduct an employment interview, he or she should be certain about what can and cannot be asked and said in the interview. This information is usually available from the human resources or personnel department or from the legal department.)

- It is legal to ask for date of birth and proof of that age—
  but illegal to show preference for younger persons in hiring.

- It is legal to ask if the person can meet the work schedule and attendance requirements—

but illegal to ask specifics about the person's spouse, the spouse's employment, or who will look after the children.

- It is legal to ask about training and experience in the U.S. military—

    but illegal to ask about reasons for discharge or about service in the military of other governments or for copies of discharge papers.

- It is legal to ask about how long the applicant plans to stay on the job or about any expected absences, providing the questions are asked of both men and women—

    but illegal to ask direct questions about previous pregnancies or possible future pregnancies.

- It is legal to ask for names the person has used with this organization or with other organizations for reference purposes—

    but illegal to ask about the origin of a name or anything about a name that would reveal its owner's marital status.

- It is legal to ask a person's height or weight *if* it has been shown that such height or weight is a requirement for the job and that no one can or has held the job without meeting the stated requirements—

    but illegal to ask about height or weight if there is no job requirement relating to these things.

- It is legal to ask if the person can be cleared to work lawfully in this country and can provide proof of this *after hiring*—

    but illegal to request proof of citizenship or ask what country the person is a citizen of.

- It is legal to ask that a photograph be supplied for the employee's record *after* employment—

    but illegal to ask for a photograph *before* hiring.

- It is legal to ask for an address where the person can be contacted—

    but illegal to ask with whom the person is living or whether the person owns or rents his or her home.

- *It is always illegal to ask questions regarding marital status, race, color, religion, creed, or sex.*

THE COUNSELING INTERVIEW

Sometimes employees have problems, and the result is that we become involved in counseling interviews. Since the problems may be emotional, these interviews will differ from the others we have. The approach will be different, too. Most often, counseling interviews come about as a result of the employee's coming to us rather than our going to the employee. Because of this, we are seen in a little different light. We don't have the same kind of control over the time or duration, topics to be discussed, and so forth, as we do in the other types of interviews. As a supervisor, we are concerned about the employee's well-being, of course, but we are also concerned with performance. If the employee's problems affect performance on the job, we have to help the person or resolve those problems in some way in order to protect the organization as well as the individual. Most personal problems are not job-related at all, but if they have a bad effect on job performance, the employee is likely to realize it. The person will know that he or she isn't working up to his or her capabilities, and this just compounds the worries, making the original problem worse. For this reason, if it is at all possible, we should help the employee solve whatever personal problems he or she brings us without any reference to job performance. Besides, this in itself may make the employee feel a little better and more capable of dealing with other things.

Interestingly enough, the employee may not even know the real reasons for the problems. Family problems may cause the person to come to work in a bad frame of mind or to interpret things in the wrong light or even to say and do things that create problems for others in the workplace. The employee may have financial problems that cause him or her to worry and fail to concentrate on the job. Lack of concentration may create safety problems or cut into production schedules. It may cause errors that show up much later in our operation. One of the serious consequences of an employee's worrying about financial problems may be that he or she will get all kinds of delusions about what his or her salary should be, how much overtime he or she should get, and what kind of intervals should be between raises. It may even affect the employee's union activities, especially if the union begins to promise great demands and rewards.

Help Out

Because of the personal nature of these interviews and the fact that the employee has come to us, we have to be very careful to treat the interviews as opportunities to *help*, not threaten, the person. We shouldn't say, "I'm glad you're here. I've been wanting to talk to you." Nothing would frighten any employee off quicker. The best thing to do is simply let the employee know we will listen and let him or her talk. We also want to convey the idea very strongly that we *want* to help. Because the employee has come to us, this is a good opportunity to get things straightened out, but we have to be careful not to mess up the chance. We have to remember that *we are not trained psychologists!* If we think we can help, we should do our very best to help. If we have *any* doubts, we should very quickly refer the employee to someone who is better trained to do the counseling than we are.

As we listen to the employee and try to decide what to advise him or her to do, we need to face the fact that we may never get either full or accurate information from the person. We may get false conclusions—conclusions based on too little information, on emotion, or on imagined facts. Because of this, we need to be careful in drawing any conclusions on our own. Probably the worst thing we can do is to form an opinion very early in the interview, then look only at the evidence that supports our opinion. But this doesn't mean that we can't recommend any action or make any suggestions. It's possible to help the employee even without getting all the information we'd like. The fact that the person doesn't leave with all his or her problems solved doesn't mean that the meeting was unsatisfactory. If we have provided the person with the opportunity to unwind, to talk, to know that someone will actually listen and not try to control him or her, we may have gone a long way toward helping to solve the problem. If the employee attacks the organization or its policies, we answer questions truthfully but avoid being defensive. We surely want to keep from getting emotional, especially if an employee is that way. We don't want to cover up the truth about the organization, an employee's work, or our feelings toward him or her. We might do more harm than good if we tell an employee that everything is rosy, knowing all the time that we are going to have to take some serious action in the near future.

When an employee comes to us with problems, there are two approaches we can take, each quite different from the other. We can assume responsibility for the problems. We can take the whole load on our shoulders, look for solutions, get information for the employee, offer to go as far as we can to do whatever is necessary to solve the problems for him or her. As undesirable as this sounds, there are times when we would go this far. When an employee comes to us apparently at his or her wit's end, or unwilling or unable to face the problem squarely, we need to step in and give support. Obviously, we don't take over permanently, but in a time of stress the employee needs to know that somebody who cares also is strong enough to accept the responsibility for his or her problem. Just as obviously, we shouldn't step in and take over the problem *just because it's been brought to us*. Part of the problem may be that the employee is unwilling to recognize the problem as his or her fault and may be trying to place the responsibility on someone else. For us to step in and take over would be the worst thing to do.

The other extreme is to let the employee take the responsibility entirely on himself or herself. We just listen. We ask some questions, but end up more or less saying, "That's interesting," and doing nothing. Again, as unlikely as it seems, there are times when this is exactly the right approach. When the employee shows that he or she has the strength to face the problem, but wants a sympathetic ear, we would do a lot of harm by taking over. All of us like to have someone to talk to now and then. We aren't necessarily looking for advice. We aren't even expecting the person we're talking with to agree or disagree with us. We simply find that we understand our problem much better at the end of the conversation, and even more so if the other party happens to ask us a pertinent question or two. So it is when an employee comes to us with a problem and appears to just want to talk. Our best response is to let him or her do only that.

Ideally, of the two options, allowing the employee to take the responsibility for his or her problems is the better one. Even if we start off by taking over, we should also immediately begin to look for ways to return the responsibility to the employee. Gradually, we shift it back by asking questions and letting the employee supply the answers instead of the other way around. As the employee begins to take the responsibility again, we keep him or her on the right track by asking the right questions—questions that simply make the person face another truth or help him or her avoid the wrong conclusion—and step in only when the employee appears to be running out of steam. Most important, we should avoid trying to be the hero and get all the credit for the solution. We're looking for the credit without knowing it when we adopt the parental attitude of "I think it'll work out all right if you just take my advice." The important thing is to get the problem solved, not to get credit for solving it. What may make the solution most effective is our ability to convince the employee that it was *his* or *her own* solution.

We've already seen that being a supervisor doesn't mean we are a trained psychologist or counselor. We aren't in a position to understand some of the more serious problems that require professional counseling, such as mental problems, drug or alcohol dependency, or deep-rooted family problems. We have to avoid becoming amateur psychologists. We know we're reaching that point when we say to ourselves or others, "You know, his problem is that he's not willing to admit he isn't acting right toward his family," or "If she would just admit to me or someone that she hasn't applied herself to the job enough to earn a promotion, she'd get over this problem." Problems are often complex, just as individuals are, and when we think we've found a simple solution to a problem that's causing some widespread difficulty, we're in over our head.

The strange thing about counseling is that most people are looking for an answer they *want* to hear rather than the one they *ought* to hear. As a result, they don't always hear things as precisely as they should. For example, if an employee is having some serious problems with a spouse who drinks, we may try to suggest some professional counseling for the employee or the spouse or both. In the conversation, the employee says, "Don't you think I should just leave and get out of this horrible situation?" Rather than cut the person off (gently) at this point—it isn't our decision to make—we may say, "That's a possibility, and I can see why you feel that way. That's not for me to say, of course." Later on, if our employee does leave his or her spouse and there is a further problem, the employee is likely to say, "But you told me you could see my point and encouraged me to do it!" No matter what we say from now on, the person will still believe we said to leave his or her spouse—because that's what the employee *wanted* to hear. The employee wanted us to tell him or her what to do, to make the decision easy, but at the same time that person had already what advice he or she wanted from us. Our best approach is to decide whether the problem is over our head—and be very humble about deciding this—and if it is, then repeat time after time, "See a professional, see a professional, see a professional." It's not a matter of not getting involved or not wanting to give advice. We are involved and we are giving advice—good advice! We're smart enough to know that we shouldn't be dealing with this kind of problem. We know that there are others who are better at it than we are and who can give professional advice and aid.

Finally, keep the employee's problems confidential, if possible. Avoid putting those problems into his or her personnel record, especially when the person has come to us expecting to get private help. If there was a discussion about performance, or the meeting resulted from a performance problem, then it may be necessary to put this in the files. If the personnel records are open to other supervisors, we should be careful not to put anything about this meeting in those records unless the employee is agreeable to it. Another caution is to avoid casually mentioning the problem to other supervisors. If we violate the confidence that has been given us, we not only stand to aggravate the problem, but we can be sure we've had our last counseling interview.

Caution

Having said all this about the counseling interview, we should offer a word of caution about doing counseling. The truth is, few supervisors are trained counselors. Dealing with very personal problems of employees is a rather touchy and dangerous undertaking. Most organizations retain professional counselors on their staffs or as consultants. Rather than get too deeply into counseling, we would be wise to recognize when the situation is really over our head. Often the employee wants very much to get a certain answer and may not hear anything else. Even if we only offer something as an option and caution the person against it, if it's what that person wants to hear, he or she does it, and it doesn't work, we will get the blame. We could even be held accountable for the bad results.

THE DISCIPLINARY INTERVIEW

Counseling interviews are difficult because they are different from other types of interviews. Disciplinary interviews are difficult because they have the potential to be very unpleasant. They are one of those necessary evils that we have as a part of our job as a supervisor. But note, the disciplinary interview is a basic requirement of our job and is rarely ever as bad as we expect it to be. The reason we have to have disciplinary interviews is that employees break rules. We have to have rules and regulations—standards of the job—but rules get broken. Not everyone meets every standard all the time. When employees fail too often or by too great a margin to meet the standard, we have to discipline them—or *change the standard*. We simply can't run an organization in which people continually fail to meet the standards set by those in a position to know what a good standard is. Nothing lowers morale more quickly or destroys our effectiveness as a supervisor more completely than allowing someone to constantly break the organization's rules. If we set a precedent by letting one person get away with something, we have little chance of stopping others who decide to try the same thing. It's equally hard on the person who wants to abide by the rules when everyone else is allowed to do otherwise. Even when it's no more than one person who habitually comes in late, if the office hours are established and accepted, then everyone should abide by them; no exceptions.

When it comes to the disciplinary interview, the simplest approach is to take a *positive* attitude toward it. For the good of all concerned, something needs to be done. If the problem is allowed to continue, nothing but trouble can result. The organization is suffering because of the situation, and to let things get worse because we dread doing something unpleasant doesn't make good sense. Not only is the organization not functioning at its best, but our job is harder because of the problem, and we, too, are failing to operate at our best. We are having to cover up or redo or make excuses or explain to others because of the situation that one employee has gotten us into, so we have every right to attack the problem head-on. We have already seen that the others in the group are going to become involved, especially if the situation is allowed to continue without corrective action, so for the good of the others in the work group, we need to do something in a hurry. Even the employee who causes the problems suffers from them. His or her career is in jeopardy, because the longer this goes on, the worse we think of the employee—perhaps even worse than he or she deserves. So regardless of how unpleasant the interview may appear, the reasons for conducting it are real enough. If we do a good job of it and get the problem solved, we will be the stronger for it, and all concerned will be happier and better workers as a result. But two things are worthy of special note here. First, no matter how much we dread the confrontation, it won't get any easier if we put it off. Second, again, this kind of interview rarely is as bad as we expect it to be.

The Process

Disciplinary interviews begin just like the other interviews we have talked about. Our first action is to put our interviewee at ease, going through the steps we have discussed. The worst thing we can do, of course, is jump down the employee's throat the minute he or she walks into the office. If we feel that our temper is going to explode, then we'd better postpone the interview until we calm down. We must continually remind ourselves that all our employees are valuable and we mustn't do anything that will cause any one of them to become less valuable. We aren't trying to win a battle—we're trying to get the organization back to running the way it should be. We aren't even trying to prove any points; neither are we trying to prove that the interviewee is wrong and we are right. We are simply trying to correct a situation that cannot be allowed to continue. Our employee must know that we are trying to be fair. From the moment we begin talking, the person must recognize this. Being fair means that we want to hear the employee's side of the matter and want to know any facts he or she might have to add to our total knowledge. This brings up an important point: we must have as much information as possible before we start the interview. Perhaps more than any other kind of interview, the disciplinary interview requires that we be fully informed. This certainly is no time to discover that we have our facts wrong or that we don't have the whole story. And it's just as important to remember to have the facts substantiated. When we say, "You've been late nearly every day this month," we aren't really making a hard, factual statement. We'd do much better to have the exact information and say, "You've been late fourteen days this month." The difference between the two statements is the difference between confidence and shaky ground.

We must also be sure that the interviewee knows that he or she is being disciplined. Sometimes we try to sneak the disciplinary comments between praising comments, and the message is lost. If we wait until the person is about to leave and then say, "By the way . . . ," and go into the reasons for our calling the person, we've done both the employee and us an injustice. The employee should know from the start what the purpose of the interview is. He or she should know that his or her behavior has been unacceptable. We should explain what the standard is and how the person has failed to meet it. Just as clearly, we should let the employee know what corrections are expected and when they should take place. Of course, this isn't merely a "tell, tell, tell" interview. As quickly as possible—when we have stated the reason for the interview—we should start to "listen, listen, listen." We want to be sure the interviewee has a chance to state his or her side of the issue. There is always the possibility that there may be some things in the person's favor that we haven't considered. If someone says, "My last boss told me it was all right," or "The other departments started doing this two months ago," we'd better be prepared to study the matter further. At least we should know about it, if these things are so.

Finally, we should deal with the employee's specific problems, not his or her total performance—unless that total performance is in question. There's little to be gained by making an employee look worse than he or she is just to prove a point. We need to be ready to admit the person's strengths and willing to give praise as the occasion arises. But we can't let the good points overshadow the bad, nor can we hide the fact that the employee is being called on to answer for his or her conduct. Like most interviews, the disciplinary one needs to terminate with the same preciseness with which it begins. The longer we drag it out, the more danger there is that we will begin to cloud the issue. Simply put, we need to deal with the problem, state the standard, state the acceptable behavior we expect from the employee, listen to all the facts, answer pertinent questions, be sure that he or she understands what happens now—*then end the interview*. If possible, we end the session on a positive note of our expectations for better performance; we end it on a pleasant note to show we expect things to work out; but above all, we end it.

THE APPRAISAL INTERVIEW

When we appraise our people, we generally end the process with an interview to discuss the matter with them. This is called an appraisal interview. It should be done periodically for the benefit of both the employees and us. They need to know their strengths and weaknesses, and we need to know how they see themselves and the job. But a word of caution is in order: if the organization has a regularly scheduled time for making appraisals, we shouldn't wait until that one certain time each year to let employees know how they're doing. If we expect smooth development of the people who work for us, we must let them know as often as possible where they need to grow. *Once a year isn't often enough.* So the appraisal interview isn't some ritual that's performed annually to satisfy some organizational policy; it's something that we do with our employees as often as we need to discuss their growth and development.

The primary purpose of the appraisal interview is to get a comprehensive look at employees as they fit into the organization now and how they will fit into it in the future. It should be one of the most enjoyable of all sessions we have with our employees, because it's an opportunity to do what we should spend a great deal of time doing—helping employees grow. For this reason we shouldn't confuse this type of interview with the disciplinary one. This isn't the time to point out the interviewee's faults; we don't save disciplinary observations to bring out at this moment. The purpose of the interview should be clear in our minds and clear to the employee. The interviewee should know why we're having the get-together and even make plans for points he or she would like to cover during the interview.

Employee Participation

Employees should be given every chance to be a part of all interviews, but especially of this one. The interviewee should know in advance that the interview is planned, that we want him or her to participate, and that we will be talking about the *future* as well as the past. Of course, each interview starts with putting the employee at ease, but it shouldn't take as long in this case as with other types of interviews. Most employees want to know how well we think they are doing and are anxious to get to the subject, particularly if they know in advance that we want to talk about their progress. As soon as we get into the subject, we should let the employee tell us how he or she sees himself or herself. It's good to allow the person to explain how he or she sees the *job* at the same time. Doing a brief task analysis will let us know what the person thinks the job is, which may explain certain shortcomings—there may be some things the employee just doesn't know he or she is supposed to do. As we begin to compare our views with those of the interviewee, we need to be careful that the person doesn't lose sight of the fact that we want him or her to be a part of the discussion. If we become too domineering, the employee will begin to think that it doesn't really make much difference what he or she thinks—we've already got our mind made up. So we try to keep the employee in the conversation throughout the entire interview. We give the honest impression that this is *the employee's* session, an opportunity to get the facts on how he or she is doing and where he or she is going. When the interviewee sees something differently from the way we see it, his or her opinion should count for as much as ours. If the person has the supporting data, then we should accept what he or she says. (Just because the employee works for us doesn't mean that he or she is less smart or less honest.)

In the appraisal interview we should, ideally, concentrate on the future as much as possible. Even when we're talking about past performance, we want to relate it to the employee's future performance. How can the person change to do things better? What is the employee doing now that is great and likely to enhance chances for promotion in the future? As much as possible, we should let the interviewee set his or her own goals and decide what actions will produce the best results, both personally and for the organization. Certainly, the interviewee should be allowed to participate in setting personal objectives and selecting any corrective action that is decided on. As we look at the interviewee's future, we help set both long- and short-range goals for him or her. The long-range ones will deal with the person's ambitions, study, and direction in the organization. The short-range ones will have to do only with the job at hand. We want to help the employee see that there is a certain amount of danger in looking too far ahead, especially if it means beginning to forget about the requirements of the present job. Too many people have lost out in the future because they didn't give enough attention to the present. Part of our obligation as a supervisor is to let the employee know how he or she is doing on the present assignment so the person will have an opportunity to make the most of the future. The appraisal interview allows us an excellent opportunity to do this, particularly if we let the employee be a part of setting his or her short- and long-range objectives.

As in any interview, we should be sure the employee knows exactly what we are saying. We should state how we see the person's job and future. As the interview draws to a close, we should begin to summarize and clear up any misunderstandings that may have arisen. If we have decided on some specific training or other course of action, we should state that clearly, also. If there is to be some kind of follow-up, then the time and place should be settled. Even if another meeting isn't scheduled, we should establish that we don't want to wait until next year to talk about the interviewee's progress and future. Also, not only should the employee feel free to talk to us, but he or she should feel free to initiate such a meeting.

Finally, we should note that sometimes the employee may take our appraisal efforts as just another chance to criticize him or her. The employee may not accept what we say or agree with our estimate of him or her. The person may rationalize and blame the organization or coworkers. If we do our best and the situation still turns out this way, then we have actually found out even more about this employee than we already knew. We now know that he or she can't take criticism and lacks the ability to see himself or herself objectively. If so, then *so be it*. We've done our part; we'll continue to do our part. We'll continue to let the employee participate in planning for his or her future. We'll continue to involve the employee in these types of interviews. We'll even look at our own information and see if it's faulty in some way. But we must still be the supervisor, and we must still hold to what we see and believe. The worst thing we can do is let employees bluff us into changing our minds or our actions. But the chances of this getting to be a real problem are pretty slim. As we have said, most employees want us to tell them how we see them, both in the job now and in the future. If we have prepared effectively for the interview, we'll be glad we conducted it and will look forward to the next one!

THE EXIT INTERVIEW

As a new supervisor, very few of us get the opportunity to conduct exit interviews, which are simply interviews with employees who have indicated in a positive way that they want to leave the organization. The purpose of these interviews isn't to try to persuade the employees to change their minds. Often supervisors do this and end up making things worse than they were when the employees decided to leave. So why have interviews with people who are leaving, especially if we aren't supposed to talk them into staying with the organization?

The reasons are pretty obvious when we start to think about all the things we can learn from such interviews. As a supervisor, we need to check our perception. How well do we know the individual who is leaving? Do we really know why the person is leaving? Do we really know what that person's relationship is with the rest of the organization? The answers to these questions should come out of the interviews—to check our perception. Another reason for exit interviews is to check our own ability as a supervisor. Have we got some weaknesses that could be corrected? Are we somehow at fault for the individual's leaving? Have we created a situation in the work group that may cause others to leave, too? This, also, should come out of the interview.

Another reason for the interview is to check the organization's policies and working conditions. Are we matching the wrong people with our jobs? Are our hiring procedures creating bad situations? Are our policies out of date or out of line with those of other organizations? Is there something wrong with our wage structure? These questions may not be answered in one interview, but clues may be seen in the things that are found out. So this is another reason for conducting exit interviews.

A final reason for these interviews is that they benefit the employee who is leaving. The person may need to get some things out in the open. He or she may feel a certain remorse about leaving, and the interview can help, as the person talks about the decision to go. Most important, the person may be heading into some future trouble that can be prevented by a calm and rational talk. All these become real, logical, and sound reasons for having exit interviews. But the results will not be satisfactory if we do a poor job of conducting the interview.

How do we conduct exit interviews? In the beginning, this interview looks similar to the others, but there are some important differences. As usual, we want to put the interviewee at ease. We want to let the interviewee know that we appreciate his or her taking the time to talk to us even though he or she is leaving the organization. We must immediately let the person know that we feel he or she can help us and we'd appreciate that help. And we want to assure the interviewee that we are not going to try to change his or her mind about leaving. We want the person to know that our every intention is to *listen*. We are looking for insight into our own problems and ways that we can improve the organization. Above all, we should put the interviewee at ease by explaining that we aren't going to pry or ask him or her to tell us all kinds of bad things about others in the group.

When an exit interview begins, *we start listening*. We ask open-ended questions designed to get the interviewee talking and *keep the interviewee talking*. We avoid interrupting and do our best not to go on the defensive. We don't want it to get to be a policy-defense interview. We correct any statements about policies that are obviously untrue, but we don't have to defend policies. No matter how much we'd like to launch into an explanation of all the good things that these policies have accomplished, this isn't a time for us to be giving out information like that. We want to keep the disagreement to a minimum, so even when we correct a statement in order to supply the facts, we do it by saying, "Well, it may have appeared that way, but actually the policy reads . . ." And when we encounter a situation in which there is no way to avoid disagreement, we need to say, "It's interesting that you feel that way," not "You're crazy if that's the way you think it is."

Exit interviews have one hazard that must be avoided. We must be sure not to let them degenerate into name-calling sessions about people in the group. Unless there is a substantial amount of evidence, there is no need to get into a discussion of specific people. Even given such evidence, there is no reason to talk about people unless there's something useful to be gained by it. If it's widely known that someone in the office or some policy in the organization is a problem, this interview probably isn't the place to discuss it. Also, it makes more sense to talk only about those things that we can do something about. If the interviewee wants to talk about something about work that bothered him or her, but it is something that shouldn't have affected the person, this, too, has no real place in the discussion.

Use the Information

In one respect, exit interviews are like all other interviews we conduct—we must learn to use the information we get. It's useless to take the time to gather information if we don't use it after we get it. Exit interviews may be the most important of all from this standpoint. Using the information from them may be the means of preventing other exit interviews in the future! We should study the information and decide what we've really learned and how we can use it. If we have found a bad situation, we should correct it. If the information tells us that something we did caused a problem, we then take the necessary steps to see that it doesn't happen again. Finally, we should review our own actions during these interviews to see if we are satisfied with the way we conducted them. We ask ourselves:

> "Did I plan it well?"
> "Did I put the employee at ease?"
> "Did it go as I planned it?"
> "Did I really accomplish anything?"
> "How did the employee feel when it was done?"
> "How did I feel when it was done?"
> "If I had it to do over again, would I do it differently?"

If the answer to this last question is yes, then we need to take whatever steps are necessary to see that we really do it differently the next time!

CONCLUSION

Successful interviews don't just happen. They are carefully planned. It is an oversimplification to say that an interview is merely a matter of two people's talking to each other, but it's important to remember that that is basically just what it is. The purposes may be different from one interview to the next, the roles played by the interviewee and interviewer may change from one interview to the next, but still it comes down to our ability to *talk with people*. There are times when we're trying to get information, as in an employment interview. Sometimes we want to give information, as in an appraisal interview. It may be that we simply need to listen, as we mostly do in a counseling interview. But whatever kind of interview we're involved in, we are still using the skills of talking with people on a one-to-one basis. We need to learn how to conduct interviews so we'll have a good idea of where we're going and when we've gotten there. We have to learn to ask questions properly, perhaps open-endedly or by using reflective-listening techniques to keep the person talking. Perhaps we will have to be very direct and let the person know where he or she is missing the mark—and what the consequences are for not making the correction. These things aren't always easy to accomplish, and to be really good at them we have to practice, study our results, and practice some more. We have to be practicing the right thing, though, because practice only makes *permanent*, not necessarily *perfect*. If we practice the wrong thing long enough, we'll get good at being bad, and it will even begin to feel natural to us.

Listening is by far the hardest thing to learn about effective communication. But in an interview, listening is most often the key to success. We can direct the interview by responding to whatever part of the interviewee's remarks we think will lead in the right direction, but this works only if we have been listening carefully to what was being said. Bad interviews result when we fail to take our turn at *listening*. But listening means more than just being quiet while the other person is talking. It's a matter of paying careful attention, understanding, and responding properly. The steps in successful interviewing are simple enough to learn, but take some concentration, mostly on setting our goals and then listening to see if we're getting the feedback that tells us we're going where we want to go. Once we've learned to be a good interviewer, it's surprising how much satisfaction we can get from conducting a successful interview. Since we're involved in so many interviews during our years as a supervisor, it behooves us to try for as much of this kind of satisfaction as we can get.

In conclusion to our discussion of civil rights and the employment interview, we can only add that employers are hiring and rejecting people every day without violating any laws or discriminating against anyone in the process. Good employees are being hired, too, and jobs are being filled with qualified people. Until we learned to understand the law and how to determine just what the job really required in the way of skills, things were pretty rough. Many unqualified people were probably hired just because the interviewer was afraid to turn them down and bring on a suit or an investigation. Those days are rapidly passing as we get smarter and learn more about how to conduct the employment interview. Above all, we want to get the best person for the job; we have no interest in discriminating against anyone. To make certain this is what happens in our interviewing, we need to study the information covered here and be sure to check with our own organization and its policies on hiring and interviewing. If there is a fault with this section, it may be that it is oversimplified. For that reason, we urge you not to depend entirely on what is here, but to continue seeking additional information and advice from within your own organization.

EXERCISES

1. Group multiple role-play: Have the group divide into subgroups of three people. One person is the interviewer, one the interviewee, and the other the observer. Those being interviewed are to play themselves. Each is being considered for a completely different assignment. The idea is to find out each person's feelings about a change of jobs within the organization that will necessitate relocating to another town. The orga-

nization will pay the moving expenses and handle the sale of real estate, but there is no pay increase. There is opportunity for advancement in a couple of years, and while no promises can be made, the chances are pretty good that a promotion will result if the employee doesn't mess up on the new job. The observer should look for the steps in successful interviewing, such as putting the employee at ease, stating the purpose of the interview, asking open-ended questions, listening, dealing reflectively with questions, summarizing action to be taken as a result of the interview, and concluding the interview on good terms.

2. Group multiple role-play: When the role-plays in exercise 1 are completed, have the participants rotate positions, with the observer now being interviewed and the interviewee becoming the interviewer. The former interviewer becomes the observer. When this is over, have the people report their successes and failures. Record the things that were difficult to do and areas where participants need to improve.

3. Subgroup exercise: In small groups discuss why disciplinary interviews are dreaded and what can be done to overcome this feeling. Decide whether there is a justification for the dread and see whether anyone has had a bad experience with an employee he or she has had to discipline. Bring the group back together and see what the small groups found out. Make a list of the most often used excuses for not doing disciplinary interviews and decide how many of these are justified.

4. Individual exercise: Ask the participants to think about themselves as they were when they started with their present organization. Recall what questions were asked and list them down the left side of a piece of paper. On the right side of the sheet, put a check mark by those things that were really important to the job the person was actually hired to perform. When all have finished, collect the typical questions and record them on the board. Save them for further use.

5. Group activity: Look at the items from exercise 4 and decide what questions participants really need to ask a person they're considering hiring. See if there are any questions that get into the interview through custom or tradition. See if any can be

eliminated just because they don't relate to the job to be done. This isn't easy and shouldn't be taken as an excuse for not asking anything! Employers do need much information, and this is the time to get it, before the employee comes to work for the organization.

6. Group activity: Examine the questions collected from exercise 4 and see how many of them might be construed as discriminatory if the person hadn't been hired. In other words, which of these questions could have been used against an organization if a person wanted to bring a charge of some kind for violating the EEOC requirements?

Chapter 12

TRAINING: THE SUPERVISOR'S RESPONSIBILITY

One of the biggest mistakes supervisors—new and old—make is to assume that training is an adjunct to our regular job, something we do only when we have plenty of time and nothing else to do. If we have this attitude, we really don't understand our job very well, since the real function of the supervisor is to get work done through other people. Taking this another step, we can say that our *prime* job is to see that our people are trained. If we have anyone under us who can't do the job because he or she hasn't been trained, then we have fallen down on *our* job as far as that person is concerned. Unless our people are properly trained, we have no real justification for appraising them or for finding fault with their work. Training, then, becomes an important part of our job, and we will do well to learn how to train others if we expect to succeed as supervisors.

TRAINING IS A SKILL

Unfortunately, many people want to classify the ability to train others as an art or a science. Maybe it is, but it is a skill first, and like any other skill, it must be learned. Sometimes we go in the opposite direction—we tend to think of training others as something we can do without any special skill. After all, we say, what's so hard about telling someone how to do something we know all about? The problem is, that's what we usually do and call it training—we tell someone how to do it, and *telling isn't training*.

Supervisors have to learn many skills. We must learn to write, speak, conduct interviews, and train our people. Unfortunately, we can do these things in such a way that it will *look* as if we're doing all right when we actually aren't. We watch people doing some training and it looks and sounds as if they're doing a good job, but we may be fooled by what we see and hear. The people being trained may not really get the message and may go away frustrated. The people doing the training may figure they have done well and go about their business thinking the employees should do their jobs satisfactorily. Later we may hear the trainers say, "Don't you remember, I told you last week how to do that?" The point is that *the employees get the blame for the poor job of training done by the supervisors*. So we must learn how to train; that is, we must learn the skill of training others.

There are some things we can put off learning, but training must be learned very quickly if we are to get the most work out of our people. Not only must we learn how to train others quickly, but we must learn how to do it *well*. Every time we do a poor job of training someone, we waste time that can't be recovered, and we also get ourselves into the dilemma of not knowing whether to train over again or let the employee go on doing the job only half-well. The truth is, we rarely repeat the training, but we do end up spending a lot of time trying to repair damage done by poorly trained employees. The worst thing that can happen, of course, is that we end up blaming the employees for not being able to do their jobs when we've really failed at ours.

But we can learn the basic skill of training others if we recognize it as a skill and work hard at learning it. We cannot assume that just because we know the job we're training the employees to do, we also know how to train someone on that job. Operating a drill press or changing the ribbon on a typewriter is quite different from *training* someone how to operate the press or change the ribbon. There are steps to training that we can identify and measure. We can tell whether or not we have done a good job, and we can improve on the skill once we learn what the skill consists of. Let's take a look at the skill in more detail and see just what it is that makes up this thing that some want to take for granted.

WHY TRAIN?

If we ask whether training is necessary, the obvious answer is, "Of course." But if we ask why we train, we get some strange answers. Some train just because there is money in the budget. Others train because the employees expect it. There are those who train because higher management has decreed that it be done. Still others train only when they have spare time; then they train to fill up the time. None of these are reasons for training. Basically, there are only three good reasons for training:

1. The employees can't do the job.
2. The employees can do the job but not well enough.
3. The employees are doing the job incorrectly.

In the first case—not being able to do the job—it may be that the employees are new and have not done it before. This is an obvious case for training, but there are those who say, "Experience is the best teacher—let them learn the hard way, like I did." This isn't a very practical approach from the standpoint of efficiency. Maybe the employees will be better able to do the job after they have made numerous mistakes, but who pays for all those mistakes? Who helps the employees unlearn all the things they learned to do incorrectly? If the employees are new, then for their benefit and that of the organization, it's our job to see that they have an opportunity to start off learning the right way to do their jobs. Only then can we get an accurate picture of how well they're performing and progressing. But it may be that the job is new and hasn't been done before by anyone in the organization. The job may involve a new procedure or a new piece of equipment. Here, again, we owe it to the employees to get them started on the right foot. Also, for the good of the new policy, let's see that the job is done correctly from the beginning. Anytime we introduce something new, there will be enough problems without our complicating things by doing a poor job of training.

The second case—training because the employees can't do the job well enough—isn't quite as simple as the first case. It may be that the employees haven't been trained and have picked up some of the job on their own. We need to speed up their production and save on wasted time. Now we are faced with the question of whether or not to train, because after all, the employees know something about the job already. We have to weigh the time and expense of training against the advantages of doing the job faster or better. The same is true even if the employees actually had some training at one time but need more in order to meet the standards set for our organization. We have to decide how much it's worth to get the improvement training can produce.

Finally, there are the employees who are actually doing the job incorrectly. This is a valid justification for training. How do we know the employees can't do the job? We may be able to tell just by the number of errors that can be traced directly to them. It may be that a survey of some kind has caused us to look more closely at each employee, and we see that some are failing to do their jobs correctly. It may even be that watching the employees work convinces us quickly that they actually don't know what they're doing. This sounds like reason enough for training, but we need to ask one basic question before we do any training: "If the employees' lives depended on it, could they do the job correctly?" If the answer to this is yes, then training isn't the solution; there is some other problem, and training won't solve it. So when we train, we must be sure to ask ourselves why we are training: to enable the employees to do the job, to enable them to do it better, or to enable them to do it correctly? We need to ask this question for *each* employee we train.

This all sounds simpler than it really is. If we aren't careful, we'll end up training someone who has had the training some time ago. To compound the problem, the employee's performance may improve for a short period right after the training, especially if he or she enjoys getting away from the job for a while. But the chances are good that the employee will just do poorly in the training session and go back to the job wondering what kind of a supervisor we are to provide training he or she has already had. Even worse, we end up giving training a bad name; because the employee can't do the job any better after the training, some will conclude that training is a waste of time.

Another potential source of trouble is training someone who isn't really going to have time to apply what he or she has learned. Maybe the employee is just a few months away from retiring or moving to another job; everyone else in the section has had the training, so we schedule him or her for it also. It's fine to worry about our employees' feelings, but if we are planning to send one person to training because we don't want to hurt his or her feelings, we need to remember that it's also good to worry about the organization's money. How can we justify spending training money when it's obvious we can't get our money back from an employee who just won't be on the job that long?

There is another time when it is a mistake to train: when we want to see an employee promoted; when we aren't training because the employee needs it or will do a better job for us, but because it will look good on the employee's record to have been through this particular training program. Unless this is a part of the employee's regular development program, we've made a mistake in training for this reason. The problem may come back to us in a strange way; it may get around that we have set a precedent that anyone who takes this kind of training expects to be promoted, or several employees may want to be sent to the training program because they think it's the way to move up. In either case, we've put an undue burden on the training program and asked it to do something it wasn't intended to do.

Finally, one other thing that gets us into trouble is to train someone we know hasn't got a chance to learn the job because of his or her background or lack of experience. Some supervisors send certain people to training programs to prove a point—that the employees are incompetent. Again, we've used training in the wrong way and have failed to do our job properly—to train the right people for the right reasons.

PREPARING TO TRAIN

Before we can do any training of our own, we must determine just what it is we want to train our employees to do. This sounds simple enough, but it really isn't. For example, we should be certain we know exactly what standard of performance we are looking for. This means analyzing the job to make sure we can train someone else to perform according to the organization's standard—that is, to do the right thing in the right amount of time with no more than the acceptable number of errors. The standard isn't what someone else has done on that same job that we thought was pretty good. It's not what has come to be accepted as the average for employees doing this particular job. It's what the organization has set as a standard for the *job itself*. We need to learn to set job standards by looking at the work, not at the employees who are or have been doing the job.

Before we train, we'd better get policy questions settled, too. We'd better find out if there are changes in the mill that will make our standards wrong. If there are acceptable deviations from the job standard, we'd better know about them before we start to train. There's no reason to be afraid to ask questions about standards, because we can never be sure that our training has really been done properly if we don't know what the standard actually is. Remember, many so-called standards exist only because everyone has just accepted them without question—maybe even perpetuating error or mediocrity in the process. This is particularly true with things like work flow. Just because filing cabinets got placed in certain spots at one time, work may continue to flow unevenly around them, despite the fact that it might be much more efficient to move them closer to the work operation. As a result of this poor arrangement, the work has suffered, but the standard has been set. If we don't watch out, we'll train to this standard. This is true with such things as forms and sales slips, too. We try to train someone to fill out a complicated form or slip without ever questioning just why the item is so complex. The truth may be that it got that way because every once in a while someone added something to it without trying to cut out anything. Pretty soon it got unwieldy, but we keep on using it as the standard and trying to train people to fill it out. A few well-chosen questions might help uncomplicate the forms. In fact, just listening to our employees might be some help. They probably know that certain things are unnecessary, but no one has ever bothered to ask them. Remember, they are doing the job, so no one else can be more familiar with what is actually being done than they are. If we can't come up with a better reason for doing something or not doing it a certain way, we should take their word for it.

It's highly unlikely that we can ever train on everything that needs attention, so we have to decide early in the game just what it is we are going to include in the training program for each of the employees. For example, for new employees, we should concentrate on those things that will be likely to come up first in their new assignments. They'll have enough to do to learn what they'll be faced with immediately without worrying about what will come up several months from now. If the job is being changed, we should concentrate on the changes, not the entire job. It's wasteful (and boring to the employees) to go through operations that the employees already understand. Even after we have decided what to train on, we should still check and see if there are any existing programs that will do the job for us. Maybe the organization already has some kind of program that will come close enough to doing our job that it wouldn't be worthwhile for us to develop an entire training program to make up the difference. It's always well to check this out before going too far. By the way, we mustn't forget to ask other departments about their training programs. Sometimes we get so out of touch with others in the same organization that we don't even know that they have the same training problems we have and may be conducting programs very similar to the ones we are preparing. We ask ourselves, "Why hasn't someone done this kind of training before?" Then we ask, "Who else has the same kind of training problems I do?" The answers to these questions should help us screen the market well enough to prevent us from reinventing the wheel.

Once we've decided what training needs to be done and why we're doing it, we must set some realistic objectives or goals for the training we are going to do. The simplest way to do this is to ask, "What is it I want the employees to be able to do when the training is over?" Basically, the answer to this question depends on the answers to the following ones:

"What actions do I want from them?"
"What standards do I plan to use to gauge their success?"
"What limitations or tolerances can I live with?"

If we've taken a good look at the job, as we suggested earlier, these things should be clear by now. We should know what a satisfactory job is, and if we don't, it will show up when we attempt to answer these questions. It's not enough to say, "We want them to understand how the framus machine works." We have to specify the action and the degree of tolerance we expect to allow. Requiring that operators produce a hundred items an hour with no more than two errors is much more specific than requiring that they understand how to use the machine. One reason training is so haphazard is that we go about it in a haphazard manner. We just suddenly find ourselves doing some training without much real planning. When we do a sloppy job of planning, we do a sloppy job of training. The planning doesn't have to be elaborate or time-consuming. A plan can be jotted down on the back of an envelope, *but it should be done*. We need to decide where the training is going to take place, who will be trained, and when it will be happen.

DO IT RIGHT

It seems ridiculous to say it, but when we train, we should do a good job of it. As silly as it sounds, though, we find that some training is better than other training; hence, some people are doing a better job than others. The reason is that we don't always know a good training job when we see one. Supervisors can be heard to say, "Don't you remember, I *told* you . . .," which means that they think telling and training are the same thing. In fact, when we watch them train, they end up doing most of the talking and the showing, then leave with a statement like, "Any questions?" The employees think they understand; the operation looked simple enough, but after the supervisor leaves, the employees find that they can't really do the job after all. They feel pretty stupid because they've just seen the supervisor do it and heard an explanation and didn't have any questions—all because *the supervisor did a poor job of training*. Since training is a skill, we can't expect to be good at it right away. We can try to learn the skill, though, and as we practice it more and more, we can evaluate the results and grow with it.

Good training follows specific steps and procedures. When we train people on the job, what *we do* will have a definite bearing on how well they can perform in the future. The most accepted process to use is a simple, three-step one that has worked well for many years. It goes like this:

Step 1
We tell them what to do.
We do it correctly.

Step 2
They tell us what to do.
We do it correctly.

Step 3
They tell us what to do.
They do it correctly.

Note the purpose of each step. In step 1, we tell the employees what is to be done so there will be no doubt about the action and so they will be mentally involved. Then we do it correctly, being sure they see each part of the procedure. Then in step 2, they are still involved mentally as they tell us what to do, and if they tell us correctly, we do it correctly again. In step 3, they tell us what they're going to do but do not do it until we have agreed that they're right. If they are, then we let them do it. Step 3 can be repeated several times for practice, but it's always a good idea to keep the employees involved mentally as much as possible. After all, this is where the memory is established. Even though we want the employees to develop good work habits, we still want them to perform from a good mental attitude. To increase this mental involvement, we can expand the three-step process to include not only *what*, but *why* and *how*. We still go through each step as described, but after going through *what*, we repeat the process by telling *how*. Then we repeat with *why* we perform the operation the way we do. In other words, the first time through we simply worry about the employees' seeing, hearing, and doing the right thing. They see how, but we don't go into it in much detail. Then we repeat the process, this time adding a description of *how* we do it—so that while doing it the employees hear a description of the correct way to perform the operation. Finally, we go over the *what* and *how* but add to it *why* we use a certain movement or tie it a certain way or move the ribbon to the left.

It should be noted that the employees may not understand the necessity of getting involved in the skills-learning process as much as this system entails. More than anything, they want to get their hands on the equipment, the computer, the cash register as quickly as possible. To oversimplify the situation: they want to get it in their hands; we want to get it in their brains! Their recall of the things *they* say is nearly three times as great as the recall of what *we* say to them. Our problem is that we, too, want to see them do it with their hands, so we may take shortcuts in this process. The temptation is always to tell them, show them, then let them do it. If we can just remember that they have no brains in their hands; their hands only do what their brains tell them to do. By having the employees tell us at least twice what they're going to do, how they're going to do it, and why they're doing it that way, we have a chance to better etch it into their brains. Then, when we leave them to it, we feel better because we know what they have in their brains.

Another temptation is, after hearing someone say something that is incorrect, to let them do it incorrectly in order to "learn a lesson from doing it wrong." This may sound logical, but it doesn't always work this way. People who do something incorrectly the first time, without knowing it's incorrect, tend to repeat that mistake in the future. When they reach a decision point and aren't certain what to do, they are most likely to do it the way they did it the first time. For that reason, we always want them only seeing and doing it correctly. At a later time, when they've mastered the skill, we can show them what will happen if they do it incorrectly. This time they'll know it's wrong, so it won't get into their brain and haunt them (and us) someday.

Another advantage of having employees do the telling a couple of times is that we get to hear the *why* part of the operation, for safety reasons. If an action could hurt the employees or the equipment, and we hear the employees twice say not to do it because of the hazard, we can have some degree of comfort when they are left alone. If they know that one key will dump a whole computer program, and they not only hear us say it, but say it themselves two times, the chances are pretty good that their brain has gotten the message about not hitting that key.

It should be obvious that when we are doing this kind of training, we have the employees use the actual equipment or something that looks just like what they will be using. Ideally, they should be trained on the equipment they use every day, right at the spot where they will do the job. If not, then we should try to find idle equipment that is like the equipment they'll be using. As a final alternative, we can use something that closely simulates their regular equipment, but we should remember that the less imagination they have to use, the better they will be trained. If they get dirty on the job, they should get dirty during the training. If they write on blue paper on the job, they should have blue paper during the training. By the way, there's a simple point that we miss a lot of the time: when we train, we never *face* the employees; we always show them from the same position they will take when they do the work. If we face them, they will see everything done backward and may become quite confused when they try doing it themselves.

CLASSROOM TRAINING

Occasionally, we will be asked to conduct some form of classroom training. It may be that we have become expert in certain fields or that we have been selected to study a particular subject and teach in an organizational school of some kind. In certain cases, we may have enough people working under us so that it is easier to do the training all at one time in some kind of classroom setting. For that reason, we will talk a little bit about how to do this type of training most effectively. There is more to teaching a group than just having a knowledge of the subject and more to it than just being able to make a good speech. The idea is to change some people's behavior on the job, which is the same reason for doing on-the-job training. Up to this point, everything we've said about preparing for on-the-job training pretty well holds true for classroom training. We have to know what it is we want the people to be able to do; there needs to be a standard; and it helps if we know the deficiencies of the people in the classroom. Once we've found out what we need to know about the goals, standards, and the performance deficiencies of the employees, we're ready to go into the classroom. Let's see what we need to know to make this a top-notch effort.

Some basic rules for classroom training will help us understand our job better. First, people learn more by participating in the learning activity than they do by being told what they need to know. We can tell them much faster if they aren't involved in saying or doing things, but they can forget just as fast! Next, we should realize that the students are more likely to remember what they figure out for themselves than what we figure out for them. This means that we need to let them "discover" some of the information for themselves, especially the conclusions. In some circles this technique is called *discovery learning*. That's a good name for it, because that's exactly what happens: we give the class members enough information to enable them to figure out the rest on their own. We lead them along with new information, building on what they already know, then stop with a question aimed at making them think about where all this is leading. At this point, if we've done the job right, the students will get a big "Aha!" reaction, and we'll have caused them to discover what it was we wanted them to learn. As a result, they'll remember it longer.

The next thing to keep in mind is that students will be more likely to remember and learn those things most closely related to their jobs. If they are given some information or shown some kind of new operation with the knowledge that they will be expected to use it when they get back on the job, they'll be much more likely to work at learning it than if they hear, "Someday you may need this, so you'd better pay attention." If we are doing a good job instructing, we will build in examples of how these things are applied and have a good storehouse of incidents in which the new material is used back on the job.

Obviously, not all students have the same background, not all have the same interest in learning, and not all have the same ability to grasp every subject. This brings up another point: if students aren't all learning the same way, *we may have to teach in different ways to reach different people.* For some, a lecture may be fine, because they've always been able to grasp concepts quickly from a lecture. For others, repetition may be important, because it takes a while for the material to soak in. Still others may require some discussion or different examples or different approaches. All these methods have to be mixed into each teaching session because we can't always tell which students are learning best in which way.

This leads us to the next point to remember in making ourselves good instructors. We'll know what's being learned by whom only when *we hear them tell us or see them show us.* In teaching jargon, this is called getting feedback. Just as we talked about the importance of feedback in Chapter 6 on communications, and for the same reasons, it's extremely important here in our teaching efforts. If we pay attention only to what *we're saying*, we won't know what the students are learning. If we get feedback from only one or two, we'll have a general idea of how well we're doing, but we won't know for sure how the class is doing until we hear all of them saying things and reacting to what we've been teaching. When we mention feedback, the idea of testing comes to mind. This isn't what we're talking about here. For example, simply having the class break into small groups and come up with an agreement on a certain question will, in a matter of a few minutes, reveal how well we've gotten our point across. If there is much discussion and little agreement, we'd better start over or review. If groups quickly come up with a common answer, we can reinforce this and go on.

While we're talking about differences among students in the classroom, we should point out that one very good way of converting differences from a problem to an asset is to have the less experienced students work with the more experienced ones, or the less interested or slower learners work with those who are more interested or quicker. This puts some of the responsibility on the better students, and they will actually learn more as they try to help one another along. Most of the time, students learn from one of their classmates as well as or better than they do from one of the instructors.

We said that good teaching is more than good public speaking. Let's make sure we understand that *bad* public speaking—mumbling, distracting mannerisms, poor use of the visual-aids equipment, etc.—has to be overcome by even better teaching techniques. We can ruin some very good instructional efforts by poor speaking efforts. Not that our students will necessarily get much more from the speaking itself if it's polished and stage worthy, but at least we won't detract from the learning effort if we make a good try at speaking well!

FOLLOW UP ON TRAINING

One final word about training: we shouldn't just train and then go off and leave it. We should follow up on what we have done and see how well the training "took." Training is more than doing it, marking the training record, then forgetting about it and the employees, and saying, "Well, that job is complete." We should go back to the employees and see how they're doing. Check their performance against the standard we set. Check error rates, look at outputs, see if the secretary's letters are better—whatever the training involved. If the employees are performing well, we can take credit for a job well done. If not, then we need to take a look at our procedures to see whether we failed to do the job properly. The rule in this case is simple: if the employees are doing something we trained them on, *we are responsible for their performance until we find out that something other than their training is keeping them from doing the job.* Of course, we are always responsible for their performance in a way, but now we look for some other cause because we are satisfied that the training has been done correctly. If we follow the proper procedures, we can be sure that the training *has* been done correctly.

DEVELOPING FUTURE SUPERVISORS

Even though we may be new on the job ourselves, we have to immediately begin thinking ahead to the time when we will be replaced because we're moving up in the organization. We don't necessarily train our own successor—those are management decisions—but we do need to think of our people as being able to fill our job or other supervisory jobs as soon as possible. We've seen that we have a responsibility both to the organization and to the employees working for us to develop whatever skills they have as best we can. This means dealing with their people and management skills as well as their job skills.

There's a basic rule about people that is remarkable: *people are the only resource that should get better with use!* Other resources wear out with use. Money, once spent, is no longer available. Raw material, once put through a manufacturing process, is committed and not useful to us anymore. Time and energy are used up. People should get better. They know more; they have more experience; and they've solved problems, which makes them more valuable when those same problems arise again. However, people don't get better just by existing. To get better, they need to be trained, developed, used, and directed. The same things—time and experience—that make them more useful can also make them less valuable. If the work time has taught them error or poor habits, then they won't be more valuable. If their experience has been unsatisfactory, either in terms of doing wrong things or in terms of developing poor attitudes, then we will find them *less* satisfactory than they were a year ago or ten years ago. If this is the case, then it's a supervisory error most likely.

As a new supervisor, we inherit employees with varying degrees and stages of development. We can thank someone for helping us become what we are, for giving us opportunities to learn supervisory skills. We now owe it to those under us to do the same for them. Not that everybody has the aptitude for being a supervisor, nor the interest in becoming one. Whatever our employees' skills and aptitudes, it is our job (our obligation) to bring them out and find ways of using them. That's why delegation is so important. This gives us the best chance to develop our people, in a "safe" environment. We give them small challenges, then larger ones, as they develop their skills. We put different people in charge of different tasks, and we have them fill in when we are away. We tell them what we expect, then see not only how well they did, but what we can do to improve on that. There's more to it than just giving them some work to do and turning them loose, then criticizing them afterward if they mess up. We let them know it is a training assignment, and we tell them what is expected. We train them or coach them so they'll know what to do and how to do it. When the task is over, we review the finished product with the employees. We go over their performance, looking for what is right as well as what is wrong. We give recognition for their good performance and constructive criticism regarding areas where they have failed to meet standards. The criticism or feedback ends with a positive note, meaning we let them know that we feel they will do it correctly next time and that we expect to give them a similar job again. Very early in our supervision we have to establish that people under us will not be known for the mistakes they make! They'll be known instead for the good they do and the potential they have for doing more. This encouragement will motivate them to want to develop rather than just keep on doing the same job they are doing, neither better nor worse.

CONCLUSION

Training is the supervisor's responsibility. That's the title of this chapter. It's the message within it. It's the conclusion we need to reach when we study training. Training subordinates to reach their potential is a serious business and one that can have serious consequences if not done correctly. The dangerous thing about poor training is that often it isn't the supervisor but the poorly trained employees themselves who get the blame. Although their records show that they were trained, their performance is suffering, and they will be rated as below-standard performers on those records. To make it worse, the employees may think they've been trained and give themselves a bad rating in their own minds, perhaps believing they just aren't capable of learning.

To try to emphasize this need to do a good job of training, let's think of it this way: it's now appraisal time. Our employees are going to be evaluated on how well they've done in their jobs over a certain period of time. There is a standard that is understood by both them and us as to how well they should be doing those jobs. We have no right to appraise them, however, if we've failed to properly train them up to that standard. Suppose we haven't trained them as well as we should have. We've put in some training time but not very skillfully, though the training time is entered on their records. Because the employees have not had the right training, they aren't doing their jobs up to standard. In the appraisal, we make an entry to the effect that their performance is below standard. How honest and fair is that? Shouldn't we instead make an entry that says, "Due to poor training, this employee has not yet been able to perform up to standard"? Of course, we aren't likely to make such an entry, but the employee will suffer from the poor appraisal for a long time to come. It may even be a permanent part of his or her record, and all because we didn't do our job well.

On the other hand, think about it from the standpoint of having done a good job. It's now appraisal time, and our employees are doing their jobs up to standard. Even though we aren't likely to say that they are doing well because we did such a good job of training, we can take satisfaction from knowing that when we did our job properly, our employees responded with good performance, and that, too, will be on their records for a long time. We can be pleased with this kind of result, especially if we get it often. And we will if we learn our training skills well!

EXERCISES

1. Half-group exercise: Divide the group into two sections. Have one section take the position that training is a skill that has to be learned; can be measured; and can be done poorly, well, or in between. Let them develop their arguments in favor of this in small subgroups within their section. One person should serve as their spokesperson. The other half of the group should operate the same way, in small subgroups and with a spokesperson for the entire section. Their position is that good training is an art that comes from being gifted as an instructor. Some few things can be learned, but for the most part a person either is a good instructor or is not, and trying to develop the skill won't help appreciably. When the subgroups have finished their activity and combined their findings within their own sections, each section's spokesperson should be briefed for a discussion as outlined in exercise 2.

2. Group exercise: The two sections should debate each other now, and a list of their points should be recorded on the board. All group members should be urged to take notes from each section's discussion and defend their own position. When the two sections have exhausted their discussion, the group as a whole should take a look at the points made and determine how valid they are. Sides should no longer be considered at this point; rather, everyone should begin to look at the points made with an eye to seeing how best to learn the *skill of teaching*.

3. Small-group activity: Divide the whole group into several small subgroups, each of which should pick a job that is common to all its members or at least familiar enough so that each member can contribute something to the discussion and exercise. The job should be a simple one, even a part of a job. Each subgroup should analyze the job it has selected a piece at a time until the job has been broken down into individual

operations. When the job is thus broken down, group members should set a standard for each of the operations. The standard should tell not only *how* the job is to be done, but *how well* or *how often in a period of time,* etc. In other words, the standard should be *measurable* and *observable*. When the subgroups have gotten this information, they should be ready to present it to the entire group, having picked a spokesperson to represent them.

4. Group activity: Using the information on standards from exercise 3, let each spokesperson present the group's findings, with the rest of the subgroup doing the defending. The idea is for the whole group to see that supervisors often try to train on things for which they haven't set a standard; hence, they shouldn't expect to do a very good job of training. (If they don't know how well they want the employee to perform, how can they know how well they've trained him or her?)

Chapter 13

HOW TO RUN A GOOD MEETING (CONFERENCE LEADERSHIP)

Much has been said—very little of it complimentary—about all of the meetings that are usually held in an organization. Committees meet, groups meet, managers meet, supervisors meet—and meet some more. There isn't much chance that we will change this, nor do we really want to. Meetings are a way of life and, to a large extent, the thread of life in most organizations. The reason we make fun of them or complain about them is that they take up a lot of our time—often seeming to waste it—and usually come at a point when we simply don't have a moment to spare. It may just be, however, that one of the main reasons we feel as we do about meetings is that we've never experienced the satisfaction of attending and being part of a well-run meeting, one that accomplished specific goals, did it quickly and efficiently, and terminated when the purpose had been achieved. It's to that end that this chapter is dedicated. We are going to try to establish the basis for conducting meetings that do precisely these things.

PREPARING FOR THE CONFERENCE

As we have said, conferences (meetings) are a way of life in the organization. Without proper control, they can run poorly and accomplish very little. Run properly, they can accomplish things that cannot be done in any other way. The first thing we must accept is that meetings have a precise purpose. They are necessary; hence, we should approach them with a positive attitude. We should also approach them with the idea of knowing what the particular purpose of any specific meeting is. Is it a *problem-solving* session? Have problems arisen that we need to attack in a group? If so, then we must approach the meeting with the information required for problem solving. We have to set it up so we can go through the steps in problem solving. Is the purpose of the meeting *decision making?* If so, we will need to remember that no one should leave the meeting without knowing exactly what final decision was reached. We will need to remember that someone has to be responsible for carrying out that decision. In other words, we must aim everything about the conference at decision making. We will have to use good decision-making techniques in the meeting. Since we are leading the meeting, we are responsible for seeing that these techniques are followed.

Is the purpose of the meeting *brainstorming?* Has someone decided that the best way to reach a solution or develop an idea or attack a problem is to have a group of people get together and do some brainstorming? If so, then we must be sure that all the conditions for brainstorming are met and that we understand the process. Will we have the necessary supplies for recording the ideas? Are we conditioned to avoid letting any negative thinking get into the session? Again, since we are conducting the meeting, it is our responsibility to see that everything goes well. But we need to establish the purpose in our mind so we can make the necessary arrangements.

Perhaps the purpose is *attitude development.* It's possible that the meeting is to be no more than a pep rally aimed at increasing loyalty or improving sales. Maybe there is a quality-control problem and this meeting is for the purpose of changing attitudes toward this matter. If so, we need to know it and to aim in that direction. Even if the meeting is just for the purpose of educating our group on a new policy or product or service, or about a new benefit plan, we should settle this in our mind and build our planning around it.

The point is that if we are going to run the meeting, we need to know its specific purpose. After all, we're asking a number of people to give up work time and come to the meeting. They have a right to expect that we are going to know what the real objective of the conference is and what they are trying to accomplish. As conference leaders, then, we ask ourselves, "What *specific activities* will take place?" This is important in arranging furniture, getting equipment, selecting rooms, etc. The activities will determine whether we will need to seat everyone in a circle, provide tables, or maybe just set up chairs facing the front. Thinking of these things ahead of time will make us look good and certainly help make the meeting a success.

But we need to know more. We should decide on the *specific timing* for the meeting—not just how long it will run but when we will have it. What day? What time of day? If it's to be a one-hour meeting, why run it at a time that would conflict with an already-established coffee break? On the other hand, if the meeting is to be a lengthy one, providing for a break in the middle might be a good way to inject some relief. Scheduling meetings at the end of the day (or week), when everyone is tired and thinking about going home, might not be the best approach if we plan to get into a brainstorming session. If we aren't sure how long the meeting will take, running it too close to lunch or quitting time may get us into trouble. Suppose it turns out we need more time! What often happens here is that when time starts to run out, and we don't want to have to call another meeting, we begin to make hurried decisions or leave some loose ends. When the meeting is over and we review our accomplishments, we discover that some important issues were overlooked or some of the decisions we made aren't really very practical after all.

Finally, on specifics, the conference leader needs to know the *specific attendance*. Not just how many are going to attend but *who*. There is always the consideration of seating, both who sits where and how many seats will be required. If we have any control over the selection of those who attend, we need to look at the meeting's specific objective. If this is to be an educational meeting, then maybe the more people in attendance the better. On the other hand, if there is to be problem solving or decision making, the number needs to be held to a minimum. The basic requirement for the latter kind of meeting is to have enough people there to represent everybody concerned, but not to weigh the discussion down with too many people from one side of the argument or from one department. Conferees don't like to be put in the position of having the meeting stacked against them in terms of numbers. They have just as much right to their opinion as others, but if the "other side" brought along more than its share of representatives, then the opposing factions are unequal. The conferees will know this in a hurry, too. The way to avoid this is to look at the list of suggested attendees and decide whether there is fair representation from all departments, groups, factions, etc. If not, a telephone call or private suggestion may be the best way to solve the problem. As we have said, these things make a lot of difference in the outcome of conferences, and if it is our conference, we should do whatever we can to control both the level of attendance and the particular people attending.

Physical Facilities

Of all the factors that can make or break a meeting, perhaps nothing has more influence than the place where the meeting is held and the equipment used in the meeting. No matter how well the leader coordinates the timing and the speaking and the interchange of ideas and the movement of information, if the room is poorly ventilated, or too hot or too cold, all this effort will accomplish very little. Actually, setting up the facilities isn't difficult when we consider some basic elements. We can divide the problem areas as follows:

- Creature comforts
- Acoustics
- Visibility
- Interference

Let's look at them individually. First, the creature comforts— those things that affect our senses, starting with the ventilation. Is the air being changed frequently enough by the ventilating system? Is there a means of regulating the temperature *in a hurry* if the room gets too hot or too cold? We want to be sure to have control of the facility, by the way, as far as the temperature is concerned. If someone in another room can regulate the temperature in our room, we've obviously got a problem. The same is true if the system is centrally controlled. If the only control we have is to open and close doors and windows, we might want to consider whatever alternative facilities are available. Many other things affect our comfort, some of which are subtle. For example, when we first sit in a molded plastic chair, it will feel very comfortable. But after a short time it becomes very uncomfortable, because it was molded for one position—and the trouble with that is we don't sit in one position very long. As soon as we change from the position the chair was molded for, we're in a chair that won't fit us. Many people find it difficult to remain comfortable very long in chairs that don't have arms. As long as there is a table to lean on it's not too bad, but when they try to lean back or relax, their arms drop to their sides in a strained way. Which brings up another problem that's easy to overlook: the height of the table relative to the chairs. If the table is too high or too low, again, the conferees will strain to get comfortable. We need to remember that these aren't problems that we can spot just by sitting down for a few moments. If we want to try out the furniture, we must try several positions—sitting with our arms on the table, then at our sides, leaning back in the chair, sitting in one position for a few minutes. How does all this feel? Remember, too, that there is such a thing as being *overcomfortable*. If the meeting is likely to produce a few periods of boredom, soft, relaxing chairs won't add to the alertness of the group.

The matter of acoustics is obviously of importance, but there are some problems that may not be apparent just from looking at a facility. For example, sound carries better in an empty room than in a full one. Even if our voice appears to carry very well in the room, we still need to know whether it will be all right when several people are present. One way to check this is to have someone stand at one end of the room with us at the other end and have the other person speak in a low voice. Not in a whisper but in a conversational tone, as if talking to someone next to him or her, because that's what people do in meetings many times—

they speak as though they were talking to someone next to them. If we can hear without any trouble, we can be a little more assured that it will be possible to hear things when the room is full. People's talking as if they were addressing someone next to them is another of our problems. Even if the room is acoustically satisfactory for someone who speaks in a normal voice, we can't regulate how loudly participants will talk. If someone talks very softly, and we know he or she will be in the meeting, we'd better make whatever plans we can to take care of the situation. *The rule is to prepare for the minimal conditions, not the normal or average conditions.*

Visibility is always a concern and one that can cause a good meeting to go sour. If the meeting is to be built around charts or movies or other visuals, and some of the people will not be able to see, then obviously they won't get much out of the meeting. But that's not the only problem. Even if the people are to be seated at a table and no visuals are to be used, they still like to see the speaker. This should be considered when the chairs are arranged or the tables set out. Many meetings are ruined because all the people are aligned along two sides of a table. Every time someone says something, everybody leans way over to try to see what is happening. Each has to lean out farther than the person in front of him or her, and pretty soon some are saying to themselves, "What's the use?"

Interference at a key point in the meeting can cause a near disaster, especially if we have spent valuable time building up our case. Just about the time we are making our final point, hoping now for concurrence from the group, the painter comes wandering through with a ladder swinging over the heads of all the people in the meeting. "Sorry, folks, but this is the only way to get to the next room to finish up the paint job there!" While we weep, the others try to remember where they were a few minutes ago. As with acoustics, we can't check for interference just by standing in the middle of the room and listening once. We have to know whether the room next door is being painted. We have to know what the hall sounds like when everyone on that floor takes a break and heads for the cafeteria at the same time. Is there a kitchen next door where dishes will be rattling at lunch period? Do they use a high-powered vacuum cleaner on the rugs every

Friday morning? These types of interference are obvious, and the person conducting the session can avoid them with a little planning and checking. But there is another kind of interference that is much more subtle. There is the secretary who brings the boss a message, or calls the boss to the telephone, or tells the boss his or her plane tickets are ready. What's important is not *why* the secretary is there but just the *fact* that he or she is. While only trying to be efficient, the secretary may be interrupting a number of work hours and hurting the meeting's chances of success. A "Do Not Disturb" note on the door can help a lot, but arrangements for someone to take messages and deliver them at break periods are a much better guarantee. An extra sentence in the meeting announcement, "If you're expecting any messages during the meeting, have them left with my secretary at ext. 7953," could solve the problem.

CONDUCTING THE CONFERENCE

Interestingly enough, our role as leader may vary from meeting to meeting and even during any particular meeting. This is why it is so important to know just exactly what the purpose of the meeting is. If we know this, then we can more easily tell what our role is. Primarily, our function is to see that somebody fills all the roles required to run a good meeting, which may mean that we will have to assume those not taken by others. If we are in charge of the meeting, the best thing we can do is assign roles effectively to others. Put someone in the initiating role, someone else in the timekeeping role; try to get others to perform the support role, etc. This way we can keep up with what is going on and know when to step in and take over a role not being handled by someone else, or we can reassign roles that are not being handled very well by others. The thing to remember is that good leaders aren't necessarily seen and heard all the time. Effective leaders simply make sure everything runs smoothly, regardless of who is seen and heard the most. So often we take the word *leader* to mean the person who stands on his or her feet or gives the direction or moves the meeting on to the next point. We may fill this role, or we may assign it to someone who we know performs that particular function especially well.

Hidden Agendas

One interesting and frustrating thing about many meetings is that there often exist undercurrents of thoughts and needs and ideas and objectives that never quite get out into the open. These have been called *hidden agendas*. Hidden agendas are simply those objectives that people bring to a meeting that may differ from the meeting's real purpose. Even though the stated purpose of the meeting may be to discuss overtime, we may really want to say a few things about work standards and may even want to get some answers on the subject. As decisions are being made, we may appear to be basing our suggestions on just plain common sense or the needs of the group, but we may have a hidden agenda that tells us that certain remarks would be more popular with the boss or make our department look better.

It is difficult to pinpoint every agenda that is brought to the meeting by each member of the group, but at least we should be aware that they are bound to be there. We should also be aware that they will affect the meeting because they tend to produce biased answers. The first time we get an answer that surprises us because it doesn't sound reasonable in terms of the discussion so far, we might want to see if a hidden agenda is at work. We should ask ourselves, "What else could make Bob say that? Has he said something else before that indicates there are forces working on him from back on the job? Is he trying to protect his job or his boss or his people?" The interesting thing is that we won't necessarily take any action to try to change the agenda Bob is working with; we'll just be sure to consider what he says in terms of what we think his needs are.

What's important is not to try to become a mind reader. We may never know exactly why people react the way they do—in fact, *they* may not even know—but if we see them beginning to fit a pattern, we should be alert enough to understand what they're doing and why. If we feel pretty sure that we know what's causing them to react the way they are, we may even make this work for us. If we have good reason to suspect that someone has a hidden agenda that will cause him or her to be very budget-conscious, we direct toward that person ideas about saving money and even draw him or her out on these points. On the other hand, we try to avoid getting such a person involved in matters that deal with cost increases. (We don't hide these matters, but we don't make great issues out of them, either.)

Feedback

One of the things that tells us that hidden agendas exist in our group is the kind of *feedback* we get from the participants. Without the proper amount of feedback, we can't tell how the group feels, what individuals are thinking, what direction we should take, or how well we are doing at directing the conference toward its goal. But while it's pretty obvious *why* we need feedback, it isn't always obvious *how we get it.* Let's look at some ways of getting feedback, remembering that the purpose is to use the information to control the meeting and reach the objectives we have set.

If the group is small, it isn't too difficult to get feedback. Usually a small group means less formality; hence, everyone is saying what he or she thinks. At least it isn't hard to get the participants to answer a question directed to them, and they may even volunteer to give their opinions. As the size of the group increases, the problems of getting feedback also increase. Now we have to use some techniques that will more or less force the participants to give us the feedback we need. This isn't so difficult, either, but it takes a little more effort. For example, we can simply go around the room and ask for comments on specific subjects. We can ask for a show of hands for both agreement *and* disagreement. (Be careful on this one. Even if no one raises a hand to show disagreement, it does *not* necessarily mean that everyone agrees. There are always those who won't hold up their hands but who still disagree. In this case we watch for those who don't hold up a hand for either yea or nay, then ask them how they feel. If nothing else, it will get them in the habit of responding one way or the other.) Since people coming to the meeting are supposed to be representing certain viewpoints, they aren't doing their job properly if they don't express themselves. We may have to help them along by asking direct questions, which we shouldn't hesitate to do. Remember, they are supposed to be there to help out, and embarrassing them isn't a problem. This doesn't mean that we *try* to embarrass them, but it does mean that we can ask them questions like, "We haven't heard from you, Jean. What do you think about this matter?" Another technique we can use is to have the participants talk in small groups and report to the whole group. This way they iron out their differences in the small sessions and not before the entire group. Often they just want to be sure they have had a chance to be heard and are just as satisfied to do it before a small group as before the whole meeting. The leader can see that good ideas get brought to the attention of the entire group by listening to the small subgroups and then, when the larger group re-forms, giving one member or another a cue such as, "Didn't I hear you saying that this wasn't really a problem in your office any more?" Do this only when they fail to raise the points you want brought out, of course. We don't ever want to suggest that we already know what we want them to say and that if they don't say it, we'll do it for them. Nothing will kill their incentive quicker.

What do we do with this feedback once we have it? We use it to control and direct the meeting. We see where the participants are and how far along they are. If they aren't doing as well as we think they should be doing, we take steps to move along faster. If they are on schedule, we make a note of it and keep on the same track. If they seem to be ahead of where we had thought they would be, we may even consider concluding the meeting early or plan additional matters to undertake in the meeting. But that isn't the only function of feedback. Here is a great way to get commitment. If we hear participants say something that we want them to stand up for when they leave, we can have them emphasize it right in the meeting. "How about going over that again, Jim. I think that's the best way I've heard that put so far." Another use for feedback is to give us a means of moving on to the next subject. When we have exhausted a subject and find it's time to proceed, the ideal way to do it is by using some of the feedback: "Okay, Mona, that really takes us to the next subject, doesn't it? The way you have expressed it is . . ." The transition is smooth, and we don't appear to be completely dominating the session. Mona gets credit for initiating something new, the group gets an introduction to what is going to be discussed, and we know things are running smoothly.

Conflict

It would be unrealistic not to mention the fact that we can occasionally expect to run into some conflict in meetings. Our first inclination when we encounter conflict is to become a little frightened. We think conflict is bad and may ruin our fine meeting. Of course, too much conflict *can* ruin a meeting, but a certain amount should be expected and planned for. We've already seen that people have hidden agendas, so we shouldn't think that the meeting alone has caused the conflict. Also, when people feel strongly enough about something to argue over it, it means they are involved and have some commitment on the subject being discussed. We should be glad this is the case and try our best to use it to our advantage.

First, we need to be sure to recognize conflict when it comes up in the meeting. Snide remarks, digs at other conferees, and other obvious signs of conflict aren't hard to recognize. More subtle signs are withdrawal, overpoliteness, too-quick commitment, and frequent efforts to go back and discuss topics that have obviously been closed. There is no reason ever to let conflict break out into open hostility such as name calling or shouting. We keep this from happening by stepping in before it gets this far. But what do we do when we step in? Do we just say, "Now let's not have any conflict"? Hardly. The best thing to do is to use the situation to our advantage by formalizing the debate, thus relieving some of the pressure, or by trying to summarize the positions of each side, thus directing the attention away from the disagreeing participants and back to us. By restating the positions, and even by throwing in more facts, we can often resolve the conflict.

But we may not want to resolve it too quickly. With it we have involvement, interest, and participation. Without it we may not have any of these things. When there is conflict, at least we know people are giving us their opinions. We also see others taking sides, thus committing themselves. We are, in a way, getting some of the best feedback we could hope for. As long as it is productive, let's keep it going. When we feel it has done all the good it can do, and may be starting to do some harm, we can step in and put a stop to it. We do this in a number of ways, either by taking a stand ourselves and asking for commitment from all concerned or by gradually working our way into the conversation and turning it around to more productive areas. Another way, which is not the best but may be necessary, is to simply point out that while the discussion is interesting, it probably isn't getting us very far. If conflict persists, we may have to postpone a portion of the meeting to a later date until the conflict subsides, or we may have to give in some, so that postponement won't be necessary. Most often, the group as a whole will put enough pressure on the individuals who are at odds so that the situation will work itself out and there needn't be another meeting.

USING THE CONFEREES

Most people who are good at conducting meetings or conferences have learned a simple skill: they use the other conferees to help make the meeting a success. *They share the leadership roles.* They recognize that it takes more than one person in a meeting to get the job done, so they don't just *allow* group members to assume various roles; they plan—and even manipulate—to get them into those roles. They've learned, for instance, that if somebody else does a good job of summarizing, they let that person do it. If somebody is conscious of the time and reminds the group about deadlines, the leader thanks the person for reminding them of the time factor and doesn't resent it at all. If somebody plays the devil's advocate, asking questions and taking the opposite side to test the ideas being discussed, they let that person do so because they need that role played and it's best played by one of the group members. Good leaders know that when people participate in a meeting and think of it as their own, they'll be much more likely to support the results that come out of it.

To best understand this, we have only to remember the last meeting we went to where the leader played all the roles. The *leader* kept us on track; the *leader* reminded us of the time; the *leader* interrupted the long-winded participant; the *leader* praised good ideas and questioned bad ones. The *leader* asked, "Will people really support that idea?" The *leader* negotiated compromise among varying positions and thoughts; the *leader* introduced new ideas when things began to wind down too soon; the *leader* brought out those who weren't talking or contributing. When we watch such a person, we might even think that he or she is doing a wonderful job. We might even consider patterning ourselves after this leader, remembering how nice it was to have everything under control. So what is wrong with this approach to conference leading? The problem is simple: it was never anybody's meeting but the leader's. The others let the leader take the initiative, sat back, and said, in essence, "What do you want me to do now?" They contributed only when they were told to and stopped when told to. They were supporting the *leader*, not the reason for the meeting. It never was *their* meeting. The end product isn't theirs, either. They won't be excited about how things go, and if things go wrong, they'll feel sorry for the leader, not for themselves and their effort.

Successful conferences, then, are the result of smart leaders' sharing the meeting *and the purpose* with the conferees. We begin the planning with this in mind and never let up. It's always "*our* meeting." It's always "*we* need to solve this problem." When we invite people, we tell them what they can contribute that others can't and urge them to do so. When they arrive, we greet each as a special person bringing ideas and solutions and an ability to tackle the problem at hand. If certain attendees have something worthwhile to report, their names are on the agenda, and we mention it at the start to give them proper recognition. We may even assign roles—such as someone to take notes and someone to serve as timekeeper—to people who are willing to play those roles. Good leaders will observe people falling into certain roles and let them do so. If someone seems talented at sensing the need for a compromise and starts working toward that end, we allow that person to go ahead without interruption. We make a mental note of this and call on this person later if it seems a compromise needs to be worked out.

The next time we attend a meeting, let's see if the roles are being shared. It's entirely possible that an effective meeting can run for its duration with the leader (the person *assigned* to the job) sitting back and doing very little. The best thing for us to do is try it ourselves. If we've been designated as the leader, we take the assignment gladly, but during the meeting see whether we can get others to play the roles we've talked about and whether this doesn't get more commitment from the people there.

Let's see how a meeting might go. The leader is Doug. The

conferees include Debbi, Phil, and Blanche. Others are there, but we won't go into their roles. The meeting has been going on for a while when we pick it up:

DEBBI: *I don't think that's going to work at all. That idea has been tried before.*

PHIL: *Well, maybe not quite like I suggested. Besides, that was some time ago, and things have changed a lot since then. I think it'll work.*

DEBBI: *I can't see how. If we go out and make a proposal like that, they'll laugh us out of the place.*

BLANCHE: *Is there some way we can wrap it in a different wrapper?*

PHIL: *What do you mean, "a different wrapper"?*

BLANCHE: *If it's a good idea but people remember the old way we did it, call it by a different name, use a different approach, give it our endorsement, let people know we've put some thought into it.*

PHIL: *Well, that seems a little sneaky . . .*

DEBBI: *Hmmm. I see what you're saying, though, Blanche. It isn't the idea that's bad, just the reputation.*

BLANCHE: *That's right. As I hear you two talking about it, I think it's something that's pretty timely. It would be a shame if we lost the value of the idea just because at another time under different circumstances a similar idea didn't get the job done.*

PHIL: *I can't argue with that. And there are some changes that need to be made. I guess I agree with Debbi that a few of the things I've proposed could be improved on. Why don't we give it a try this way?*

DEBBI: *If we make the right changes, I think I'd be willing to give my support all the way.*

So what did we learn? Where was the leader? We never did hear from Doug. Why not? Simple. He wasn't needed. Things were going too smoothly for him to mess it up by barging in and doing what the others were doing very well themselves. Note that there was some giving in, some compromising, some delving into history, some negotiating going on. There was a plan of action being developed. And more than anything else, there was some commitment going into the final product of the meeting. This isn't to say that the leader couldn't and shouldn't have stepped in if things had gotten out of control or if there didn't seem to be any direction. But when we have somebody like Blanche doing such a masterful job—perhaps without ever thinking about it—we should stay out!

LEADERSHIP ROLES

We've talked a lot about the leadership roles people play. Here's a brief summary of these roles and the function each performs. Think about them the next time a meeting comes along and see whether anybody but the leader is playing them. In fact, let's see if we can play some of them when we're not the nominal leader—not to take the role away from the leader but to give all the help we can.

- *Harmonizer.* Keeps the atmosphere friction-free; looks for points of agreement rather than stirring disagreement. Will recognize supporting statements from different participants and bring them out.

- *Compromiser.* Will work for agreement by using trade-offs. Recognizes when people are willing to give in on certain points and which things they feel strongly about. Serves as a moderator in negotiation.

- *Conscience.* Reminds the group of the goal and makes an effort to keep the discussion moving. May use chastisement to move toward the goal. Expresses discomfort when the group is needlessly hung up on an unimportant point.

- *Gatekeeper.* Understands the process of moving a group off dead center. Will use techniques of questioning or repetition or reflection to get things going. Knows when the group is ready to move to another point.

- *Catalyst.* Asks creative and even uncomfortable questions to get the group thinking. Will be able to bring in reticent participants by arousing emotions or getting them involved in one of the issues.

- *Summarizer.* Keeps group members aware of where they are. Marks their progress with a summary or feedback on decisions. Recognizes when there is repetition or discussion of topics already settled and moves the group on with a good transition statement. May take notes for the group or even work at the easel to summarize.

ENDING THE CONFERENCE

Just as it is important to know how to plan, start, and conduct a meeting, it is important to know how and when to end one. Why should this be a problem? Isn't everyone anxious to get out of the meeting and back on the job? Yes, probably so, but that's the trouble; we let them go before we have taken care of some important matters. For example, when it appears we have covered all necessary points and reached the proper solutions, we're ready to adjourn, aren't we? *No*, not yet! Does the group *know* what the conclusions are? Do the people know what we have agreed to do and say? Do they know who's supposed to do what? These things have to be taken care of or all our efforts may go for naught. Maybe just a summary statement is all we need. "So this is what we've agreed to do: First, we will tell . . ." By stating these things clearly and concisely, we are asking for commitment and consent. If we have watched the meeting closely, there shouldn't be any misunderstanding. But we state the agreements anyway, so there will be no doubts. We also state the action we have planned and who has the responsibility for taking the action. We make sure all participants understand their roles and are committed to carrying them out. If another meeting is required or some reporting period is necessary, this should be definitively settled. If certain people are to finish certain actions before the next meeting, a schedule should be worked out and the timetable agreed upon. If we suspect that one or more of the people don't really know what they're supposed to do or aren't committed, this is the time to get it straight. Once the meeting is over, it's going to be difficult to take care of these things.

FOLLOWING UP ON THE MEETING

It would seem that after all that has been done so far to make this a successful meeting, surely there is nothing left to do. Maybe not, but don't be too sure. There are at least three things that need to be done before we can call it a completely successful session. First, we need to check on the actions of all those who had things to do and deadlines to meet. Are they staying on schedule? Are they doing what the group at the meeting really decided on? Have they run into problems that were not anticipated? Just natural common sense tells us that we will need to do these things and get answers to these questions. Second, we should report the action of the conference to those who must be advised. The report need not necessarily be a long set of notes or minutes but should contain enough information so that those who could not attend or who will be affected by the results will know what was done and what was planned. Finally, we have to take a look at the meeting from the standpoint of improving our own ability to conduct meetings. How did we do? Were there things that should have been handled differently? Will we make the same mistakes again, or do we see how we went wrong? Did we handle the conflict well? Did we recognize the support we were getting from some of the conferees? (And did we make use of it?) As a new supervisor, we may make some mistakes in conducting our first meetings; this is expected and acceptable. However, if we don't look at our actions and our mistakes with a view toward doing better the next time, our next mistakes are inexcusable!

CONCLUSION

Someone has described a conference as a "meeting with a purpose." That's as good a definition as we can think of to describe the attitude we should have toward a conference. Some dread going to conferences; some dread conducting them. We should understand that the conference isn't just another meeting with no purpose, but, rather, a gathering together of specific people for a specific purpose at a specific time. If we can't identify the purpose of the conference, then by the definition we've just given, it isn't a real conference. It's a purposeless collection of people who will waste the organization's time and may even make insignificant decisions about unimportant things. When we put a stated purpose on the gathering, it becomes a full-fledged conference and deserves all the attention we can give it to make it a success. And that's what it takes to make a conference a success: *all the attention we can give it.* Good conferences aren't measured by how well we handled the talkers or by how close we came to the announced quitting time—but by their results. True, how we handled the conference will have some effect on the results, but there's a lot more to it than that. Results will depend on how well the conference was planned, how well we did in selecting conferees, how well they understood and played their roles in the conference, and how well we did in sharing the various functions of conference leading. If we ended up playing all the roles, from gatekeeper to summarizer, *we* may have had a good conference, but it's doubtful that anyone else did.

The logic behind a good conference is pretty simple. *Conference* implies a group of people *conferring.* The process goes like this: We select some people to come together to confer because a problem exists and they are the ones who are concerned with the problem or who have some information that will help in solving that problem. Our job as conference leader is to use those people in such a way that there won't be a problem after we've had the conference or after we carry out the action decided on by those attending. This means that we use these resources to do what they can do best: solve the problem at hand. If further action is required, we make sure to get their commitment to the solution by involving them in both the strategy of problem solving and the necessary action. As we said in Chapter 7 on planning and organizing, the planning isn't complete until the plan has been acted on. We should never leave a conference without all participants knowing exactly what is expected of them and when they are to complete what they have agreed to do. Finally, it is important to conduct the follow-up we mentioned. See to it that they do their part. That's *our* part!

EXERCISES

1. Individual activity: Have each member of the group think of the last meeting he or she attended. Try to pinpoint the date, who attended, and what the purpose was. Individuals should think of a specific meeting, not a collection of past meetings they've attended. Once they've picked a specific meeting, they

should make a list of things that helped the meeting go well and things that kept it from running well. They should set up their notes as follows:

Things That Helped	Things That Hindered
1.	1.
2.	2.
(etc.)	(etc.)

2. Group activity: When the individuals have finished exercise 1, they should report their results and have them recorded. This will give rather long lists of things that help and things that hinder the success of a meeting. These lists are valuable, and each person should keep a copy of them for future use. For now, though, let the group decide what the conference or meeting leader could do to overcome the hindrances listed. Many steps are obvious, such as set an agenda or set starting and stopping times. Others are more subtle. These, too, should be listed on the board and made a part of the observers' permanent notes.

3. Group activity: Looking again at the list generated from exercise 2, have the group discuss how many of the hindrances could have been overcome by the *participants*, apart from whatever the leader could have done. Brainstorm a list of things participants can do in any meeting to make it better, even if the leader isn't doing a very good job.

4. Individual activity: Each person should think of a meeting he or she will be having in the near future. It may be a large one or simply a staff meeting with a few people attending. Take several minutes to answer the following questions:

What is the purpose of the meeting?

What is the expected product?

Who should attend?

When should they be notified?

How should they be notified?

Are some people more important to the meeting than others?

Is the seating arrangement important—and if so, where will participants sit?

Can certain leadership roles be assigned to some of the people—and if so, to whom?

What time is the meeting scheduled?

What time should it be over?

How much leeway is there?

(This information need not be fed back to the entire group. Small subgroups can review one another's responses and compare their progress.)

Chapter 14

PROBLEM SOLVING

Problem solving, like most of the other topics discussed thus far, is a skill. There are specific steps in the process that, when properly followed, pretty well guarantee success. The difficulty often comes when we start to look at the process, because the steps *sound* complicated. Actually, the process is simple, and it is the one we use most of the time in making our personal decisions. When we consider buying a car, a house, or a boat, we go through these steps. We don't necessarily go through them *consciously*, but we deal with each of the issues nevertheless. As we discuss the steps, then, it's a good idea to think about how we use them in solving our everyday problems. If we already use the process, we might ask, "Why talk about it here?" Well, because although we use the process or its steps on *big* problems, we fail to use it on the small ones that often can grow into big ones if they aren't handled correctly. Also, for some reason, we don't always apply the process to the job, even though we use the ideas in our own affairs. (For example, we realize that we quite often have to resort to buying things on credit—and in the process end up paying more money for them—but we fail to see that the organization we work for runs into the same problem, i.e., not enough cash to pay now and save money later.)

The suggestion here is to start developing the habit of using the specific steps on small problems until we automatically go through the steps in any problem situation. We will look at the steps, see how they work, and give some examples; then it will be up to us as supervisors to apply the process on our own. Again, let's emphasize: the steps just *sound* complicated; they aren't really all that hard to understand and apply!

DEFINING THE PROBLEM

The first step in problem solving is to be sure we are attacking the *right problem*. An employee comes to us and claims to be tired of working on a certain job. If we take that at face value and start to solve that problem, we may find that we are solving the wrong problem, and maybe creating another. In reality, the employee may be fed up with us as a supervisor, or have had about all he or she can take from the employee who works across the aisle, or be making more mistakes than necessary because he or she hasn't had enough training.

How do we know whether we are trying to solve the right problem? The best way is to do what the doctor does when examining a patient—get all the symptoms together and see what kind of picture develops. This way we won't be treating just a symptom, but the real problem. Once we identify the symptoms, we start to ask, "What are the things that could produce these symptoms?" If employees are doing poor work, that may be a symptom of poor attitudes, which may be a symptom of poor supervision or perhaps poor working conditions. Are there other signs, such as a high turnover rate, absenteeism, or tardiness? Are some of the employees performing all right, while others aren't? Have these same employees performed better in times past? Only after we are satisfied with the answers to these questions can we be sure we are solving the correct problem and not just treating a symptom. Once we are sure we know what the problem is, it's a good idea to state it for our own clarification. "Reduce the loss of production time. Reduce the error rate. Increase the overall production rate for the group." Note that it's *not* the time to say, "Reduce the error rate caused by union intervention." This assumes that we already know the cause of the problem, which may be the case, but it's a good idea to get a few more facts before stating this—which brings us to the next step in the problem-solving process.

GATHERING INFORMATION

The information-gathering stage is an important one, but one that's often taken too lightly. After all, we've spent all this time defining the problem, so haven't we got enough information? No, not at this stage. We aren't ready to solve the problem yet. We just want to get as much information as we can to help us be sure we really are solving the right problem, then to help us pick up some ideas on how to solve the problem. Once we've gathered as many facts as seem to be available *in the time allowed us to look*, we take one last look and see if we really are on the right track. Have we discovered that every supervisor before us has had the same problem with the same employees on the same job? This doesn't make the problem go away, but it does put it in a different light.

Note that we emphasized getting as many facts as time allows. One of the important decisions we must be able to make is when to stop looking and start solving. In other words, we must recognize that to go any further would take more time and effort than the problem deserves. We might like to have production records going back for ten years, but if compiling such figures would take weeks of digging by a number of employees, we need to be able to measure its value against the cost of obtaining it. On the other hand, if the information is available right in the files, we can't use the excuse, "It'll take too long to look it up." Note, again, we aren't looking for a solution yet, so any information should be gathered with an open mind. It would be improper of us to gather only the information that will help us prove a point rather than solve the real problem. If we go into the problem-solving process with preconceived notions of what we are going to do anyway, then following a systematic procedure is an exercise in futility.

It is essential during this information-gathering stage to get specific rather than general information. We need to find out who or what, how many, how much, where, when, how long, etc. We will find that this kind of information is harder to get than are general comments, but much more reliable in the long run. For example, it's not enough to hear "She's late all the time." We need to ask, "How many times in the last month?" We shouldn't accept information like "This machine is costing us a fortune in repair bills." Such information will sink our argument one of these days, for if we don't ask, our boss might: "How much is a fortune?" Admittedly, generalities and opinions are much easier to get, and we probably make more friends when we ask people their opinions instead of making them dig up *specific* information. But we are trying to solve a *specific* problem, and we are hoping to recommend that *specific* action be taken. If all of this is based only on opinions, then we aren't likely to come up with the best solution available. By the way, when we're getting this information, we should make some kind of mental or written note on just how reliable the information really is. If some information is questionable, we should so note it, because otherwise we may base decisions on that information as if it were completely reliable. If we know that there is some doubt as to the validity of the information, we'll treat it with caution later on. If not, we may forget and create for ourselves a little grief that could easily have been avoided.

FINDING THE CAUSE

The reason we have placed such emphasis on the fact that we aren't yet ready for the solution is that at this point we are ready to identify the *cause*. Only when we have found the cause can we select an appropriate solution. Using the information we have gathered, we look at all the possible causes. If we decide that the poor work output is the result of inadequate training, not sloppy work habits, then we have some valuable data to use toward identifying the proper solution. However, we may find that we need more information or a different kind of information to get rid of the cause.

The difficult thing to remember is that causes aren't always easy to find. Rather than say that the cause isn't obvious, we should say that the cause that seems obvious may not be the real problem. If we have a problem because one of the workers in the office is being snippy with people in other departments, the cause may not be his or her bad attitude; it may be that we haven't made the assignment completely clear, and the worker is protecting his or her job in what seems the safest way—by keeping others away from it. An employee who is afraid that the job he or she has is not as important as other jobs will do his or her best to make it seem important, even if it comes out as trying to make life miserable for other people. "I'm sorry, but I'm too busy to help right now," or "Did the boss tell you to handle that? That's my job, and I don't want you messing it up." The cause may be poor supervision, poor definition of work responsibility, inadequate work, or several other things. But if we've gotten enough information, we should have a pretty good idea at this stage just what the real cause of the problem is.

After we are sure we have the cause isolated, it's still a good idea to make a quick check of history. Did this same thing cause the same problem at some other time? Has this same problem been caused by a shift change or a changeover to new equipment before? Have we always had this problem when we put in new equipment? There are a couple of good reasons for checking history when we have identified the cause. First, has someone identified this as a cause before and tried to solve the problem by eliminating the cause? Did the problem go away? Did it turn out to be more expensive to solve than the solution was worth? Did the solution turn out to solve only part of the problem? Are the basic ingredients still there; that is, the same people, the same office, the same equipment? If they are, did the solution just fail to take effect, or has something else—some new ingredient—entered the picture?

The second good reason for checking history is to find out if there is any record of the problem's *going away by itself*. Some problems are like that. When there is a change in the office routine, trouble develops. We know we should do something but aren't sure just what. Then, before we know it, the problem has disappeared! The danger in this kind of thinking is that most of us tend to expect that *all* problems will go away sooner or later. This just isn't so. Many potentially good supervisors have fallen by the wayside waiting for problems to vanish. Even many problems that seem to leave come back in another form—often a much more horrible form, at that. So we can't wait just because some problems do go away. But we can find out if this particular problem is caused by this particular thing that has a history of repeating itself, then going away. For example, when it's time to replace a typewriter in the office, we can be sure that there will be someone who isn't happy with our selection of who gets the new machine, no matter how fair our decision is. (Employees don't always want fairness—they sometimes want new typewriters!) A check with supervisors who have been around for a while will tell us what to expect when the new typewriter decision is made. This same check may tell us that it's all right that some of the employees are miffed; they always are, and their discontent will wear off by itself. If we are satisfied that this is right, and that the new typewriter caused the problem, then we can be equally satisfied that time will heal the problem just as well as any other solution we might pick. Of course, if we know enough about the situation before we select the new typewriter or the person getting it, we may take steps to keep the problem from arising.

FINDING ALTERNATIVE SOLUTIONS

Now comes the tricky stage. We have already determined the cause and are going to try to find the best solution—the solution that will eliminate whatever is causing the problem. The reason this is tricky is that it is the last time we can really use much imagination or ingenuity. What we want to do now is think of several possible solutions, not just one. We want the *best* one, and there is a way of getting it. The process is to *brainstorm*—that is, to think of as many alternatives or options as possible without making any efforts to evaluate them, or decide on one, or throw any of them out as not being feasible. The most important thing is that we must not think, "Well, I'm sure *that* won't work, so I'll discard the idea right now." About the only rule is to concentrate on those solutions that will most likely remove the cause we have identified. If there is doubt, *keep the idea around* anyway, unless the doubt is very strong. (We might even ask ourselves, "Why did I think of this in the first place? There must be some reason it came to mind, so I'd better hang on to it for a while.")

The problem with evaluating too early is that we may overlook some good ideas just because we don't get around to thinking about them! We hit on an idea that sounds promising and we go with it, thereby never even thinking of alternatives that might have been better in the long run. To make matters worse, the idea we picked to solve our problem may end up being less effective than hoped, either because it had some flaws in it or because it wasn't as practical as it sounded to us in the beginning. By the time we find this out, we may have used up too much time or gone too far to consider other options. We may even find ourselves committed to this approach and have to support it, knowing it isn't the best possible solution to our problem.

After we have spent some time listing (either mentally or on paper) all the ideas we can think of, we should take a last look at them and see if anything else comes to mind. This will tell us whether we've paid too much attention to a single line of thought. Often ideas cause us to think of other ideas, so the time may be well spent. By the way, this is a good place to ask, "How do I know when I have enough options to choose from?" The answer is that we have to look at the problem and decide *how much time it's worth*. The bigger the problem or the more complex it is, the more time we can devote to solving it. Two things are sure: we can spend too much time by just going on looking for more alternatives, and we can be pretty sure that we will reach the saturation point on productive ideas after a while—in other words, we will reach a point at which expending the amount of time no longer produces the same quality of alternative.

An advantage of listing the options we have looked at is that at some point, when we are trying to justify the solution we chose, we can say, "Well, I considered these other options, but here is why I picked this one." If we have done a good job of thinking out our decisions, we can show why the way we took is better than the alternatives we rejected. Of course, if for some reason there is a need to select one of the other options (company policy, budget considerations, etc.), then it's also good to be able to say, "I considered that, too, and if we go that route, then here are the things that will have to be done . . ." A final advantage is that it's sometimes possible to sell an idea by showing what the alternatives are. If someone doesn't like what we have chosen, it's good to be able to say that the alternatives are thus and so. It's just a lot better for us to list the options than for someone else to ask, "Why haven't you considered . . . ?" It weakens our decisions if we have to say that there are things we haven't considered, even if they turn out later to be bad alternatives.

PICKING A SOLUTION

Now that we've gone through all of this, how do we go about picking the best solution from the options we have listed? There are some definite steps, and we need to consider them now. First, we must use a *systematic* approach. It would be a shame to go this far in such a careful manner and then lose all of the advantage by not using the same careful approach in picking the best alternative. The approach should be a screening process to look at each of the options we have identified and see whether they meet certain criteria. If so, then we can use them; if not, then we can eliminate them one by one.

First, we ask whether the alternative we are looking at is really *possible*. We said earlier that we didn't want to rule out any ideas at that point, but now we begin to be very critical. Now is the time when we decide whether or not the idea really will work. Is it within the capability of our group, our talents, our budget? Next, we ask if the alternative is actually *workable*. Even if we have the capabilities, will it in fact work under the conditions that exist in *our* work situation? Will our people accept the idea? Will this option fit into our way of doing things, considering the routine, our interfacing with other work groups, etc.? Then we ask ourselves whether the alternative we are considering is really a *probable* solution. After all is said and done and we are ready to use it, are we willing to stick our neck out and promote this as a solution? Will the boss accept the idea? In other words, what is the *probability* that the idea will work and will be used? Finally, we ask the obvious question: is the idea *applicable* to this problem at this time under these circumstances?

This last question is the most critical of all. We must be sure that the solution applies to the real problem, the one we finally settled on. As we study each alternative to see whether or not to use it, we want to know not only whether it applies to the specific problem but whether it solves *all* of it. We should be comfortable with an alternative that gets this far in the testing, and we will be if we are sure it fits the problem and will solve all of it. Because of the systematic approach we have used, we have eliminated most of the bad solutions by now. The way to evaluate the ones that are left is to put them to one more test. We have, of course, placed certain "must" conditions on each of these solutions. Any option we picked had to meet these musts. But in the process, we also discovered that they met certain "nice" conditions, some more than others. Although we realize we can't expect everything, there are things that would be nice to have along with the solution. One way to pick the best alternative, once we have narrowed the options down this far, is to look at the nice benefits we get from each one. Those that meet all the musts and provide the most or best nice outcomes become the most attractive to us. It is from this list that we pick the final solution. Stated simply, we pick the one that not only will solve the problem we have stated, but also will give us the best side benefits. We have to be careful here, though, because we don't want to become attached to an idea just for its side benefits. We could end up defending it beyond its merit, when another option might solve the problem just as well, be more popular with other people, and perhaps be the most practical one to pick—*all because of some side benefit we feel so strongly about.*

Once we have chosen an alternative, and it has been checked out according to the suggestions here, we need to *state it very clearly.* For the benefit of all concerned, we should make sure that everyone who hears about the solution knows exactly who is going to do what and what it will take in terms of people, money, and time. If we have decided to move certain people to new locations, we should specify which people, where they will go, and what will be their job responsibilities when they get there. If we have decided to go into overtime, we should state how much overtime will be required, who will work it, and how much it will cost. Remember, early in this chapter we said that this would sound complicated but really isn't—so all of this doesn't have to be put down in elaborate form. Once those concerned have been told, the information should simply be available if someone asks. It can be in our head *if we really have thought out the problem.*

PUTTING THE PLAN TO WORK

This brings us to the point of implementing the solution. How do we go about introducing the new idea? Surely this shouldn't be a problem. It often is, though, and many plans fall through at this point. Again, certain questions must be asked. We have to anticipate problems and try to decide ahead of time how we will handle them. For example, we should ask ourselves, "Who will likely resist this solution?" If we anticipate that one of the old-line workers will try to kill the idea, we should take steps to prevent this, even if it means going to that worker and getting him or her to help introduce it or give us some suggestions on ways to make it work. We need to decide what risks are involved in trying this new or different idea and who will likely misunderstand what we are trying to do. Is our boss in agreement? Will he or she back us up when questions arise or opposition appears? After we've tried to anticipate who will be affected and what problems this will cause, we should see whether we have considered all possible risks, resistance, and resentments. If so, it's time to carry out the plan we've chosen.

Before we do that, though, we need to assure ourselves that we know what we're talking about. Going through these steps should give us the confidence to proceed with the solution to the problem. We mention this at this point for two reasons: First, as a new supervisor, we aren't always accepted for what we know or do. We are still thought of as new and thus not as capable of thinking the great thoughts that others with more time and experience can think. While this isn't true, it doesn't keep people from feeling that way, so it has to be considered. Second, we should not be afraid to push our ideas. By going through the steps we've discussed, we have become very familiar not only with the problem but also with the alternatives for solving it. In a way, we have become experts on this small portion of the operation, and this should overcome the lack of confidence that others have in us and that we have in ourselves. This is pretty important to the outcome of the plan!

CARRYING OUT THE PLAN

Now comes the important part of making our plan operate. We have spent valuable time arriving at what we think is the best solution to the problem. We have confidence that it is going to work. But it won't work by itself! If the plan is poorly carried out or not done the way we've specified, the results will make the solution *look* like the wrong one, even if it's not. Surely the solution deserves as much careful attention in the implementation stage as it did in the selection and planning stages.

Carrying out the plan means more than just putting it to work or telling someone else to do the job. It means keeping track of the progress, watching how well things are going, even making adjustments along the way. We must be careful to avoid being so committed to the plan that we can't see things that are going wrong. Our commitment should be to the *job*, not to our plan. Again, this doesn't mean that we have to spend a lot of time sitting around watching everything that happens. If we have confidence in the plan, we should be able to let it run its course fairly well. But occasional spot-checking should tell us whether we are really solving the problem. If we have reassigned some of the workers to different jobs, then we can tell a great deal by looking at production figures on a sampling basis. If the sales territory has been changed, then occasionally checking the present results against previous ones will tell us all we need to know about the plan we are trying out.

While we are watching the plan in operation, it's a good idea to keep an eye out for potential trouble. We've already talked about making a note of where we might expect opposition or misunderstanding. Since we know this ahead of time, we have some good checkpoints. The trick is to figure out when trouble is brewing so we can head it off and not wait until things are in bad shape to step in. The skill of anticipating trouble is a hard but valuable one to learn. Most trouble can be stopped more easily when it first starts than after it's gone on a while. If we suspect that someone is going to misunderstand or not like the solution we are instituting, we'd better make sure that the person doesn't get too many opinions formed before we deal with his or her misunderstandings. It will be a lot harder to change the person's mind than to help the person make up his or her mind in the first place.

Part of the reason for watching the progress of our solution is to check on our own problem-solving ability. We will need to know—sometime in the future—just how well we did at defining the problem, selecting alternatives, and picking the right option. Not only will we want to know how well we did at this, but we will want to get a look at the *value* of the solution. As we think about our future problem-solving efforts, we will want to ask ourselves, "Was all of this done efficiently, or did I spend a lot of time coming up with a solution that is now falling apart at the seams? Further, did I do a poor job of anticipating where the trouble would come from?" All this leads us to the final step—that of following up on the solution after the plan has been put to work and all the smoke has cleared.

FOLLOWING UP ON THE SOLUTION

The simple question we ask now is, "Did the solution really work?" The answer will tell us most of what we want to know. No matter how well thought out the plan was or how well we implemented it, if it didn't solve the problem, it really wasn't very good. But if it worked and we got the side benefits we thought we would get, then we have to say that the solution was a good one. If possible, we should try to find out *why* the solution worked. This may seem strange, but there is always the possibility that the problem disappeared in spite of what we did rather than because of it. All this means is that we take a look and try to determine whether other factors were at work at the same time that may have had an effect on the outcome of the problem-solving effort. While this isn't worth a lot of time, it's worth at least a little to keep us from getting caught thinking we have solved a problem by ourselves when what someone else did had as much to do with the outcome as what we did.

As we mentioned earlier, we should always be looking for flaws in the solution. How might we have prevented the negative things that happened? Were there obvious signs that we missed, or was the error unavoidable? Would it have been worth the extra time to look longer for possible trouble? This is simply hindsight, but it's valuable. It can keep us from making the same mistakes twice. It can help us measure our own ability at problem solving. It can be of help to future problem solvers, because if we have a good idea of what happened, they can learn from both our successes and our failures. Of course, all of this presupposes that the problem is dead, not just sleeping. Sometimes problems disappear for a while just because we have done something different; then, as soon as things settle down, they creep up on us again.

Part of following up on the solution includes finding out just exactly how much it took to make the solution work. How much did it really cost? How much overtime did we really put in that was directly related to our solution? Is the job actually *more* complicated as a result of our action? These are fair questions to ask, and we may well need the information to support our next idea. If we have exceeded our estimated expenditure, it's a lot better for us to catch it than for someone else to. Also, when we find out exactly what the costs were in terms of money, material, and people, we can honestly answer the question, *"Was it worth it?"* This can be done only when all the facts and figures are in.

CONCLUSION

In the beginning of this chapter, we said that the suggested method might seem complicated. What we have tried to do is lay out the entire problem-solving process. It will be a rare day when we use each of these steps to its fullest extent. No matter. The idea is to see that the approach to problem solving is systematic and not haphazard. Breaking it down into steps, as we have done here, shows more clearly that there is a beginning, a middle, and an end. The middle is only one step, picking a solution. What comes before and after determines how well the chosen solution is going to work. Briefly, here are the steps as they have been given:

1. Defining the problem
2. Gathering information
3. Finding the cause
4. Finding alternative solutions
5. Picking a solution
6. Putting the plan to work

7. Carrying out the plan
8. Following up on the solution

It wouldn't hurt us to write these steps down and tape them somewhere around our desk. When we start to solve a problem, we can take a look at the list and ask, "Where am I right now in the problem-solving process?" If we can't decide where we are, we'd better not be too confident of our solution. But if we're lucky (or just happen to be doing a good job), we can find out exactly where we are in the process and continue in full assurance that we're heading down the right road. We should have no fear that our solution will be the wrong one!

EXERCISES

1. Subgroup activity: Using the steps in problem solving shown at the end of this chapter, have groups of no more than four people go through the following problem.

   Bill John is an accountant with a large firm. For some time now he has been doing some freelance work on the side, keeping books for small businesses and doing tax returns. Next Saturday, he has a chance to do a job in a distant city, a drive of about ninety miles. The Johns have two cars, one with an automatic transmission and the other with a standard shift. His wife, Betty, never learned to drive a standard shift, so she drives the automatic and he drives the standard. The standard needs new tires for highway driving, but the old ones still have in-town miles left on them. The automatic has new tires, but they won't fit on the standard. It is Thursday when Bill finds out about the job in the distant city. When he calls his wife to tell her about it, he asks her what she has planned, if anything, for Saturday. Her reply is that she plans to take the new neighbor, Sally Thorne, shopping.

   At this point, we stop and let the subgroups work on the problem. When they are finished, they should read out their answers to the entire group. A record of the answers should be kept.

2. Group activity: Using the same information given in exercise 1, have the group members determine what they *don't* know in

order to adequately solve the problem. How much information would be required to actually solve the problem? Suppose they found out that Sally Thorne didn't have a car? Would this help? And suppose they found out that the local bus doesn't go to the shopping center on Saturdays? They still don't have all the information. What else is needed? Have the group brainstorm exactly what must be known in order to identify a truly adequate solution. (It's interesting how many might have suggested going ahead and buying the tires for the standard-shift car as a solution. While this has some merit, it's the kind of thing we often do in problem solving if we don't have all the information we need—which is frequently the case!)

Chapter 15

ORAL AND WRITTEN PRESENTATIONS

As supervisors, we have to present solutions to problems we have solved or communicate our ideas up or down the line. We may do this either orally or in writing. Whichever the case, the acceptance of the message can depend as much on the quality of our writing or speaking as on the message itself. It's too bad that we sometimes lose an argument or get poor results because we fail to do well at putting our position in writing or standing in front of people speaking. Obviously, we can't become great writers or speakers by reading one chapter in a book. But we can take a look at what we're *really* trying to do when we write or speak. Before going further, though, it would be a good idea to review the chapter on communications (Chapter 6), because we will need to apply some of the basics of communication in order to understand what is said here.

WATCH STEREOTYPES

Perhaps the most common mistake we make in trying to improve
our writing or speaking is to assume that there is just one right
way to write or speak. We fail to realize that there are many
acceptable ways to express ourselves. In writing, we can phrase
what we say in several quite appropriate ways and still reach our
audience. We search for the correct form to use in writing a letter,
for example, not realizing that anyone who says that there is only
one way to set up a letter is misinformed. In fact, if we stick to
some kind of stereotyped form in our writing, we may be stereo-
typing *ourselves*. We may be admitting that we have no imagination or that we are very formal, even when the occasion calls for an
informal approach. We may be giving the impression that we are
stodgy or old-fashioned and that we lack the flexibility required to
suit a particular situation. Whether in speaking or in writing, there
is plenty of room for imagination, which means that the person
who always says something just a certain way or appears to be just
the perfect orator may not be the best communicator. The truth is,
the polished orator will probably be out of place in the kind of
speaking situations we get into in our supervisory role. There is
really just one basic standard for writing or speaking: *get the
message across.*

HAVE A PLAN

There is a three-point plan of action that never fails. If we know
these three things, we should be able to handle any kind of situation in which we are trying to get a message across to someone
else, whether by speaking or by writing. They are:

1. Know your subject
2. Know your audience
3. Know yourself (capabilities)

Let's look at each of these and see what they mean to us as
supervisors.

Know Our Subject

What does it mean to know the subject? It means we should research it until we are sure we have a complete understanding of what we are about to write or say. Even if we aren't expected to be an expert, we should at least know enough to see that our words and phrases are used correctly. This doesn't mean that we research the topic to death. It means that we simply learn as much as we are supposed to know, plus perhaps a little extra (but never a little less). Of course, if we are regarded as an expert and others are looking to us for all the answers, then we do, in fact, have to do a great deal of research.

Perhaps a better way to think of it is to know what is important and what isn't. Rather than becoming an authority on a whole subject, we figure out what part is important to the audience or the reader and concentrate on that. We may even have to educate the audience that certain things *are* important. We also figure out what part is important to the project we're working on. Maybe the audience is interested in more information than the project requires. Maybe people think it would be interesting to pursue some issues that really aren't pertinent to solving the problem at hand or that do not contribute to the overall project. If so, we simply have to avoid the trap and get to the important points, even though our audience thinks it wants something else. Of course, this means we must explain why we are leaving other things out and be ready to defend our position.

The audience isn't all that may cause us to add to the information we cover. We have our own pet subjects and like to ride certain horses to death every time we get a chance, so we have to control ourselves as well. One of the best ways to regulate ourselves and our audience is to be familiar with the subjects that relate to the one we're writing or speaking about. Not that we have to become an expert—we just need enough knowledge so that we can tell how some of the related material might affect the outcome of the project being discussed or so that we can answer some of the questions that might be asked later. We shouldn't pose as an authority. We shouldn't try to bluff on the subject. We should simply try to familiarize ourselves with enough of the information to give us a pretty good picture of those things that relate to the subject at hand. (Later on, as we grow, we can take on more and more related subjects, but in the beginning it's better to be good at what we're talking about than to try to spread ourselves too thin.) Organization is the key here, because as we begin to organize and tie up loose ends, we see where related subjects fit in and where the weak spots are.

Know Our Audience

Knowing the audience isn't as simple as it might appear. As we've already said, if what we want the audience to have differs from what the people think they need, then we've got to tell them *in terms that are meaningful to them*. Even though we're expressing our own thoughts and ideas on the subject, the way we express them must be in terminology the audience will understand. Ideally, we should start off by making it clear that what the audience is getting is what it has asked for. This way at least the members are tuned in, whether they're getting the information exactly as they expected it or not. The way to appeal to the reader or listener is the same: "Here is the information you asked for." "You asked me to speak on . . ." At least we ought to start by saying, "You will be glad to know . . ." Whatever we do, we should use the name of our reader or listener, and the second person, rather than *I* or *me*. This helps keep it friendly, especially if we avoid stock phrases such as "Enclosed please find . . ." or "A funny thing happened on the way to make this speech . . ." Using phrases like this may say something about us that we don't want said. *And stopping is just as important as starting*. Nothing can be kinder or friendlier than stopping when we have said all we have to say. But if we aren't careful, we fall into some bad habits. "If I can be of further help to you in this or any other matter, please do not hesitate to call on me," and "In closing, let me reiterate what I've already said." Such phrases often kill whatever good might have been accomplished.

Know Ourselves

The most important thing to know is ourselves. What are our capabilities? If we have the ability to talk and write on a subject, we shouldn't sell ourselves short. We're writing or speaking because we know enough about the subject to do just that, and that's reason enough. We have a chance to sell ourselves, too, and that's an opportunity we should take advantage of. We also have a chance to prove a point that we've come up with. It may be a solution or an idea, and whatever it is, if we have done the research, we should not be willing to let someone else try to explain it just because we think we lack the ability to do so. It's often true that good ideas go down the drain because we fail to take advantage of the opportunity to promote them ourselves. We either let the idea go altogether or entrust it to someone else, who may not have the whole story or who may lack the interest to sell the idea.

But we also need to know our limitations. Even if we are willing to make the speech or write the letter, we should speak or write within our abilities. If we can't tell jokes, we shouldn't try. Use a substitute, such as a short anecdote from the newspaper, or just play it straight—that nearly always works! If we can't be an orator, we shouldn't try. We should just tell it simply, quickly, and stop when we're through. If we aren't familiar with certain words or phrases, we leave them alone. We're better off not using them than using them incorrectly. And if *we* aren't sure about them, our audience may not be, either. But just as we need to know our limitations, we need to do something about them. We should be constantly striving to do better than the last time. Each time we write or speak, it's a good idea to add one new challenge or trick of the trade. Try a little humor, add a dash or semicolon to our letter. When someone says, "You did a fine job," determine to do even better next time. If we feel we didn't do too well, decide what we did wrong and then look for an opportunity to try to do better, not just stop with a failure.

Note that skillful communication is pretty important to the new supervisor. The ability to express ourselves in writing or by speaking before a group is an asset that never goes out of style. At every level in the organization, we are called on to tell someone something. *The telling is just as important as the finding out what to tell.* Very little will call attention to us and to what we know as much as the ability to say it or write it. A good oral briefing or a crisp, accurate report is an exciting thing to those who are short on time and need to get their facts in a hurry. If we are able to provide them with this service, we will certainly be rewarded for it. The higher we go in the organization, the more useful this skill becomes, so the better we get, the more we improve our likelihood of advancing. Chances are fairly good that whenever two near-equals are being considered for a job, the one who can communicate better will win out.

TIPS ON WRITING

Generally, there are just three reasons we ever write anything: to *inform*, to *request*, and to *substantiate* or document. When we write to inform, we are doing so because someone needs some information we have and has asked us to supply it, or we have some information the other person should be using and we want him or her to have it. The recipient may not know he or she needs the information, and we may have to sell him or her on accepting it, but at least we must recognize that a particular letter is for the purpose of giving someone some information. Writing to request information is quite different from writing to give information. Our approach is different in that we have to be much more specific to be sure to get just what we require. Even in requesting information, there can be two motivating reasons. First, we could want the information because we are going to use it; second, we could want it because someone has asked us to get it for him or her. In the first case, we have only to determine exactly what we want and why we want it, then ask for it. In the second case, it's a little harder. We have a communications problem at both ends. We not only have to fathom someone else's needs and make sure we aren't asking for the wrong thing, but we also have to be sure we are getting it in good, usable form. This means we have the problem of determining what the users are going to do with the information. If they are going to use it exactly as we get it to put into a report, then we must make sure to give it to them in near-final form. If they're going to extract parts of the information and use them with other information, then we need to put it in a form that allows them to find things in it very quickly. Then, of course, we have the job of communicating this need to the people we are getting the information from; hence, another communications problem.

The third reason for writing is to substantiate or document a conclusion or decision we have made. In this case, we have to be sure to use all the rules of good communicating, because we are really in the selling business now. This is especially true if we are writing to substantiate someone else's idea or conclusion. This happens when the boss tells us to write a letter to a client to explain what we have decided on a matter.

So we have three reasons for writing: to *inform*, to *request*, and to *substantiate*. It's simple to find out which reason we are writing for, but too many times we forget to do it. It's much easier to find the right words if we know why we are writing. It's also easier to proofread our writing when we know exactly why we're writing in the first place. We say to ourselves, "Did I make it perfectly clear what I wanted, or does the receiver have to guess and read between the lines? Did I spend so much time leading up to the subject that the reason for writing got lost?" It's always a good idea to put ourselves in the reader's shoes and see if we can determine what the letter or report is all about. The simplest way to check our writing is to see whether we got to the point quickly. It's just as bad to put in too much background information as to put in too little. If we spend too much time leading up to the reason for writing, the reader may have left us before we get to it. The best way is to open with the purpose of the letter:

> "Here's the answer you asked for on the framus machine . . ."
>
> "Can you tell us how many of these you will need in the next year?"
>
> "We recommend canceling the project immediately."

With lead-in sentences like these, the reader won't have to guess why we're writing the letter or report. This doesn't mean we should be blunt or tactless, just obvious. We spare the details until we have established our reason for writing. But we also get to the point clearly. We don't use obscure words or phrases that are familiar only to us or to our organization. We state the purpose early; we don't bury it in the third paragraph somewhere between background detail and unimportant information. The reader should be able to tell at a glance what he or she is supposed to do, by the way.

> "Will you send me five copies?"
> "Wait until Friday—I'll call you then."
> "Take the necessary steps to purchase the property."

All this comes early and clearly in the report. Any supporting data comes at the end of the report or as an attachment to the letter.

Finally, here's a helpful tip: to learn to write, *we must write!* We must practice, reread whatever we've written that didn't get the message across, then practice writing some more. We should read other people's writings and reports and analyze them. We should tear them apart, ask ourselves why they worded them as they did, notice the good things they have done—*then imitate the good things.* Most effective writers freely admit they started out by imitating people who were already successful, so there's no shame in recognizing and copying a good writing style. If there are people in the organization who have a reputation for writing well, study what they've written, see what it is that makes their material precise or easy to read, then try to do likewise.

SIMPLIFYING OUR WRITING

There is no doubt that writing comes easier for some than for others. Suppose we're one of those for whom it doesn't come easily. Can we reach the point where it will come easily and naturally? Probably not, if we don't write all the time. Does that mean we should just give up and not try to write? Not at all! It means we should strive to be an adequate writer, just as we should strive to be an adequate speaker. As a supervisor, we have to be able to put things into written form. We have to write clearly and concisely, and what we write needs to be expressed in such a way that it cannot be easily misunderstood. (Remember the rule: if it can be misunderstood, it will be!) So how do we become adequate? By following some simple rules and practices, a number of which we list here.

- *Talk about it first.* We ask the question, "Why am I writing this?" Having gotten a clear answer for this, we ask another: "What do I really want to say?" That may sound too simple, but if we talk about it, even to ourselves, we'll find out the answer quickly.

- *Talk to the receiver on paper.* All this means is that we imagine the person sitting across the desk from us, listening to us as we talk through the message. We don't put anything into the letter we wouldn't say; that is, we don't use the clichés, the jargon, or the gobbledygook that haunt much business writing.

- *Write to express, not to impress.* In the long run, the best letter or document of any kind is the one that people can understand quickly. We all get letters so full of big words and long sentences that we have to read them several times to grasp the meaning. Then we call the sender to make sure we understood what was being said. The person may have been trying to impress us, but the impression was far from flattering! We would have been much more impressed with a letter we could read once and understand the first time!

- *Short is better.* Since words are codes for expressing ideas and facts, the more words we have, the greater the opportunity for misunderstanding. Sentences, paragraphs, and letters that are brief are the easiest to understand. We shouldn't shortchange the person on the other end by not giving enough information, but we'd rather he or she had to call for more data than for an explanation of what we said.

- *Say it first and last.* The kindest thing we can do (to save the reader's time) is to open the letter with the purpose in the first sentence, as mentioned earlier. "We need assistance on the committee," or "Here is the information you requested about . . ." If we want the person to remember and to take action, the last thing we say can emphasize the purpose, too. "We look forward to your answer about working on the committee," or "We hope the information is sufficient." Studies show that people are more likely to recall the first and last things they read in a letter.

- *Stop when it's over.* When we've finished, we don't have to add a formality about providing assistance or "not hesitating to call on us." When we've made it clear what we're writing about (giving information or seeking help), we don't need to tack on another statement saying we'll be glad to help. We've already demonstrated that in our letter. We just say it and quit—doing the reader a favor!

- *Read for meaning, not for glory.* Before signing the document, we read it once from the *reader's* point of view. Suppose we had gotten this letter; would we understand what it says, knowing no more than the receiver knows? We can save ourselves a lot of grief by doing this. Rewriting or editing a letter or document takes less time than correcting errors that arise from misunderstandings.

- *Don't strive for perfection.*   There's no such thing as a perfect letter, and we don't need to try to produce the first one! When we've been through these steps and are fairly satisfied, let the letter go. The small changes we might make at this point will never be noticed by the reader, and we can use the time more productively doing something else.

TIPS ON SPEAKING

We can't learn to speak well just by reading about it, but there are some things to look for and do that will improve our ability as a speaker if we take advantage of the knowledge we've gained. All the suggestions we made about preparing obviously apply here, and how well we have done these things will largely determine the success or failure of our speech. But even the best preparation won't make us a competent speaker. Above all, we must learn to *practice, practice, practice.* We don't have to practice every word we're going to say, but we do need to work on phrases and try different combinations of words in order to get the most out of the words and phrases we use. Since we're more likely to be frightened at the beginning, we should practice our opening remarks until they're as precise as we can make them. If we start off well, the rest will come easier. Our confidence will be higher, and the audience's reception will be better. Another way to build our confidence is to test our ideas on other people. We shouldn't bore them or ask them to listen to the entire speech, but at least try to get them to react to our key points and ideas. Do they understand what we're driving at? Do they see the logic we're using? Do they have some pretty good arguments for why we should say it differently?

When we start to speak, we must be alert to the audience's reaction. Do the people seem receptive? Are they bored? Is there anyone in the group who looks friendly and appears to be nodding agreement? (If so, it will build our confidence to direct our attention to him or her frequently to see how we're doing. Be careful, though; this person may not be a good gauge of the thinking and feeling of the entire audience.) One way to keep the audience with us is to get feedback. Look our listeners in the eye when we've made a good point and try to get them to nod, smile, or frown. Don't be afraid to ask them to hold up their hands or even stand up to indicate whether they are on one side or the other of an argument. This way we've made it clear that we're talking *to* and *with* them, not *at* them. And since we want to talk to them, we look at them, not at the ceiling, the floor, or our notes. Look around the group; don't talk to just one side of the room or to a few people in the front row.

There's nothing wrong with using notes—in fact, the audience expects it. But we need to use them well or not at all. Notes are just that: *notes*. They're not our speech written out. Very few people can get away with writing out their whole speech, then making it appear casual and natural. Certainly we can't do it if we are just learning to speak, so it's all the more important for us to make good use of our notes. But if our notes are not much shorter than the speech, we're really only going to end up reading the speech. If so, then why not simply send all the members of our audience a copy of the speech and save them some time? The rule for making notes is to include only the key points and phrases in them, plus any statistics or figures we must remember. Again, practice will reduce the need for notes.

Another thing that will help us eliminate the need for notes is to have some good speaking aids. Unfortunately, this introduces another dimension to our speaking, and one that can also be misused. The trouble is that we tend to use things like visuals, charts, chalkboards, or easels as crutches rather than as aids. We depend on them to help *us*, not the audience. Just because we can get a lot of figures on a projected visual doesn't mean the audience is going to remember it all or even give it attention for very long. There's nothing exciting about looking at a screen full of statistics for several minutes while a speaker reads and comments on them. If the aid doesn't make the point any clearer, don't use it. But some aids are vital. There's hardly any better way to show a relationship of parts to the whole than to use a pie chart or similar "whole" type of graph. Of course, we remember what we see much longer than what we hear, so good visuals are necessary to aid in retention. Also, visuals can save us a lot of words if we use them at the proper time and in the proper way. (It would take many words to describe a cow, but a picture could get the message across in a hurry!) One important consideration is that if we decide to use a visual and think it will help the audience get the message quickly and clearly, then we should make sure the audience can *see* the visual. The audience isn't likely to be very receptive when we say, "If you could see this, you'd note that it has two small holes."

WORDS OF CAUTION ABOUT SPEAKING

In spite of the fact that most of us try to improve our speaking skills, there is a danger in becoming *too* good! It can happen that as we get better, people are more enraptured with our style than with our message. We find that people tend to relax, with the idea that we're so good, we'll take care of their learning, too. In other words, as we get more charismatic, people focus more on our performance than on what we're saying. If we are serious about communicating ideas and facts to them, we need to let the message get through without hiding it behind our "golden-throated oratory." People will pay more attention to us if we can come through with sincerity. They need to hear us talk *with* them, not *to* them. That's hard to do. It means we have to appear human. We have to let them know that we don't have all the answers while convincing them that we do know enough to justify our speaking to them.

Of course, if our goal is to persuade them to our viewpoint, it may be that we want to use our most powerful speaking skills, overcoming some of the weaknesses in our ideas. We need to practice and emphasize our strong points with fervor. This is the time to use our best platform skills. On the other hand, if our arguments are clear and persuasive in themselves, we'll want to let the arguments do the work. We'll need to speak clearly and concisely and even slowly, so the facts will soak in and be digested. This is a good time to repeat for emphasis. It's a good time to review the bare essentials, after we've made our points in detail. If part of our goal is to educate, we may have to set aside time for questions and answers. Here again, there are some cautions. If we open the floor for questions, we run several risks:

- *Getting off the subject.* The devil's advocate may attack at any point in the presentation, even reopening topics we've already covered. There may be someone who has a hidden agenda and wants to talk about something unrelated to the matter at hand. We'll have to be prepared to deal with this swiftly and politely, but in a way that avoids giving the impression that we will cut off anyone who doesn't ask the right questions.

- *Getting a question that is beyond our ability to answer.* There is always the possibility that someone in the audience knows as much as we do (or more) about the subject we're discussing. In all sincerity, or with malice aforethought, the person may ask something that exceeds what we know or what we want to talk about. If this happens, we can turn it back to the audience or even back to this person by asking, "Anybody have a thought about that?" Or we may simply say, "That's a little beyond what I wanted to get into today. Maybe we can talk about that later."

- *Getting a question about one of our pet peeves.* We always run the risk of somebody asking a question that's right up our alley of biases. We can't resist getting on our soapbox and expounding on the subject for a long time. And that's the problem: we don't have a long time. We can either say, "I'm afraid I'd better stay away from that" (thereby letting the audience know about our strong feelings), or we can just give a brief answer and avoid going into detail about precisely what has aroused our strong feelings.

- *Getting a rambling question.* There are those who ramble and give answers as they ask their question or haven't thought out their question very thoroughly. When they ask the question, it is difficult to understand, and we may fall into the trap of answering the wrong question or rambling ourselves. The best approach is to clarify the question before offering an answer. "Would you mind putting the question into one sentence?" or "Let me make certain I have the question right," then don't go on until the person has agreed that this is the correct question.

There are other hazards to opening the floor for questions, often including the lack of time. But a question-and-answer period is when the speaker gets feedback on how his or her remarks have been received, so it's worth thinking about. There are other pitfalls in public speaking, too, but the foregoing will serve as guidelines for our attempts to improve. What it all comes down to is that we need to be good speakers and good writers, because writing and speaking are the main ways that what we know gets out to those who don't know.

CONCLUSION

A final tip for those of us who find ourselves in the situation of having to write something or speak before a group of any size: *be friendly on purpose.* Write and speak with a smile. Let our writing show we are friendly by our use of personal pronouns and people's names. Refer to things that the readers are familiar with rather than examples that relate only to our experience. With our speaking, too, remember that pleasantness is contagious. We can get away with a lot by saying it in a friendly way. This will come as we speak and write more and more, which is what we should do: speak and write more and more. To do our job well, we must steadily develop this side of it. Many books and self-help programs are available. We need to take advantage of them as well as to practice by accepting every opportunity to write and speak that comes our way. If we do poorly, it's a sign that we need practice, not a signal to stop doing it altogether. If we do well—and we will if we keep trying—then we will be more likely to sell our ideas *and ourselves.*

EXERCISES

1. Individual activity: Each person in the group should write the boss a memorandum about the activity that he or she has been engaged in so far in the study of this book. It should be no longer than fifty words and consist of no more than two paragraphs. It may be edited and doesn't have to be copied over. When all have finished, they should be ready to read their memos to group as a whole or to other individuals in the group.

2. Small-group activity: Form subgroups of no more than four

people. Let each person read his or her memo to the other members of the subgroup. Those members should look for unnecessarily long paragraphs, cumbersome words that don't sound like everyday English, and stock phrases. When all the memos have been read by their writers and comments made by the rest of the subgroup, each person should have at least five minutes to redo his or her memorandum.

3. Individual activity: Let each person count up the number of words in the memo he or she wrote for exercise 1; next, do the same for the memo written for exercise 2; then subtract the smaller number from the larger. If it turns out that the second memo had *fewer* words than the first one, put a plus sign in front of the result, because that's a positive step forward. If it turns out that the second memo had *more* words than the first, put a minus sign in front of the result, because that's a negative step backward. The idea is to see how many words have been *saved* in rewriting. Everyone in the group should read out the results so that a total for the group can be obtained. (The object is for these people to see how many words they can save when writing only a fifty-word memorandum, and to imagine, then, what they'll do day after day in writing letters if they learn the right lessons from this chapter!)

4. Group activity: Brainstorm a presentation that this group might make on how to save words and express the meaning more clearly in their writing. This will be an oral presentation. Using the rules of good speaking, decide on the opening remarks, how to catch and hold the audience's attention, and what illustrations to include. The body of the speech should be outlined, showing the points to be made, and the suggested action should be presented close to the end. The conclusion must be emphatic and dramatic. It should actually be worked out, with the entire group developing a closing sentence for the speech. (While the speech probably won't be given, it's good material for someone who wants to pursue the subject further.)

Chapter 16

TEAM BUILDING

Much has been said about team building. Team building is often seen as the panacea of organizational organization. It is believed by some that the installation of some form of team-building program will suddenly (or quickly, at least) transform loose-knit work groups into finely tuned, highly efficient, re-markably productive, machinelike operational entities. On some few occasions, this has happened to a small degree, but not without tremendous effort, expense, and time on the part of all levels of management and well-trained production people. Not that teamwork isn't nice—it is—and it is essential to a successful organization. The reason it hasn't worked as an overall program in most cases is that such programs expect too much, too fast, of too many people who just aren't ready for such a massive change.

In this chapter, we won't deal with programs, but rather with the work group immediately under the supervisor reading this book. We won't talk about an organization-wide team-building effort; we'll only discuss what we can do to mold a group of people with different goals, different agendas, different degrees of maturity, different backgrounds, skills, and capabilities, different experiences, and different motivations. That's a pretty big order in itself. Is it possible? We'll see that we can do a great deal as an individual supervisor to accomplish this, even if the organization isn't practicing or even supporting a team-building effort.

DEFINITIONS AND REQUIREMENTS

Now let's decide just what it is we mean when we talk about a team and a team-building effort. Three things make up the definition of team building. First, the overall picture: *developing a group of people into an intradependent entity striving toward a common goal.* Second, the individual responsibility: *getting them to accept individual as well as group responsibility for their performance in meeting these common goals.* Finally, the responsibility of the group and the supervisor to each other in reaching the goal: *getting and using the group's inputs on changes, improvements, and time and labor requirements to meet the common goal efficiently and effectively with the resources available.* That's a lot of words. What do they mean? Essentially they mean shifting and sharing responsibility as a group to get to where the organization wants the group to be.

People tend to be more motivated when they have a part in what they are doing. When the boss says something like, "What do you think about how to get this done?" to the group in a staff meeting, the individuals automatically begin to develop a proprietary feeling about the assignment. This notion is discussed in detail in the chapter on motivation. The idea of team building isn't new, it's just that we're gradually developing ways to shift not only the *responsibilities* from management to the workers, but even *authority* in many cases (see Chapter 9 on delegation). It's pretty obvious that people are much more effective when they work together and function as a team than when they act according to their own individual desires and intuitions. It should be equally obvious that this isn't a natural approach, for most of us have strong independent feelings. This inclination makes our job tough when we try to meld this independent group into a working-together entity.

Requirements for Success

For team building to be a success, the work group must meet some requirements; otherwise the supervisor trying to get the group together shoulders a tremendous burden. First and foremost, group members need to have a high level of maturity. Maturity in this case isn't about either age or experience. It is the ability to put the organization, and even other workers, ahead of personal desires and agendas. It means controlling jealousy or envy and the need to win arguments. It means putting in a little extra effort that may not reap any immediate rewards, but will help get the ox out of the ditch. There are many examples of team-building attempts that failed simply because no one bothered to consider the group's maturity level. (Another tough job for the supervisor, which we'll talk about later in the chapter.) In addition to maturity, the group must possess job skills or have the means of getting them as needed. Both skills training and workers' experience are involved here. The supervisor needs to be a good trainer and to have a good understanding of workers' past performance history. The final requirement for success is that all people concerned must have a clear knowledge and understanding of the group's goals, as well as a sincere belief in them. At this point the organization's ability to communicate at all levels comes into play. The supervisor in particular must be able to fit the group's goals into the overall organization's goals, communicate these goals to the work group, then get the group's input as to how to meet them. *This process takes a lot of skilled communication!* (We'll learn more about this later in this chapter.)

Signs of Immaturity

A word here about immaturity. Often we think of immaturity as related to age or experience, but it knows no age or experience limits. Frequently, new employees show a great deal of maturity, whereas older, experienced employees often exhibit little maturity. As a new supervisor, we can look for some of these obvious signs of the lack of maturity needed for building good teamwork:

1. **Lack of respect for others.**   This is exhibited through ridicule

of others' comments or ideas in meetings and general lack of attention or interest in others' ideas.

2. **Selfishness.** One person's getting a new desk, or a new tool, or even his or her own pencil sharpener can cause wholesale panic among the employees.

> *"Why did she get that instead of me?"* or,
>
> *"I need one of those more than he does!"* or,
>
> *"Why does he always get the best tools? He doesn't deserve any more than we do."*

All these statements are actually saying, "Hold on, we aren't ready to talk about team building yet!"

3. **Backbiting, carping, sniping, and the like.** These are sorry little words that best describe some immature offices or workplaces.

> JOE: *Hey, what did you think about the boss's reaction to Jim's idea for rearranging the furniture?*
>
> BILL: *So, what's the big deal? If he'd do more work around here instead of always trying to get on the boss's praise list, things would be a lot better.*

By itself, it doesn't sound so bad, but when this type of talk surfaces constantly in reaction to anything and everything, it shows that the group has a long way to go to become mature enough to work well together.

4. **Politics rule the roost.** "It's a whole lot easier to have a firm conviction after I know what the boss thinks." If our people are saying that about us, then we may lack the maturity to take on a team-building effort. There's the matter of buttering up to the boss, too:

> ALICE: (In a meeting with the boss and Judy) *I thought we could just go ahead and start on the new roll, since the old one is about worn out.*
>
> BOSS: *I thought we had agreed to use up the old one to save a little money?*
>
> JUDY: *Yeah, that's what I understood, too. I told Alice that you'd said that but I guess she thought she had a better idea.*

5. **Blame is more important than solution.** It's a pretty un-healthy environment when the first thing we hear after a mistake has been made is, "Okay, who did this?" instead of, "Okay, how can we get this working again quickly?" After employees have heard the search for blame for years, it be-comes ingrained in them to think blame first, solution second. In many workplaces people are known for the mistakes they made, rather than for their accomplishments, even years after an infraction.

6. **Feelings are worn on the sleeves.**

> AL: *Nobody really appreciates my work around here.*
> BILL: *Tell me about it! All I did was come in three minutes late and the boss chewed me out like I'd committed murder!*
> AL: *What did he say?*
> BILL: *Well, it wasn't what he said; it was the way he said it.*
> AL: *Did he scream at you?*
> BILL: *Well, no. But it was the look he had. I could tell he was mad.*
> AL: *Yeah, people have such a bad attitude. Like Sue yesterday.*
> BILL: *Why? What's her problem?*
> AL: *I was just trying to offer a little correction and she got all bent out of shape.*

This dialogue is repeated in many ways when people have low levels of maturity. They take everything personally, and getting their feelings hurt serves as a way to excuse them-selves from things they are doing wrong. After a while, people are afraid even to talk to each other.

There are other signs of immaturity, of course, but these examples are typical. When the workforce acts like this, the environment needs to be changed before team building can take place.

THE SUPERVISOR'S ROLE IN TEAM BUILDING

No matter what the organization does to build teamwork, it is up to us, the immediate supervisor, to make it a reality. Naturally, it's much easier and effective if higher management is helping, not hurting the process! But although it's tough when we have to buck higher management, even then team-building efforts can be made to work. First of all, to get things going we need to understand the team concept. We can play favorites by giving some people easier jobs or giving less discipline for failure to meet standards. We don't need to praise everyone's good work, but we need to use good skills in making corrections. We have to recognize differences among people in their skills levels, past experiences, and motivation. We also must be aware of the differences in *maturity levels* among workers and in differences in ability and even willingness to work together as a team.

Next, success may well mean that we have to rethink some old ideas and practices and learn to live with some entirely new concepts. The idea of thinking in terms of *group* as opposed to *individual* will come hard, for us and for the hourly workers, too. As we've said, most of us are used to thinking about individual performances, individual rewards, and individual accomplishments, not group accountabilities. Not only do individuals want recognition, but they have learned quickly to shift blame to someone else. "It's not my fault!" is something children start saying almost as soon as they can talk. Relearning must take place gradually, not all at once; it must take place in small bits, not big chunks.

A third thing we must do to make team building work is to learn about people, which means developing people skills. Although understanding people is a lifelong task, we can learn some basic things fairly quickly that will go a long way in helping us with team building. One basic fact is that people want recognition for what they do. Learning to say, "That looks good!" is simple, but essential to survival, and can be applied to individual or group accomplishments, as we'll see later in this chapter. People are much more likely to repeat doing what feels good to them, and it feels good when someone says we've done a good job— providing, of course, we've really done a good job! Whether we did something on our own or as a part of a team, it feels good to be recognized.

Something else we need to learn is that different people need different kinds and degrees of recognition. People who are consistently successful don't need to be told very often that they've done a good job, nor do they need to be told about little things; but they do need to hear about large accomplishments. On the other hand, people who haven't much history of success need reinforcement often, and even about small things. Of course, there are many other people skills, and we hope this book will pass along more of them.

Another role we undertake in team building is coordination. At times we serve as more a buffer zone than a sieve. Although it is important not to block necessary information flow from higher management to the workers, at times the coordination of team building requires that some things do not flow down. When higher management doesn't respect our efforts to build a team and demands to know, "Who's responsible for this mess?" it may be important to try not to involve the group. In fairness to higher management, this situation doesn't arise as often as it is talked about; for the most part, middle management respects requests from first-line supervisors not to disturb the team effort.

On the other hand, it's just as important to be the sieve that facilitates information flow up and down when it's essential to group accomplishments. Our boss needs to know what's going on and needs to approve of the goals and, for the most part, of the means we will use to meet those goals. Further, the group cannot be shielded from changes in organizational goals, or budgets or production requirements. It is important not only for the group to know about the changes, but also for it to be a part of the solution to any resulting problems.

We must also coordinate with our peer supervisors. Others must know that we are doing things as a team, not individually. Our peers and their people can't undermine this effort by going to our employees and expecting to get their attention ahead of the group effort. If the group is working on a project, solving a maintenance problem, or working together on a short deadline, our peers shouldn't expect to get a light bulb changed right away—unless the group as a whole is consulted and decides it's a big enough emergency to warrant an exception.

Our final area of coordination is with and between subordinates. Although good teamwork results in the group's making most of its own decisions under our management, and requires good communications between participants, it is our responsibility as the immediate supervisor to see that this is really happening. We, too, must be sure not to violate the team approach by pulling an individual for another assignment without the group's getting in on the decision.

SIMPLIFY THE PROCESS

Teamwork is a frame of mind, a belief, and a commitment, not just a program. It represents a commitment to a specific, agreed-upon goal. It represents a commitment to a group, as well, that says the group's goal is more significant than our own goals, at least in the short run. More than that, teamwork entails a belief that the goal is worthwhile. We must believe in the goal of the group primarily because we shared in the formation of it, helped put the plan together to meet it, and are offering our energy and expertise to reach it. We think it's the thing to do right now. And because we helped develop it, and we understand how we plan to meet the deadlines, make the numbers, finish the product, or whatever it is we're attempting, we have a proprietary interest in the goal. All these factors simplify the process.

Know the Goal

Our past experience probably wasn't like this. Without team building, we did what we were told, often without knowing the reasons or sharing in the vision of the finished accomplishment. We probably simply came to work, did our thing, went home, came back the next day, did it all over again, and had no feeling of completion. When whatever we were doing was finished, we started something else, without knowing the goal. Now we know where we're trying to go; we have known from the beginning, and we even helped formulate the process of getting there. We'll know when we're there, and we'll share in the victory with others on the team.

Treat Subordinates as Members

As the supervisor, we simplify the process by treating our subordinates as members of the team—always. That can be tricky. We begin by recognizing them as individuals, with individual worth, individual and unique skills and abilities that can be combined with others, who have other skills, to make a workable team. We must also see them as contributing more than their job. We must see them as a current resource, with capabilities for even greater contributions in the future. Further, we value them for more than just their skills and experience. We want our employees to realize that they have a mind, a thinking capability that can figure out how to get things done. When they get together with others with thinking capabilities, we have a problem-solving team that is much more able to solve problems than is any one person.

Let Them Have It

A final step we can take toward simplification is to turn things loose once the process starts. Again, past experience makes this difficult for us. We are likely to consider that our job as supervisor is to see that everything is done properly, which can only happen if nothing gets delegated—or so it seems. New (or poor) supervisors frequently comment to newly formed teams, "Now, remember, this is your project. You make all the decisions, set the timetable within the parameters we've discussed, and do your own thing. It's all yours! The only thing I ask is that you don't send anything out without me checking it first." As we noted in the chapter on delegation, it's only delegation if we truly turn things loose!

DON'T OVERDO THE PROCESS

Not everyone in our work group is going to be able to do everything. If we recognize this up front, we will have less trouble. Instead of letting everyone try to be an expert, we use the true experts whenever possible. Let the experts remain experts. Let them do what they do best, while sharing the thoughts and ideas of others. We don't allow nonexperienced, noninformed members to have inputs equal to those of the recognized experts. That would be unfair to the uninformed and demeaning to the experts. We always point out the experts in the formation of the teams, but make sure that all opinions are still welcome and explain that questions are important and comments imperative if the members of the team are really going to be contributing members. There's nothing wrong with having the experts train others, so that more people will have the skills. In this way, individuals can grow while working as a team. The key is to use everybody's inputs, no matter how big or little their contribution may be.

One thing that does happen in team building is overdelegation. The boss pulls a disappearing act and is never around for questions. We must be there if the team needs help, but not simply to solve all its problems. This is especially important at the beginning of a team assignment. It is all right to tell people what to do occasionally, of course. And if the solution is obvious and the team is stuck, we are obligated to give them the benefit of our expertise. When we do so, it should go like this:

TEAM: *We're really stuck on this.*
SUPERVISOR: *What have you done so far?*
TEAM: *We've thought about it and tried to plug in several solutions, but nothing seems to work.*
SUPERVISOR: *What have you tried?*
TEAM: *Well, here's the worksheet. You can see the approaches we've tried. None of them got the problem solved.*
SUPERVISOR: *Did you check the computer printout to see if the data are current? Sometimes the night shift's results haven't been put in yet.*
TEAM: *Hey, that's a thought. We didn't know that.*
SUPERVISOR: *Why don't you give that a try? If it doesn't work, get back to me and we'll see if something else is needed.*
TEAM: *Thanks, we're out of here!*

We handled this situation without detracting from the team's responsibilities. There was no use in the employees' floundering around until they stumbled onto the right solution. We saved time, and the team was still in control of the project. Most important, the team remained responsible for the end product and getting there. One problem that often works against the team process is that some people use being a member of the team as an excuse to escape responsibility. It's up to us to keep pushing the team, always letting people know it's their job, not ours, to get to the end of the task. Note that this conversation began with a question, "What have you tried?" If the team hasn't tried anything, our best approach is to send the team members away with an admonition to go a little further and see what they can come up with.

We will be successful as far as team building is concerned if we learn to play many roles, to wear different hats. First, we must always be the *boss*. This is not an assertion of authority; it's just that the group wants the security of knowing that somebody's driving the bus, that somebody is in charge. The team needs to know that somebody can make the final judgments, the final call, somebody can see that things happen to support the team's actions—all things only a supervisor can do. Sometimes, we must be a *coworker*. Even though it's our job to get the jobs done through others, at times we have to jump in and help out—when there is an emergency, when deadlines are at stake, when someone is sick—not for long, but long enough to get over the crisis. At other times we must act as an *advisor*. We have experience, knowledge gained from higher management, and a better overall view of the organization, all of which make for a good advisor. We give advice when needed, and not with superiority or with the appearance of knowing it all, but as one who can contribute just the right thing at the right time. Finally, sometimes we must just sit back and observe. When things are going right, plans have been made and approved, the team is on schedule, each member is doing his or her job well, then the best thing we can do is *nothing*. At such times we simply observe, be proud, and enjoy the moment.

TEST FOR MATURITY

As we've seen, not every group is ready to be a team. Working together with other people toward a common goal requires maturity in several areas. Because it isn't usual for us to work together, we lack the simple experience of working as a member of a team. For most people, sharing responsibility for a common goal and giving up full control over what needs to be done is new and possibly uncomfortable. Groups have personalities, just as people do. The people in the group give it the personality. If many of the group members are self-centered or self-serving, the group will develop a selfish personality, especially toward other groups. If many of the people are overly protective of the feelings of others so that they won't voice their disagreement about decisions made in the group, outsiders can use and abuse the group to their purposes. This group will get the reputation of not being able to get much done. In these kinds of situations, maturity is a problem. The group is too immature to put the task ahead of the individuals in the group. The truth is, the people in the group are just too immature to get the job done. A mature group overcomes conflicts, or at least learns to negotiate successfully to resolve them. Its members accept each other in the group role, knowing what each one can best contribute.

Just as a group's personality is reflected in its functioning, so are the personalities of the individuals in the group. Most people have a hard time sharing both glory and blame. The natural tendency is to take the glory and give away the blame. In a group, people must share both. A person can get only a portion of the glory for a job well done and must accept a fair share of the blame for any failure. That takes maturity. As we've seen, a close look at a person's reaction to criticism will give us a good picture of that person's level of maturity.

Another test of maturity is to determine how well potential team members can work with people they don't particularly like. Everybody has the right to dislike someone else, but no one has the right to let that dislike keep him or her from working successfully with another person. A mature person can work through his or her feelings about others on the job. He or she can put the job ahead of those feelings and learn to respect or accept others' ideas and opinions. People who can't do this on a day-to-day basis rarely are successful on a team.

MEETING EGO NEEDS

We have an important role to play in keeping the egos of all the team members satisfied. Our tendency is to praise the group for its total contribution and success. This needs to be done, but doing it doesn't meet the ego needs of the individual group members. Remember, it's hard for people to accept only part of the credit for what is happening. We have to find ways to give the individuals some personal recognition, too. Simply saying in passing, "Hey, Sue, I liked the way that poster turned out you drew for the group," will go a long way in meeting the individual's personal need for recognition.

Team building requires meeting people's ego needs on three different levels:

- *Individuals within the team.*   Letting the individual know how he or she is measuring up to the others on the team.

- *Team compared with other teams.*   Letting the team know how it compares with other teams, such as the night-shift team.

- *Teams compared with other departments.*   Letting the whole department know how it stacks up against another department or division, or even the competition.

HAZARDS OF TEAM BUILDING

We've seen the advantages of team building, and we've seen that it takes a lot of work to succeed with team building. Team building also has its drawbacks and hazards. Let's look at some of those hazards. First, we may put too much emphasis on the teams and their successes, ignoring some talented individuals. We may miss out on the potential of some workers by not providing opportunities for them to grow or training for other tasks. It's easy to get lost in a team, especially a strong-willed team with autocratic leadership. It's easy to feel superfluous in a team activity under the same conditions. Also, people can develop a lack of individual responsibility and accountability. They may get used to passing along some or all of the blame for problems to others when working on a team. Then, when they are working on their own, they don't accept accountability for their own actions. We begin to hear things like:

> "It's not my fault; I did my part."
> "I didn't know that was my job."
> "Nobody told me how to do it."

Another hazard of team building is that authority figures may emerge. It is a fact of group dynamics that nothing gets done until some authority struggles work themselves out. We have to keep close tabs on what is happening at the beginning of the team efforts to make certain that one or two people don't dominate the team. If necessary, we should step in and talk privately with those who seem determined to run things their way. We don't want to be harsh, but should simply caution that the activity must involve the entire group and that one or two people should not make all the decisions. Sometimes an authority struggle or something else that causes dissension gives rise to antigroup cliques that work against the group's efforts. People in these cliques may think of themselves as devil's advocates, but in fact they serve as a roadblock and a detriment to accomplishment of the overall goal. Here, again, we may have to step in and do some regulating if the group can't resolve the differences. A note: The group will have enough trouble working toward a common goal without having to resolve all these personality problems. It behooves us to try to help out in these situations as much as possible. We can help the team do its job by keeping the path swept clean of personalities, egos, and cantankerous people!

A final hazard should be mentioned. We've been talking about team building in a small way, under one supervisor—us. We started off by saying that even if higher management isn't trying to encourage team building, we can still make it work by following the suggestions here. It is pretty obvious, however, that there is a limit to how much pressure and interference the group can stand from upper management. When the big boss starts criticizing individuals in the group, imposing deadlines or quotas that are beyond the team's capacity, or pressuring us to become more autocratic, things are going to fall apart. This is rare, but it may happen. At that point, we are in an untenable position and we must recognize that the team process isn't going to work. For that matter, nothing else will work, either. There is no easy solution, except to try to salvage what we were able to accomplish. Remember that when our boss isn't a good boss, it's the problem of the boss the next level up. He or she is the person who will have to know what's going on and deal with it. Fortunately, this is not a commonplace occurrence.

CONCLUSION

Teamwork is gradually imposed, but usually worth the effort for a first-line supervisor. It isn't easy to make it work; it brings with it hazards and shortcomings; but it will work. People nearly always rise to the occasion when they know what is expected. They like to be a part of the decision-making process. We hear it said that people resist change, but that's not the problem. Mostly, *people resist being changed.* If we let people in on the process from the beginning and allow them to make some of their own choices in procedures and directions, they'll make the team work because it's theirs, rather than something imposed on them. In the end, good, old-fashioned, people-skilled, motivating supervision is still the most effective way to get the job done, with or without teams. It's just easier when people are working as a team!

EXERCISES

1. Debate/Discussion: Form two subgroups. Group one takes the position that everybody is mature enough to belong to a team, and therefore all work should be done with formal teams; people's personal egos shouldn't get in the way of the good of all. Group two takes the position that people have too many personal and hidden agendas to surrender themselves to the control and threat of a team format; things always work better when a boss assigns work and each individual does what he or she is assigned.

2. Individual assignment, then whole-group discussion: Have individuals make a list of all the requirements for a good team operation. After a few minutes, break into subgroups of three or four members and see which subgroup can come up with the longest list. Have each group record its list on easel paper; then hang the lists up around the room. Each group has a member read its list for the whole class to discuss. Each subgroup should defend its own list.

Chapter 17

SELF-DEVELOPMENT AND EVALUATION

It would be easy to stop the book at this point with just a few words of exhortation about personal growth and development. But as a new supervisor, we need to know how and where to develop ourselves. As we get embroiled in the everyday problems of the job, we forget to look at ourselves to see if we are any better at what we're doing than we were a few months ago. In fact, we forget just what areas we are supposed to improve in. Little problems seem like big ones when they are with us, so we spend all our time worrying about them and fail to realize that good supervisors have to think about the future as well as the present. Not only do we need to worry about the long-range objectives of the organization, but *we need to think about some long-range objectives for ourselves*. This isn't to say that we should spend all our time worrying about the next job or our "big promotion"; we simply have to realize that we really aren't going to be of much value to ourselves or to the organization if we fail to grow to our full potential. But how do we develop ourselves, and what are the areas that should receive priority? The answers to these questions will make a big difference in where we will be ten years from now and what we will be doing then.

HOW DO WE DEVELOP?

How can we improve ourselves if we have all the problems of the job to worry about? The chances are that we are going to be so busy we can't take time out to train ourselves or even do much planning about the future—*and here we have the first indicator that we need some development.* If we can't get the job done in the time allotted to us and still find some time to look to next week and next year, we may need to examine the way we are doing our job. Are we really organized in our work effort? Are we spinning our wheels doing things that should be delegated to others? Are we doing things over because they weren't done right the first time? Are we spending too much time on small, insignificant details, thereby letting problems grow bigger? There are some pretty good signs to show us how well we are doing. Let's consider some of them.

First, there's the matter of not having enough time. One sign that we aren't organizing our efforts very well is that we're working without taking time to plan. It's a vicious cycle, because the less time we have, the less we plan, and the less we plan, the more time it takes to do the job, so we run out of time. This goes on and on until finally we're swamped with work and have no time to plan it. The results are that we don't do a very efficient job of what we do and we may even overlook doing things that should be done. But how do we get out of such a dilemma? Well, one way is to turn the process around by stopping the cycle. We can start to do so by taking even five minutes at the beginning of the day to try to put our affairs in order. If we don't do this, we'll probably do the first task that comes up, whether it's important or not. Five minutes of deciding what needs to be handled first and what can wait will save us from getting behind on important things. Another five minutes will allow us to decide what *we* must handle and what *we can delegate* to someone else. Another telltale sign that we need to watch for in our supervisory job is the tendency to justify doing more and more of the job ourselves "because I can do it in less time than it takes to explain or train someone else." When we get into this cycle, we're doing more and our people are doing less. They're not happy because they see us doing work that they could and should be doing. We're unhappy because we're doing work we shouldn't be doing, and we may even decide that our people are lazy or have a poor attitude because they aren't doing more— *all because we haven't taken the time to plan our work very well.*

Remember, these are indicators that we need to develop; they're not cures. The matter of how we develop is just as important. So far, we've seen that one way is to force ourselves to do five or ten minutes of planning and delegating. Another way is to give ourselves a little instant success. We need confidence in ourselves, and this comes from accomplishing something. Even if it isn't the biggest or most important job we've ever done, just finishing a task—and stopping long enough to take note of it—will boost our confidence a lot. How can we use this technique to our advantage? One simple method is to make a list of what we have to accomplish in a period of time: a day, a week, or two weeks. (If our confidence is fairly low, a day works best.) We list the things on a page or two and number them as they are listed. During the day we mark them off one at a time as we complete them. A good way to mark them off is with a transparent felt-tip pen. This tells us what job we did and that it has been accomplished. Seeing the broad strokes of the felt pen gives us a boost, because we realize that as hectic as the job has been, we've still gotten a few things done. The next day, or at the end of the day, we make a new list, taking the tasks done off the list and adding new items for the upcoming day.

Two things become pretty obvious as we follow this procedure: one is that it shows us how much we are really doing, and the other is that it gives us an excellent opportunity to plan and organize our work. As we look over what we have to do, we may notice some duplication of effort. We may see that someone in the office can do two or three of the items because they are closely related. Also, as we list the things to be done, we have a chance to set some priorities. Naturally we want to do the important tasks first, so they should be near the top of the list. As we write down the jobs, though, we often discover that we've missed some things that should be at the top of the list. If we hadn't made the list in the first place, we'd have overlooked something important or tried to do it in a hurry at the last minute, in either case doing less than what is expected of us. One caution here: getting the right "size" is important. Writing down something that's going to take two or three days isn't going to give us much confidence; it will have just the opposite effect. If we see that the list is short and each item takes a day or more, we need to list some of the parts of the job that can be done separately and then cross these off as we accomplish them. This serves also to organize the large tasks into small, logical steps, helping us do a better job overall and still giving us frequent successes.

Another way we can develop is to watch others. First, we watch our boss or someone else who is getting a lot of work done in the same time we're working. We study people's behavior, their pattern, their organizing. We try to figure out what it is that makes them able to get as much done as they do. We can even discuss the subject with them. Don't make it a flattery session, though. They probably get a lot done because they make good use of their time; we don't want to be guilty of taking up too much of their time with our poor organizational habits. The way to discuss the subject is by asking the right questions, not by asking other people to solve our problems. We watch people work, then ask them why they did certain things. "Why did you call the meeting right at that time? What advantage did you gain by having the meeting at all?" Of course, we need to make it completely clear that we aren't questioning their wisdom, just trying to improve on our own. To enhance our perception, we can attempt to anticipate what their answers will be. We try to figure out the reasoning behind what was done, then see how close we are to the reasons they give. As we get closer and closer, we can see that our judgment is getting better. We're probably making better decisions on our own job now.

Next, we make a conscious effort to judge the abilities of the people under us. We see how well they accept the responsibilities we give them and deliberately give them more as they prove themselves capable of handling them. We aren't just trying to get more work out of them; we're trying to expand their ability to handle more important assignments. Appraising others isn't the easiest thing to do; neither is delegating. Our ability to do these together, though, is a measure of our success. There are some who fear giving up responsibility and authority to those under them. Some fear that their subordinates will somehow get the credit and maybe even the job. Such lack of confidence in oneself is a sign of poor leadership and immaturity. One of the common traits of most good leaders is that they gather around themselves those who will assume responsibility when it is given. We should bear this in mind when we consider whether or not to let someone else do some of the work or make some of the decisions. Some people fear giving up any responsibility and authority for an even less noble reason: they are afraid that if the job is done wrong, they will have to take the blame. The truth is, that's the whole point—that we are willing to take the blame in order to protect people under us and give them the confidence to take the necessary risks until they have convinced themselves that they can do well on the job. This doesn't mean that we are going to let them think that everything went well when it didn't. It means that we will be a buffer between them and higher management. It means that we will know and tell them that they did the job well or poorly, but for a while at least, they are safe under our protection. Once they feel this, they should respond with good, creative decision making. But if we don't create this kind of atmosphere, we will be stuck with the work ourselves and the problem we're talking about—not having enough time to do our job.

Personal Development

There is more to developing than just becoming more effective on the job. We also need to make ourselves more well-rounded. This includes becoming better informed on what's going on in the community, in the country, and in our profession. It includes becoming better readers and writers. We need to relate better to the world so we can relate to our people, who come from various walks of life and various backgrounds, sometimes from different parts of the country. How do we do these things? We do them by *making a conscious effort to improve.* Let's consider some things that will help.

First, we must do some self-analysis—not the psychological kind of analyzing, but the measuring of our abilities and short-comings. We need to decide what we do well, what we do poorly, and what we can't do at all. We even need to decide what we like to do, what we don't like to do, and where we see possibilities for improvement. Next, after we've taken a realistic look at ourselves and are confident that we know ourselves pretty well, we need to look at our biases and our mental blocks. Do we balk at the thought of giving a talk in front of people and then conclude that we really don't have to do that anyway? Do we hate to read and then tell ourselves that we can learn more from watching television? Do we dislike writing much more than our name and then resign ourselves to the idea that we will never be able to write because we just don't have the gift for it? These are all biases that, if not overcome, will hurt us in the long run.

Having looked at our likes and dislikes and concluded that we need to improve on some of the things we don't like to do, we take the next step of picking our priorities. We decide what we want to improve on in one of several ways. We determine which one is the most valuable to us in our job or family, or which one will help us the most in doing other things we need or want to do. We can decide which we're the worst at or which will take us the longest to develop the skill for. We can see which one will be the easiest for us to develop, giving us a boost sooner when we start our redevelopment program. Or we can undertake several improvement projects at once. If our confidence is high enough, this is fine; but this route can also discourage us the fastest if we don't develop as quickly as we'd like.

Whatever the project we pick, we need to set some goals and make some realistic plans for accomplishing these goals. It is not enough for us to say, "I'm going to get better at this during the next year," without saying how much better or how we're going to get better. Let's look at some specific things we can improve on, some of the things many people are weak on, and some things that we've already mentioned. Take writing, for example. Many people hate to write, don't feel they're good at it, and find it takes a threat of death to get them to sit down and compose even a memo. But all of us need to be able to write satisfactorily if we ever expect to do our job well. Even if all we have to do is tell the incoming supervisor something that happened on the night shift that requires attention, we must write it clearly and concisely. So how do we learn to write? *One simple way is to write!* We find that people who force themselves to write, even only frequent letters to their grandmothers, get better at it, especially if they go back and read what they've written before they send the letters.

Another way to improve our writing is to study what others have written. If we work for someone we think writes well, we should study carefully samples of that person's writing. The idea isn't to copy somebody's style but to see just what makes the other person an effective writer. (By the way, there's nothing wrong with copying a good style. It's just that we need to feel comfortable with the way we write, and following somebody else may be awkward for us.) Nevertheless, we study a letter or a memo or a report until we see what the writer is doing that we are failing to do. Maybe it's nothing more than using short sentences. Maybe he or she is picking simple, precise words. Maybe the person is limiting the length of the paragraphs. Whatever it is, we can see that the writer is doing something we aren't. Try reading the other person's letter once, getting the idea of the message, and then putting it aside and writing the same information in our own words, without copying his or hers. Then look at the original letter to see where the writer did better than we did.

If we're serious about improving our writing, we can even take a course to help us. There are seminars or short courses that sometimes last no more than two or three days. Almost all community colleges, and even vocational schools, offer night courses in writing. One course should be sufficient to teach us what we need to know to get on the road to better writing. The advantage of taking a course is that we get pointed in the right direction, so that we will be practicing the correct things rather than repeating the same mistakes we now make. If we don't take a course and don't have access to a good book on how to write better, at least we can *read*. As we'll see later, reading helps us to improve in all kinds of ways, including in our writing.

Let's look at another area in which we might need to improve. Suppose we have decided to get over the fear of speaking in front of others. We have convinced ourselves that we have as much to say as the next supervisor, but we don't have the confidence to get up and talk, even in a small, informal meeting. What can we do? Again, there are places where we can get training, speech classes, or even speech teachers. Most towns and many organizations have Toastmasters groups. Colleges offer night classes, weekend sessions, and other seminars that include lessons on speaking in front of others. No matter where we go or who trains us, the main thing we'll have to do is finally get up and talk before a group. It's like driving a car; we can read all the books on the subject, look at movies, and listen to lectures, but we won't learn to drive until we get behind the wheel and go out into traffic. It will be hard the first time, the second time, the third time, and maybe even several more times; but it will get easier each time.

We mentioned broadening our perspective about the world around us. How do we do that? Again, the answer most people offer is *reading*. Sometimes people seem to avoid reading, letting the television tell them everything they need to know. They seem to forget that television is primarily an entertainment medium, not an informing one. Not only does it fail to tell us all the things we need to know, but it also misinforms us. Fiction doesn't tell us about problems in the local community or how businesses are really run. We won't be a better supervisor because we see how some writer presents a story about problems in a mill or plant. We won't do our job better because we've seen a comedy about how bad supervisors treat workers, even if the story is what is sometimes called true to life. We will be better informed if we read an article on the business page about a new industry moving into town or about trends in our industry. We'll be better informed if we pick up a weekly business magazine from the newsstand and find out something about the way inflation is effecting change in the business world.

If nothing else comes from reading, we can make ourselves more disciplined by taking time every day to read something that has some meat in it. Some people have been successful in business because they forced themselves to read something they otherwise wouldn't have read. There is some merit to that. Try picking up a magazine or a section of the paper and finding something that *doesn't sound interesting*. Read it for ten minutes. It may surprise us to discover that we actually learned something, and what's even better, we'll find we can use that information in a conversation one day soon. Television can help us become informed if we discipline ourselves in what we watch, but it can also ruin our incentive to read if we get hooked on it. What we're saying is, learn to read better by reading more. Not only will we be better readers, but we will also be better-informed and better-disciplined readers!

THE NEXT JOB?

There are two reasons for developing ourselves—to do better in our present job and to be ready for the next one. It is important to keep them in this order—the present job, *then* the next one. This may sound simple enough, but many good supervisors fail to get promoted because they get so interested in the next job that they forget to deal properly with the present one. We think, talk, and plan about the job we hope to get, letting the details of the present one slip. The first thing that happens is that our interest also begins to wane, and pretty soon disaster strikes. An important assignment gets only meager attention. Details are overlooked, and wrong decisions are made. Errors creep in, and higher management gets involved in finding out what happened. And we, who were potentially able to take on more than we now have been assigned, find that we're losing some of the work we used to have because someone up the line doubts our ability to handle even our present job. Some have said, "Do well on the present assignment, and the future will take care of itself." That's pretty good advice, except that it doesn't include all that's necessary to get ahead. It assumes that the requirements for the next job are the same as those for the present one. This may not be true. If not, then it's good to develop in those areas where we are weak. If the next level above us requires considerable report writing and we don't think we're very good at it, this is one place we can start. We can look around for chances to learn more about report writing, and we can look for opportunities to do some report writing on our present job. We can start off by making short reports on things the boss has asked about, then work up to longer and more complex ones. Just doing reports is a good way to learn, but we should do some studying and developing on the side so the experience will be meaningful. We follow the same routine in the other areas where we think the requirements of the next job exceed our present capabilities. The advantage of this approach is that it will actually make us look better on our *present* assignment rather than as if we have abandoned any interest in it. While we are improving in our existing job, and improving our reputation at the same time, we are also preparing ourselves to take over a more responsible task when the opportunity arises.

One final word about the next job: let nature take its course; don't try to help it too much. Very few people can show where they have been successful at plotting their careers job-for-job. Most successful people will tell us that they got the job by being in the right place at the right time *and* by being ready when the occasion presented itself. It's not all luck, but luck surely plays a part. Our job is to be prepared when the luck breaks for us. This means that we not only have developed ourselves to take over the added responsibility but also have covered the present job quite adequately. What this says, perhaps, is that in a real sense *we help make our own luck*.

We need to remember that the ways to develop ourselves are too numerous to mention here. We could spend a lot of time just telling about how to grow through reading the right books and magazines. There are night schools and self-help courses. Programs are available within many organizations. But these are obvious to most of us, so we won't go into them here—not because they aren't good and profitable, but because they are the obvious things to do when we talk about self-development. We've tried to talk about some of the less obvious ones that can go along with these approaches. It might be said, and with accuracy, that part of how we tell whether or not we are capable of taking on the next higher assignment is to assess our ability to identify the areas and ways of developing ourselves. If we are a successful supervisor—new or old—we will be sensitive to our own needs for development and will find ways to make the necessary improvements. Perhaps more important, we will see it as a challenge, not a chore. We will do it and call it fun, not exhausting drudgery. Good supervision can be learned. If we take the time to back off and look at ourselves and where we are going, we'll see that we have already come far. It may have been hard work, but that's not all it was; there was probably a great deal of pleasure in making the trip. The rest of the way is even better!

CONCLUSION

We've already said that appraising our people is a hard job. A much harder job is *appraising ourselves*. Looking with objective eyes at our own strengths and weaknesses is close to impossible for most of us. One problem is that we know our *motives*, and when we know that they were good in a certain situation, even though we didn't perform too well, we tend to overlook our weaknesses in that situation. If we're going to improve ourselves, we'll have to be willing to see both the good and the bad in ourselves. We can't be too hard on ourselves—nor too easy. We look at areas like time management, delegation, training, communication, and interpersonal skills and imagine that we are appraising ourselves. We look for a standard, then our *performance* against that standard—not our intentions. We also have another question to answer: do we want to be better? That sounds like a ridiculous question, but many of us reach a plateau and decide—admitting it or not—that we really don't want to expend the effort or time to raise our performance level any higher. If we make this decision, we ought to be sure to keep it in mind and not end up somewhere down the line saying, "I could have had that promotion if I'd wanted it," or "I wonder why the organization hasn't treated me better."

On the other hand, if we really are serious about being good supervisors—and that certainly is true of anyone who has read this far in this book—we set some targets for ourselves, decide what must be overcome in order to reach them, and go about getting there. If we look at ourselves and decide that a certain target is too far beyond our reach *at this time*, then we set another, short-range target and head for it. Also, if we decide that there are things in the way that aren't under our power to control, then we change our target. Notice that we've used the word *target* often. We need a target to shoot at, a goal to strive for. It's more than saying, "I'd like to be a better communicator someday." We have to be specific enough to say, "I'd like to be a better listener someday." We have to define both the weaknesses that are keeping us from getting there and the goal itself. When we begin to approach our goal, we have to make these decisions all over again or we'll end up just drifting along, not getting any better or any closer to any goal. A Hindu proverb says, "If we don't know where we're going, any road will get us there." That's true of our self-development. The idea is to set a target, then direct our energies toward reaching it, remembering that the vast majority of the successes we have aren't because of somebody else; they're because of us. We don't need "pull" from somebody else in the organization to get ahead. We usually just need a little "push" from within ourselves.

EXERCISES

1. Group activity: The entire group should brainstorm a list of things that should be considered in evaluating present skills. What needs to be examined? (The list should be recorded, but heavily refined, so that it isn't too long and impossible to deal with.) Next, consider how future chances for advancement can be determined. What can people look at in their own lives and jobs? The group should come up with a refined list of these things, too, and record it where everyone can see it.

2. Individual activity: Each person should look at the list from exercise 1, examining his or her present skills. Spend a few minutes with the list and decide whether it is really a usable list or too nebulous to be meaningful. Take some time on this before going on to the next exercise.

3. Group activity: Now that everyone has had a chance to use the list worked up in exercise 1, see what reaction people had. Brainstorm ways of refining the list some more until everyone is happy that it will now give useful data.

4. Individual activity: Each person should now try to use the second list from exercise 1, the one dealing with things that people need to look at in their lives and jobs in order to determine their future opportunities and direction. Spend some time on this, trying to make it a meaningful activity, then go on to exercise 5.

5. Group activity: When everyone is finished with exercise 4, the group should evaluate the list, as in exercise 3. Again, the object is to refine the list so that it is an aid in determining where people are going and what is needed in order to get there. Each person should take both lists with him or her and review them at least once a year to measure progress.

EPILOGUE

Here we are at the end of another book on how to be a better supervisor. What have we learned? Only time will tell. What have we tried to offer? A supermarket designed to lay out the possibilities for growth and development. This is not to suggest that everything in the book is applicable to every new supervisor; the suggestions here are just that and no more—suggestions. The new supervisor will be no worse for having considered them; there is even the possibility that something that has been said will cause him or her to get a new idea, a new perspective on an existing problem. If the suggestion and the resulting idea pay off, then not much more is needed to justify the time it's taken to read the book.

Let's repeat what was said earlier: this isn't a rule book; it's a guidebook. The ideas and suggestions have all been tried by someone, someplace, at some time with enough success to justify their being in this publication. Whether or not they work for you is not a measure of your effectiveness or your abilities—more likely it's proof that supervising people is complex and deserves all our efforts and skills. If we are willing to put all our energies into the job and to learn the skills, then there can be only one result—we'll end up being good supervisors. There may be better rewards, but this one should suit most of us for a long time to come!

INDEX